Mastering Software Testing with JUnit 5

Comprehensive guide to develop high quality Java applications

Boni García

BIRMINGHAM - MUMBAI

Mastering Software Testing with JUnit 5

First published: October 2017

Production reference: 1231017

Published by Packt Publishing Ltd.
Livery Place
35 Livery Street
Birmingham
B3 2PB, UK.

ISBN 978-1-78728-573-6

www.packtpub.com

Credits

Author
Boni García

Reviewers
Luis Fernández Muñoz
Ashok Kumar S

Commissioning Editor
Smeet Thakkar

Acquisition Editor
Nigel Fernandes

Content Development Editor
Mohammed Yusuf Imaratwale

Technical Editor
Ralph Rosario

Copy Editor
Charlotte Carneiro

Project Coordinator
Ritika Manoj

Proofreader
Safis Editing

Indexer
Aishwarya Gangawane

Graphics
Jason Monteiro

Production Coordinator
Shraddha Falebhai

About the Author

Boni García has a PhD degree on information and communications technology from **Technical University of Madrid (UPM)** in Spain since 2011. His doctoral dissertation was focused on test automation for web applications. He is an author of more than 30 research papers, including international conferences, journals, and magazines.

At the time of writing this book, he was working as a researcher at **King Juan Carlos University (URJC)**, and also as assistant professor at **Digital Art and Technology University (U-tad)** in Spain. He has participated in different research initiatives. For instance, he is member of Kurento project, where he has created a testing framework for WebRTC applications. He also participates in the coordination of ElasTest, a project aimed to create an elastic platform for end-to-end testing of different types of applications.

Boni is an active member on the free open source software community with a big emphasis on software testing and web engineering. Among others, he is the owner and main developer of the *WebDriverManager* and *selenium-jupiter* projects (JUnit 5 extension for Selenium).

First of all, I would like to thank my girl, Verónica, for her essential support while writing this book. Without you, this manuscript would have been simply impossible. But, most importantly, thank you for sharing your life with me. I would also like to thank to my sisters, Yoly and Inma, for all their help, not only with this book, but in life in general. Thank you for being always there. In addition, I want to dedicate this book to my nieces, Andrea, Silvia, and Laura, who are the most amazing people in the universe (at least the part I know). I also would like to remember here my parents, Pablo and Dolores. There is nothing I would like more than if you were here. I know that a part of you is living with us, in your daughters, grandchildren, and myself. I miss you so much. Finally, I also want to dedicate this book to the most important person in the world, my little boy, Pablo. Son, whenever you read this, I want you to know that I learned what happiness really means by looking into your eyes. I would like to believe these words can travel in time and space to give you a big hug anytime. Remember that your parents love you more than anything.

About the Reviewers

Luis Fernández Muñoz in the last 25 years he has been serving as a Professor and Researcher at **Technical University of Madrid (UPM)** and **King Juan Carlos University (URJC)**, both in Spain. he has also collaborate as Consultor and Trainer in different public and private national and international institutions. His main expertise comprises all the software engineering disciplines, from coding and testing, to analysis, design, architecture, and project management, usually around C++/Java and Web/JEE technologies.

As a Consultor in private companies, he has participated in different projects as different roles, from management to development of code and tests. In the different areas he has worked, he highlight cloud computing, combat simulation and physical activity expert systems, among others.

Additional, my entrepreneur spirit took me to become in the one of co-founders of TS Company, an UPM startup with 25 employees in only four years.

He has developed my research endeavor in the Natural Computing Group, in which he made his PhD dissertation focused on Parallel Algorithms for the Application of Evolution Rules in Endomembrane P Systems. After that, he has directed some others PhD dissertations. Thanks to all of this, he has participated in more than 60 publications, in conferences, journals, and several research projects.

This versatile career has given me the opportunity of learn by reading and listening to relevant people in the field, which is one of his main hobbies. Deep reflections, discussions and building the mental structure of conceptual ideas rigorously, but his way, is his motivation challenge. Traveling, chatting, and venturing -without losing his mind- is the way he enjoy's the best in life.

Ashok Kumar S is an Android developer residing in Bangalore, India. A gadget enthusiast, he thrives on innovating and exploring the latest gizmos in the tech space. He has been developing softwares for all Google related technologies, and he also a Google certified Android developer. A strong believer in spirituality, he heavily contributes to the open source community as an e-spiritual ritual to improve his e-karma. He regularly conducts workshops about Android application development in local engineering colleges and schools. He also organizes multiple tech events at his organization and he is a regular attendee of all the conferences that happen on Android and Java related technologies in the silicon valley of India (Bengaluru). He also runs a YouTube channel, called `AndroidABCD`, where he discusses all aspects of Android development, including quick tutorials. Having 4 years of professional experience. Currently working with Dunst Technologies Pvt Ltd as full-time Sr. Mobile Engineer. He has extensively worked on Android Native applications ranging from Enterprise applications to commerce application. I spend most of my time in exploring brilliant architectures and libraries. I have a strong interest in code quality, testing, and automation, and all three. he is a speaker at Android conferences that happen's in Bengaluru, Apart from all of it, I am also a photographer, A storyteller.

www.PacktPub.com

For support files and downloads related to your book, please visit www.PacktPub.com.

Did you know that Packt offers eBook versions of every book published, with PDF and ePub files available? You can upgrade to the eBook version at www.PacktPub.com and as a print book customer, you are entitled to a discount on the eBook copy. Get in touch with us at service@packtpub.com for more details.

At www.PacktPub.com, you can also read a collection of free technical articles, sign up for a range of free newsletters and receive exclusive discounts and offers on Packt books and eBooks.

https://www.packtpub.com/mapt

Get the most in-demand software skills with Mapt. Mapt gives you full access to all Packt books and video courses, as well as industry-leading tools to help you plan your personal development and advance your career.

Why subscribe?

- Fully searchable across every book published by Packt
- Copy and paste, print, and bookmark content
- On demand and accessible via a web browser

Customer Feedback

Thanks for purchasing this Packt book. At Packt, quality is at the heart of our editorial process. To help us improve, please leave us an honest review on this book's Amazon page at https://www.amazon.com/dp/1787285731.

If you'd like to join our team of regular reviewers, you can e-mail us at customerreviews@packtpub.com. We award our regular reviewers with free eBooks and videos in exchange for their valuable feedback. Help us be relentless in improving our products!

Table of Contents

Preface

Humans are not perfect thinkers. At the time of this writing, software engineers are human beings. Most of them. For that reason, writing high-quality, useful software is a really difficult task. As we will discover in this book, software testing is one of the most important activities carried out by software engineers (that is, developers, programmers, or testers) to warranty a level of quality and confidence in a given piece of software.

JUnit is the most used testing framework for the Java language, and one of the most remarkable in software engineering in general. Nowadays, JUnit is much more than a unit testing framework for Java. As we will discover, it can be used to implement different types of tests (such as unit, integration, end-to-end, or acceptance tests) using different strategies (such as black-box or white-box).

On September 10, 2017, the JUnit team released JUnit 5.0.0. This book is mainly focused on this new major release of JUnit. As we will discover, JUnit 5 has supposed a complete redesign of the JUnit framework, improving important features, such as modularization (JUnit 5 architecture is completely modular), composability (the extension model of JUnit 5 allows to integrate third-party frameworks in the JUnit 5 test lifecycle is an easy way), and compatibility (JUnit 5 supports the execution of JUnit 3 and 4 legacy tests in the brand-new JUnit Platform). All of it, following a modern programming model based on Java 8 and compliant with Java 9.

Software engineering involves a multidisciplinary body of knowledge with a strong impetus for the change. This book provides a comprehensive review of many different aspects related to software testing from, mainly following an open source point of view (JUnit is open source from its inception). In this book, in addition to JUnit, you learn how to use third-party frameworks and technologies in our development process, namely, Spring, Mockito, Selenium, Appium, Cucumber, Docker, Android, REST services, Hamcrest, Allure, Jenkins, Travis CI, Codecov, or SonarCube, among others.

What this book covers

Chapter 1, *Retrospective On Software Quality And Java Testing*, provides a detailed review of software quality and testing. The objective of this chapter is to clarify the terminology of this domain in an intelligible way. Moreover, this chapter provides a summary the history of JUnit (version 3 and 4) and also some JUnit enhancers (for example, libraries that can be used to extend JUnit).

Chapter 2, *What's New In JUnit 5,* first introduces the motivation to create a version 5 of JUnit. Then, this chapter describes the main components of the JUnit 5 architecture, namely, Platform, Jupiter, and Vintage. Next, we discover how to run JUnit tests, for example, using different build tools such as Maven or Gradle. Finally, this chapter is the extension model of JUnit 5, which allows extending the core functionality of JUnit 5 by any third party.

Chapter 3, *JUnit 5 Standard Tests,* gives a detailed description of the basic features of the new JUnit 5 programming model. This programming model, together with the extension model, is called Jupiter. In this chapter, you learn about the basic test lifecycle, assertions, tagging and filtering tests, conditional test execution, nested and repeated tests, and finally how to migrate from JUnit 4.

Chapter 4, *Simplifying Testing With Advanced JUnit Features,* provide a detailed description of the JUnit 5 features, such as dependency injection, dynamic tests, test interfaces, test templates, parameterized tests, compatibility with Java 9, and planned features for the for JUnit 5.1 (not released yet at the time of this writing).

Chapter 5, *Integration Of JUnit 5 With External Frameworks,* talks about the integration of JUnit 5 with existing third-party software. This integration can be done in different ways. Typically, the Jupiter extension model should be used to interact with external frameworks. This is the case of Mockito (a popular mock framework), Spring (a Java framework aimed to created enterprise applications based on dependency injection), Docker (a container platform technology), or Selenium (test framework for web applications). In addition, developers can reuse to Jupiter test lifecycle to interact with other technologies, for example, Android or REST services.

Chapter 6, *From Requirements To Test Cases,* provides a set of best practices aimed to help a software tester to write meaningful test cases. Considering the requirements as the basis of software testing, this chapter provides a comprehensive guide for coding tests avoiding typical mistakes (anti-patterns and code smell).

Chapter 7, *Testing Management,* is the final chapter of the book, and its objective is to guide the reader to understand how software testing activities are managed in a living software project. To that aim, this chapter reviews concepts such as **Continuous Integration (CI)**, build servers (Jenkins, Travis), test reporting, or defect tracking systems. To conclude the book, a complete example application together with different types of tests (unit, integration, and end-to-end) is presented.

What you need for this book

In order to understand the concepts presented in this book better, it is highly recommended to fork the GitHub repository, which contains the code examples presented in this book (`https://github.com/bonigarcia/mastering-junit5`). In the author's opinion, touching and playing with the code is essential to achieve a quick hands-on understanding of the JUnit 5 testing framework. As introduced before, the last chapter of this book provides a complete application example covering some of the most important topics of this book. This application (called *Rate my cat!*) is also available on GitHub, in the repository `https://github.com/bonigarcia/rate-my-cat`.

In order to run these example, you will need JDK 8 or higher. You can download the Oracle JDK from its website: `http://www.oracle.com/technetwork/java/javase/downloads/index.html`. In addition, it is highly recommended to use an **Integrated Development Environment (IDE)** to ease the development and testing process. As we will discover in this book, at the time of this writing there are two IDEs fully compliant with JUnit 5, namely:

* Eclipse 4.7+ (Oxygen): `https://eclipse.org/ide/`.
* IntelliJ IDEA 2016.2+: `https://www.jetbrains.com/idea/`.

If you prefer to run JUnit 5 from the command line, two possible build tools can be used:

* **Maven:** `https://maven.apache.org/`
* **Gradle:** `https://gradle.org/`

Who this book is for

This book is targeted for Java software engineers. For that reason, this piece of literature tries to speak the same language than the reader (that is, Java) and therefore it is driven by working code examples available on the aforementioned public open source GitHub repositories.

Conventions

In this book, you will find a number of text styles that distinguish between different kinds of information. Here are some examples of these styles and an explanation of their meaning. Code words in text, database table names, folder names, filenames, file extensions, path names, dummy URLs, user input, and Twitter handles are shown as follows: "The `@AfterAll` and `@BeforeAll` methods are executed only once".

A block of code is set as follows:

```
package io.github.bonigarcia;

import static org.junit.jupiter.api.Assertions.assertTrue;

import org.junit.jupiter.api.Test;

class StandardTest {

    @Test
    void verySimpleTest () {
        assertTrue(true);
    }

}
```

Any command-line input or output is written as follows:

```
mvn test
```

New terms and **important words** are shown in bold like this: "**Compatibility** is the degree to which a product, system or component can exchange information with other products".

Warnings or important notes appear in a box like this.

Tips and tricks appear like this.

Reader feedback

Feedback from our readers is always welcome. Let us know what you think about this book-what you liked or disliked. Reader feedback is important for us as it helps us develop titles that you will really get the most out of.

To send us general feedback, simply email `feedback@packtpub.com`, and mention the book's title in the subject of your message.

If there is a topic that you have expertise in and you are interested in either writing or contributing to a book, see our author guide at `www.packtpub.com/authors`.

Customer support

Now that you are the proud owner of a Packt book, we have a number of things to help you to get the most from your purchase.

Downloading the example code

You can download the example code files for this book from your account at `http://www.packtpub.com`. If you purchased this book elsewhere, you can visit `http://www.packtpub.com/support` and register to have the files emailed directly to you.

You can download the code files by following these steps:

1. Log in or register to our website using your email address and password.
2. Hover the mouse pointer on the **SUPPORT** tab at the top.
3. Click on **Code Downloads & Errata**.
4. Enter the name of the book in the **Search** box.
5. Select the book for which you're looking to download the code files.
6. Choose from the drop-down menu where you purchased this book from.
7. Click on **Code Download**.

Once the file is downloaded, please make sure that you unzip or extract the folder using the latest version of:

- WinRAR / 7-Zip for Windows
- Zipeg / iZip / UnRarX for Mac
- 7-Zip / PeaZip for Linux

The code bundle for the book is also hosted on GitHub at `https://github.com/bonigarcia/mastering-junit5`. We also have other code bundles from our rich catalog of books and videos available at `https://github.com/PacktPublishing/`. Check them out!

Errata

Although we have taken every care to ensure the accuracy of our content, mistakes do happen. If you find a mistake in one of our books-maybe a mistake in the text or the code-we would be grateful if you could report this to us. By doing so, you can save other readers from frustration and help us improve subsequent versions of this book. If you find any errata, please report them by visiting http://www.packtpub.com/submit-errata, selecting your book, clicking on the **Errata Submission Form** link, and entering the details of your errata. Once your errata are verified, your submission will be accepted and the errata will be uploaded to our website or added to any list of existing errata under the Errata section of that title.

To view the previously submitted errata, go to https://www.packtpub.com/books/content/support and enter the name of the book in the search field. The required information will appear under the **Errata** section.

Piracy

Piracy of copyrighted material on the Internet is an ongoing problem across all media. At Packt, we take the protection of our copyright and licenses very seriously. If you come across any illegal copies of our works in any form on the Internet, please provide us with the location address or website name immediately so that we can pursue a remedy.

Please contact us at copyright@packtpub.com with a link to the suspected pirated material.

We appreciate your help in protecting our authors and our ability to bring you valuable content.

Questions

If you have a problem with any aspect of this book, you can contact us at questions@packtpub.com, and we will do our best to address the problem.

1

Retrospective On Software
Quality And Java Testing

In order to make an apple pie from scratch, you must first invent the universe.
- Carl Sagan

The well-known testing framework JUnit has come a long way since its inception in 1995. On September 10, 2017, an important milestone in the project life cycle took place, i.e. the release of JUnit 5.0.0. Before going deep into the details of JUnit 5, it is worth reviewing the status quo of software testing, in order to understand from where we have come, and where we are going. To that aim, this chapter provides a high-level review of the background of software quality, software testing, and testing for Java. Concretely, the chapter is composed of three sections:

- **Software quality**: The first section reviews the status quo in quality engineering: Quality assurance, ISO/IEC-2500, **Verification & Validation (V&V)**, and software defects (*bugs*).
- **Software testing**: This is the most commonly performed activity to guarantee software quality and reduce the number of software defects. This section provides a theoretical background of software testing levels (unit, integration, system, and acceptance), methods (black-box, white-box, and non-functional), automated and manual software testing.
- **Testing frameworks for the Java Virtual Machine (JVM)**: This section provides a summary of the main features of the legacy versions of the JUnit framework (that is, versions 3 and 4). Finally, a brief description of alternative testing frameworks and enhancers to JUnit is depicted.

Software quality

Software is the collection of computer programs, related data, and associated documentation developed for a particular customer or for a general market. It is an essential part of the modern world, and it has become pervasive in telecommunications, utilities, commerce, culture, entertainment, and so on. The question *What is software quality?* can generate different answers, depending on the involved practitioner's role in a software system. There are two main groups of people involved in a software product or service:

- **Consumers**: are people who use software. In this group, we can differentiate between *customers* (that is, people responsible for the acquisition of software products or services) and *users* (that is, people who use the software products or services for various purposes). Nevertheless, the dual roles of customers and users are quite common.
- **Producers**: are people involved with the development, management, maintenance, marketing, and service of software products.

The quality expectations of consumers are that a software system performs useful functions as specified. For software producers, the fundamental quality question is fulfilling their contractual obligations by producing software products that conform to the **Service Level Agreement (SLA)**. The definition of software quality by the well-known software engineer Roger Pressman comprises both points of view:

An effective software process applied in a manner that creates a useful product that provides measurable value for those who produce it and those who use it.

Quality engineering

Quality engineering (also known as quality management) is a process that evaluates, assesses, and improves the quality of software. There are three major groups of activities in the quality engineering process:

1. **Quality planning**: This stage establishes the overall quality goal by managing customer's expectations under the project cost and budgetary constraints. This quality plan also includes the strategy, that is, the selection of activities to perform and the appropriate quality measurements to provide feedback and assessment.

2. **Quality Assurance (QA)**: This guarantees that software products and processes in the project life cycle meet their specified requirements by planning and performing a set of activities to provide adequate confidence that quality is being built into the software. The main QA activity is Verification & Validation, but there are others, such as software quality metrics, the use of quality standards, configuration management, documentation management, or an expert's opinion.

3. **Post-QA**: These stage includes activities for quality quantification and improvement measurement, analysis, feedback, and follow-up activities. The aim of these activities is to provide quantitative assessment of product quality and identification of improvement opportunities.

These phases are represented in the following chart:

Software Quality Engineering Process

Requirements and specification

Requirements are a key topic in the quality engineering domain. A requirement is a statement identifying a capability, physical characteristic, or quality factor that bounds a product or process need for which a solution will be pursued. The requirement development (also known as requirements engineering) is the process of producing and analyzing customer, product, and product-component requirements. The set of procedures that support the development of requirements, including planning, traceability, impact analysis, change management, and so on, is known as requirements management. There are two kinds of software requirements:

- **Functional requirements** are actions that the product must do to be useful to its users. They arise from the work that stakeholders need to do. Almost any action such as, inspecting, publishing, or most other active verbs can be a functional requirement.

- **Non-functional requirements** are properties, or qualities, that the product must have. For example, they can describe properties such as performance, usability, or security. They are often called *quality attributes*.

Another important topic strongly linked with the requirements is the specification, which is a document that specifies in a complete, precise, verifiable manner, the requirements, design, behavior, or other characteristics of a system, and often the procedures for determining whether these provisions have been satisfied.

Quality Assurance

Quality Assurance (QA) is primarily concerned with defining or selecting standards that should be applied to the software development process or software product. Daniel Galin, the author of the book *Software Quality Assurance* (2004) defined QA as:

> *Systematic, planned set of actions necessary to provide adequate confidence that the software development and maintenance process of a software system product conforms to established specification as well as with the managerial requirements of keeping the schedule and operating within the budgetary confines.*

The QA process selects the V&V activities, tools, and methods to support the selected quality standards. V&V is a set of activities carried out with the main objective of withholding products from shipment if they do not qualify. In contrast, QA is meant to minimize the costs of quality by introducing a variety of activities throughout the development and maintenance process in order to prevent the causes of errors, detect them, and correct them in the early stages of development. As a result, QA substantially reduces the rates of non-qualifying products. All in all, V&V activities are only a part of the total range of QA activities.

ISO/IEC-25000

Various quality standards have been proposed to accommodate these different quality views and expectations. The standard **ISO/IEC-9126** was one of the most influential in the software engineering community. Nevertheless, researchers and practitioners detected several problems and weaknesses in this standard. For that reason, the ISO/IEC-9126 international standard is superseded by the **ISO/IEC-25000** series of international standards on **Software product Quality Requirements and Evaluation (SQuaRE)**. This section provides a high-level overview of this standard.

The ISO/IEC-2500 quality reference model distinguishes different views on software quality:

- **Internal quality**: This concerns the properties of the system, that can be measured without executing it.
- **External quality**: This concerns the properties of the system, that can be observed during its execution.
- **Quality in use**: This concerns the properties experienced by its consumer during operation and maintenance of the system.

Ideally, the development (*process quality*) influences the internal quality; then, the internal quality determines the external quality. Finally, external quality determines quality in use. This chain is depicted in the following picture:

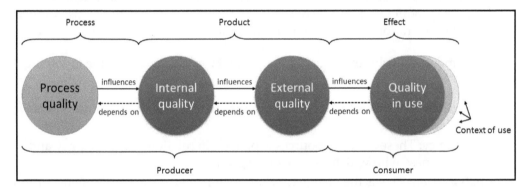

ISO/IEC-2500 Product Quality Reference Model

The quality model of ISO/IEC-25000 divides the product quality model (that is, the internal and external attributes) into eight top-level quality features: *functional suitability, performance efficiency, compatibility, usability, reliability, security, maintainability,* and *portability*. The following definitions have been extracted directly from the standard:

- **Functional suitability:** This represents the degree to which a product or system provides functions that meet stated and implied needs when used under specified conditions.
- **Performance efficiency:** This represents the performance relative to the amount of resources used under stated conditions.
- **Compatibility:** This is the degree to which a product, system or component can exchange information with other products, systems or components, and/or perform its required functions, while sharing the same hardware or software environment.

- **Usability:** This is the degree to which a product or system can be used by specified users to achieve specified goals with effectiveness, efficiency, and satisfaction in a specified context of use.
- **Reliability:** This is the degree to which a system, product, or component performs specified functions under specified conditions for a specified period of time.
- **Security:** This is the degree to which a product or system protects information and data so that persons or other products or systems have the degree of data access appropriate to their types and levels of authorization
- **Maintainability:** This represents the degree of effectiveness and efficiency with which a product or system can be modified to improve it, correct it, or adapt it to changes in environment and in requirements
- **Portability:** This is the degree of effectiveness and efficiency with which a system, product, or component can be transferred from one hardware, software, or other operational or usage environment to another

On the other hand, the attributes of quality in use can be categorized into the following five characteristics:

- **Effectiveness:** This is the accuracy and completeness with which users achieve specified goals.
- **Efficiency:** These are the resources expended in relation to the accuracy and completeness with which users achieve goals.
- **Satisfaction:** This is the degree to which user needs are satisfied when a product or system is used in a specified context of use.
- **Freedom from risk:** This is the degree to which a product or system mitigates the potential risk to economic status, human life, health, or the environment.
- **Context coverage:** This is the degree to which a product or system can be used with effectiveness, efficiency, freedom from risk, and satisfaction in both specified contexts of use and in contexts beyond those initially explicitly identified.

Verification and Validation

Verification and Validation -also known as Software Quality Control- is concerned with evaluating that the software being developed meets its specifications and delivers the functionality expected by the consumers. These checking processes start as soon as requirements become available, and continue through all stages of the development process. Verification is different to validation, although they are often confused.

The distinguished professor of computer science Barry Boehm expressed the difference between them back in 1979:

- **Verification**: *are we building the product right?* The aim of verification is to check that the software meets its stated functional and non-functional requirements (that is, the specification).
- **Validation**: *are we building the right product?* The aim of validation is to ensure that the software meets consumer's expectations. It is a more general process than verification, due to the fact that specifications do not always reflect the real wishes or needs of consumers.

V&V activities include a wide array of QA activities. Although software testing plays an extremely important role in V&V, other activities are also necessary. Within the V&V process, two big groups of techniques of system checking and analysis may be used:

- **Software testing**: This is the most commonly performed activity within QA. Given a piece of code, software testing (or simply testing) consists of observing a sample of executions (test cases), and giving a verdict on them. Hence, testing is an execution-based QA activity, so a prerequisite is the existence of the implemented software units, components, or system to be tested. For this reason, it is sometimes called dynamic analysis.
- **Static analysis**: This is a form of V&V that does not require execution of the software. Static analysis works on a source representation of the software: either a model of the specification of design or the source or the program. Perhaps, the most commonly used are inspections and reviews, where a specification, design, or program is checked by a group of people. Additional static analysis techniques may be used, such as automated software analysis (the source code of a program is checked for patterns that are known to be potentially erroneous).

It should be noted that there is a strong divergence of opinion about what types of testing constitute validation or verification. Some authors believe that all testing is verification and that validation is conducted when requirements are reviewed and approved. Other authors view unit and integration testing as verification and higher-order testing (for example, system or user testing) as validation. To solve this divergence, V&V can be treated as a single topic rather than as two separate topics.

Software defects

Key to the correctness aspect of V&V is the concept of software defects. The term **defect** (also known as *bug*) refers to a generic software problem. The IEEE Standard 610.12 propose the following taxonomy related to software defects:

- **Error**: A human action that produces an incorrect result. Errors can be classified into two categories:
    1. Syntax error (program statement that violates one or more rules of the language in which it is written).
    2. Logic error (incorrect data fields, out-of-range terms, or invalid combinations).
- **Fault**: The manifestation of an error in the software system is known as a fault. For example, an incorrect step, process, or data definition.
- **Failure**: The inability of the software system to perform its required functions is known as (system) failure.

 The term *bug* was first coined in 1946 by the software pioneer Grace Hooper, when a moth trapped in rely of an electromechanical computer caused a system malfunction. In this decade, the term *debug* was also introduced, as the process of detecting and correcting defects in a system.

In addition to this level of granularity for defects, it is also interesting to contemplate **incidences** as symptoms associated with a failure perceived by the software consumer. All in all, error, faults, failures, and incidences are different aspects of software defects. A causal relation exists between these four aspects of defects. Errors may cause faults to be injected into the software, and faults may cause failures when the software is executed. Finally, incidences happen when failures are experienced by the final user or costumer. Different QA activities can be carried out to try to minimize the number of defects within a software system. As defined by Jeff Tian in his book *Software Quality Engineering* (2005), the alternatives can be grouped into the following three generic categories:

- Defect prevention through error removal: For example, the use of certain processes and product standards can help to minimize the injection certain kinds of faults into the software.
- Defect reduction through fault detection and removal: The traditional testing and static analysis activities are examples of this category. We discover the specific types of these mechanisms in the body of this chapter.

- Defect containment through failure prevention: These activities are typically out of the scope of the software system. The objective of containment is to minimize the damage caused by software system failures (for example, walls to contain radioactive material in case of reactor failures).

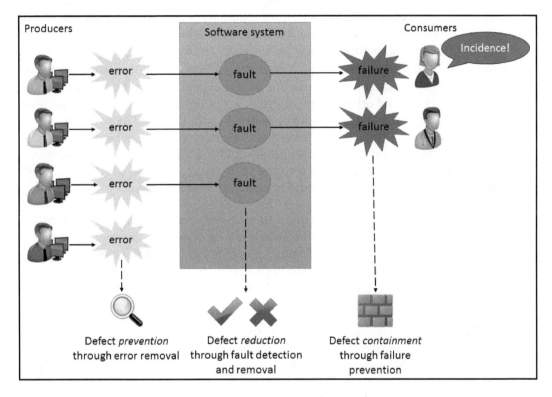

Software defect chain and associated QA activities

Static analysis

Static analysis of a software piece is performed without executing the code. There are several advantages to software analysis over testing:

1. During testing, errors can hide other errors. This situation does not happen with static analysis, because it is not concerned with interactions between errors.
2. Incomplete versions of a system can be statically analyzed without additional cost. In testing, if a program is incomplete, test harnesses have to be developed.
3. Static analysis can consider broader quality attributes of a software system, such as compliance with standards, portability, and maintainability.

There are different methods that can be identified as static analysis:

- **Inspection** (first proposed by Michael Fagan in 1976) are examinations of software artifacts by human inspectors aimed at discovering and fixing faults in the software systems. All kinds of software assets are subject to be inspected, for example the specification, design models, and so on. The primary reason for the existence of inspection is not waiting for the availability of executable programs (such as in testing) before starting performing inspection.

- **Review** is the process in which a group of people examine the software and its associated documentation, looking for potential problems and non-conformance with standards, and other potential problems or omissions. Nowadays, reviews are frequently carried out for new code before being merged in a shared source code repository. Typically, the review is done by a different person to the code author within the same team (**peer review**). This process is quite expensive in terms of time and effort, but on the other side, when correctly performed, it helps to ensure a high internal code quality reducing potential risks.

> A **walkthrough** is a special form of review. According to IEEE Standard for Software Reviews, a walkthrough is a form of software peer review in which a designer or programmer leads members of the development team and other interested parties through a software product, and the participants ask questions and make comments about possible errors, violation of development standards, and other problems.

- **Automated software analysis** assesses the source code using patterns that are known to be potentially dangerous. This technique is usually delivered as commercial or open source tools and services, commonly known as **lint** or **linter**. These tools can locate many common programming faults, analyze the source code before it is tested, and identify potential problems in order to re-code them before they manifest themselves as failures. The intention of this linting process is to draw a code reader's attention to faults in the program, such as:
    1. Data faults: This may include variables declared but never used, variables assigned twice but never used between assignments, and so on.
    2. Control faults: This may include unreachable code or unconditional branches into loops.
    3. Input/output faults: This may include variables output twice with no intervening assignment.
    4. Interface faults: This may include parameter-type mismatches, parameter under mismatches, non-usage of the results of functions, uncalled functions and procedures, and so on.

5. Storage management faults: This may include unassigned pointers, pointers arithmetic, and so on.

Halfway between static analysis and dynamic testing we find an especial way of software evaluation, called **formal verification**. This kind of assessment provides mechanisms to check that a system operates according to its formal specification. To that aim, software is treated as a mathematical entity whose correctness can be proved using logical operations, combining different types of static and dynamic evaluation. Nowadays, formal methods are not widely adopted mainly due to scalability problems. Projects using these techniques are mostly relatively small, such as critical kernel systems. As systems grow, the effort required to develop a formal specification and verification grow excessively.

Software testing

Software testing consists of the dynamic evaluation of the behavior of a program on a finite set of test cases, suitably selected from the usually infinite executions domain, against the expected behavior. The key concepts of this definition are depicted as follows:

- **Dynamic**: The **System Under Test** (SUT) is executed with specific input values to find failures in its behavior. Thus, the actual SUT should ensure that the design and code are correct, and also the environment, such as the libraries, the operating system and network support, and so on.
- **Finite**: Exhaustive testing is not possible or practical for most real programs. They usually have a large number of allowable inputs to each operation, plus even more invalid or unexpected inputs and the possible sequences of operations are usually infinite as well. Testers must choose a number of tests so that we can run the tests in the available time.
- **Selected**: Since there is a huge or infinite set of possible tests and we can can afford to run only a small fraction of them, the key challenge of testing is how to select the tests that are most likely to expose failures in the system.
- **Expected**: After each test execution, it must be decided whether the observed behavior of the system was a failure or not.

Software testing is a broad term encompassing a wide spectrum of different concepts. There is no universal classification for all the different testing forms available in the literature. For the shake of clarity, in this book we classify the different form of tests using three axis, namely testing level (unit, integration, system, and acceptance), testing methods (black-box, white-box, and non-functional testing), and testing types (manual and automated).

Next sections provide more details about all of these concepts, which are summarized in the following diagram:

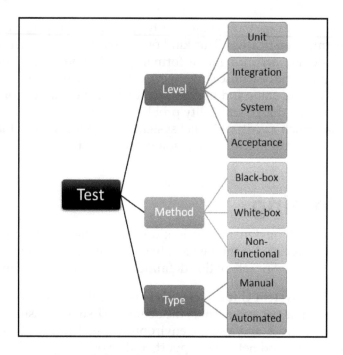

Taxonomy of software testing in three categories: levels, methods, and types

For example, as we will discover, a JUnit test that exercises a method in a class according to its functional behaviour can be seen as an automated unit black-box test. When a final consumer uses a software product to validate if works as expected, according the taxonomy before we can see this as a manual black-box acceptance test. It should be noticed than not all possible combination of these three axes is always meaningful. For instance, non-functional tests (example, performance) is typically carried out automatically and at system levels (it would be very unlikely to do manually or at unit level).

Testing levels

Depending on the size of the SUT and the scenario in which it is exercised, testing can be carried out at different levels. In this book, we classify the different testing levels in four phases:

- **Unit testing**: Here, individual program units are tested. Unit testing should focus on the functionality of objects or methods.

- **Integration testing**: Here, units are combined to create composite components. Integration testing should focus on testing components, interfaces.
- **System testing**: Here, all of the components are integrated and the system is tested as a whole.
- **Acceptance testing**: Here, consumers decide whether or not the system is ready to be deployed in the consumer environment. It can be seen as a high-level functional testing performed at system level by final users or customers.

 There is no universal classification in the many different forms of testing. Regarding testing levels, in this book, we use the aforementioned classification of four levels. Nevertheless, other levels or approaches are present in the literature (for example, *system integration testing* or *regression testing*). In the last part of this section, we can find a review of different testing approaches.

The first three levels (unit, integration, and system) are typically carried out during the development phases of the software life cycle. These tests are typically performed by different roles of software engineers (that is, programmers, testers, QA team, and so on). The objective of these tests is the verification of the system. On the other side, the fourth level (acceptance) is a type of user testing, in which potential or real users are usually involved (validation). The following picture provides a graphical description of these concepts:

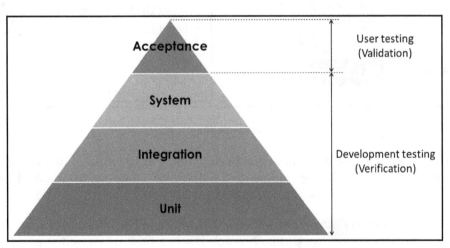

Testing levels and its relationship with V&V

Unit testing

Unit testing is a method by which individual pieces of source code are tested to verify that the design and implementation for that unit have been correctly implemented. There are four phases executed in sequence in a unit test case are the following:

- **Setup**: The test case initializes the *test fixture,* that is the *before* picture required for the SUT to exhibit the expected behavior.
- **Exercise**: The test case interacts with the SUT, getting some outcome from it as a result. The SUT usually queries another component, named the **Depended-On Component (DOC)**.
- **Verify**: The test case determines whether the expected outcome has been obtained using assertions (also known as predicates).
- **Teardown**: The test case tears down the test fixture to put the SUT back into the initial state.

These phases and its relationship with the SUT and DOC is illustrated as follows:

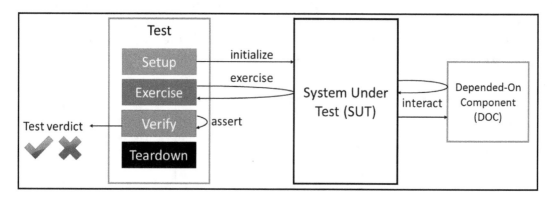

Unit test generic structure

Unit testing is done with the unit under test in isolation, that is, without interacting its DOCs. To that aim, *test doubles* are employed to replace any components on which the SUT depends. There are several kinds of test doubles:

- A **dummy** object simply satisfies the real object API but it is never actually used. The typical use case for dummy objects is when they are passed as parameters to meet the method signature, but then the dummy object is not actually used.
- A **fake** object replaces the real object with a simpler implementation, for example, an in-memory database.

- A **stub** object replaces the real object providing hard-coded values as responses.
- A **mock** object also replaces the real object, but this time with programmed expectations as responses.
- A **spy** object is a partial mock object, meaning that some of its methods are programmed with expectations, but the others use the real object's implementation.

Integration testing

Integration testing should expose defects in the interfaces, and the interaction between integrated components or modules. There are different strategies for performing integration testing. These strategies describe the order in which units are to be integrated, presuming that the units have been separately tested. Examples of common integration strategies are the following:

- **Top-down integration**: This strategy starts with the main unit (module), that is, the root of the procedural tree. Any lower-level module that is called by the main unit should be substituted by a test double. Once testers are convinced that the main unit logic is correct, the stubs are gradually replaced with the actual code. This process is repeated for the rest of the lower-unit in the procedural tree. The main advantage of this approach is that defects are more easily found.
- **Bottom-up integration**: This strategy starts the testing process with the most elementary units. Larger subsystems are assembled from the tested components. The main advantage of this type is that test doubles are not needed.
- **Ad hoc integration**: The components are integrated in the natural order in which are finished. It allows an early testing of the system. Test doubles are usually required.
- **Backbone integration**: A skeleton of components is built and others are gradually integrated. The main disadvantage of this approach is the creation of the backbone, which can be labor-intensive.

 Another strategy commonly referred in the literature is **big-bang integration**. In this strategy, testers wait until all or most of the units are developed e integrated. As a result, all the failures are found at the same time, making very difficult and time-consuming to correct the underlying faults. If possible, this strategy should be avoided.

System testing

System testing during development involves integrating components to create a version of the system and the testing the integrated system. It verifies that the components are compatible, interacts correctly, and transfer the right data at the right time, topically across its user interfaces. It obviously overlaps with integration testing, but the difference here is that system testing should involve all the system components together with the final user (typically impersonated).

There is an special type of system testing called *end-to-end testing*. In this approach, the final user is typically impersonated, that is, simulated using automation techniques.

Testing methods

Testing methods (or strategies) define the way for designing test cases. They can be responsibility based (**black-box**), implementation based (**white box**), or **non-functional**. Black-box techniques design test cases on the basis of the specified functionality of the item to be tested. White-box ones rely on source code analysis to develop test cases. Hybrid techniques (grey-box) testing designs test cases using both responsibility-based and implementation-based approaches.

Black-box testing

Black-box testing (also known as **functional** or **behavioral** testing) is based on requirements with no knowledge of the internal program structure or data. Black-box testing relies on the specification of the system or the component that is being tested to derive test cases. The system is a black-box whose behavior can only be determined by studying its inputs and the related outputs. There are a lot of specific black-box testing techniques; some of the most well-known ones are described as follows:

- **Systematic testing**: This refers to a complete testing approach in which SUT is shown to conform exhaustively to a specification, up to the testing assumptions. It generates test cases only in the limiting sense that each domain point is a singleton sub-domain. Inside this category, some of the most commonly performed are *equivalence partitioning* and *boundary value analysis*, and also logic-based techniques, such as *cause-effect graphing*, *decision table*, or *pairwise testing*.

- **Random testing**: This is literally the antithesis of systematic testing -the sampling is over the entire input domain-. *Fuzz testing* is a form of black-box random testing, which randomly mutates well-formed inputs and tests the program on the resulting data. It delivers randomly sequenced and/or structurally bad data to a system to see if failures occur.
- **Graphic User Interface (GUI) testing**: This is the process of ensuring the specification of software with a graphic interface interacting with the user. GUI testing is event-driven (for example, mouse movements or menu selections) and provides a frontend to the underlying application code through messages or method calls. GUI testing at unit level is used typically at the button level. GUI testing at system level exercises the event-driven nature of the SUT.
- **Model-based testing (MBT)**: This is a testing strategy in which test cases are derived in part from a model that describes some (if not all) aspects of the SUT. MBT is a form of black-box testing because tests are generated from a model, which is derived from the requirements documentation. It can be done at different levels (unit, integration, or system).
- **Smoke testing**: This is the process of ensuring the critical functionality of the SUT. A smoke test case is the first to be run by testers before accepting a build for further testing. Failure of a smoke test case will mean that the software build is refused. The name of *smoke testing* derives electrical system testing, whereby the first test was to switch on and see if it smoked.

- **Sanity testing**: This is the process of ensuring the basic functionality of the SUT. Similarly to smoke testing, sanity tests are performed at the beginning of the test process, but its objective is different. Sanity tests are supposed to ensure that the SUT basic features continue working as expected (i.e. the *rationality* of the SUT), before conducting more exhaustive tests.

 Smoke and sanity testing are usually confusing terms in the software testing community. It is commonly accepted that both kind of tests are performed to avoid wasting effort in rigorous testing when these tests fail, being the main difference their target (critical vs. basic functionality).

White-box testing

White-box testing (also known as **structural** testing) is based on knowledge of the internal logic of an application's code. It determines if the program-code structure and logic is faulty. White-box test cases are accurate only if the tester knows what the program is supposed to do.

Black-box testing uses only the specification to identify use cases, while white-box testing uses the program source code (implementation) as the basis of test case identification. Both approaches, used in conjunction, should be necessary in order to select a good set of test cases for the SUT. Some of the most significant white-box techniques are as follows:

- **Code coverage** defines the degree of source code, which has been tested, for example, in terms of percentage of LOCs. There are several criteria for the code coverage:
    1. Statement coverage: The line of code coverage granularity.
    2. Decision (branch) coverage: Control structure (for example, if-else) coverage granularity.
    3. Condition coverage: Boolean expression (true-false) coverage granularity.
    4. Paths coverage: Every possible route coverage granularity.
    5. Function coverage: Program functions coverage granularity.
    6. Entry/exit coverage: Call and return of the coverage granularity.
- **Fault injection** is the process of injecting faults into software to determine how well (or badly) some SUT behaves. Defects can be said to propagate, and in that case, their effects are visible in program states beyond the state in which the error existed (a fault became a failure).
- **Mutation testing** validates tests and their data by running them against many copies of the SUT containing different, single, and deliberately inserted changes. Mutation testing helps to identify omissions in the code.

Non-functional testing

The **non-functional** aspects of a system can require considerable effort to test. Within this group it can be found different means of testing, for example, performance testing conducted to evaluate the compliance of a SUT with specified performance requirements. These requirements usually include constraints about the time behavior and resource usage. *Performance testing* may measure response time with a single user exercising the system or with multiple users exercising the system. *Load testing* is focused on increasing the load on the system to some stated or implied maximum load, to verify the system can handle the defined system boundaries. *Volume testing* is often considered synonymous with load testing, yet volume testing focuses on data. *Stress testing* exercises beyond normal operational capacity to the extent that the system fails, identifying actual boundaries at which the system breaks. The aim of stress testing is to observe how the system fails and where the bottlenecks are.

Security testing tries to ensure the following concepts: confidentiality (protection against the disclosure of information), integrity (ensuring the correctness of the information), authentication (ensuring the identity of the user), authorization (determining that a user is allowed to receive a service or perform an operation), availability (ensuring that the system performs its functionality when required), and non-repudiation (ensuring the denial that an action happened). Authorized attempts for evaluating the security of system infrastructure is often known as *penetration testing*.

Usability testing focuses on finding user interface problems, which may make the software difficult to use or may cause users to misinterpret the output. *Accessibility testing* is the technique of making sure that our product is accessibility (the ability to access the system functionality) compliant.

Testing types

There are two main types to carrying out software testing:

- **Manual testing**: This is the process of assessing the SUT is done by a human, typically a software engineer or the final consumer. In this type of testing, we can find the so-called *exploratory testing*, which is a type of manual testing in which human testers evaluate the system by investigating and freely evaluating the system using its personal perception.
- **Automated testing**: This is the process of assessing the SUT in which the testing process (test execution, reporting, and so on) is carried out with special software and infrastructure for testing. Elfriede Dustin, in her book *Implementing Automated Software Testing: How to Save Time and Lower Costs While Raising Quality* (2009), defined **Automated Software Testing** (**AST**) as the:

Application and implementation of software technology throughout the entire software testing life cycle with the goal to improve efficiencies and effectiveness.

The main benefits of AST are: anticipated cost savings, shortened test duration, heightened thoroughness of the tests performed, improvement of test accuracy, improvement of result reporting as well as statistical processing, and subsequent reporting.

 Automated tests are typically executed in build servers in the context of **Continuous Integration** (**CI**) processes. More details about this are provided in chapter 7, *Testing Management*.

AST is most effective when implemented within a *framework*. Testing frameworks may be defined as a set of abstract concepts, processes, procedures and environments in which automated tests will be designed, created, and implemented. This framework definition includes the physical structures used for test creation and implementation, as well as the logical interactions among those components.

Strictly speaking, that definition of framework is not very far from what we can understand by library. In order to make the difference clearer, consider the following quote from the well-known software engineering guru Martin Folwer:

> *A library is essentially a set of functions that you can call, these days usually organized into classes. Each call does some work and returns control to the client. A framework embodies some abstract design, with more behavior built in. In order to use it you need to insert your behavior into various places in the framework either by subclassing or by plugging in your own classes. The framework's code then calls your code at these points.*

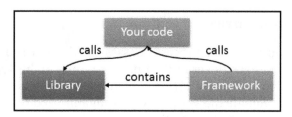

Visual explanation of the difference between library and framework

Frameworks are becoming more and more important in modern software development. They provide a capability highly desired in software-intensive systems: reusability. This way, large applications will end up consisting of layers of frameworks that cooperate with each other.

Other testing approaches

As introduced at the beginning of this section, there is no an universal definition for the different forms of testing. In this section we review some of the most commonly varieties of testing available in the literature not covered so far. For instance, when the testing process is performed to determine whether the system meets its specifications, it is known as *conformance testing*. When a new feature or functionality is introduced to a system (we can call it a build), the way of testing this new feature in known as *progression testing*. In addition to that, to check that the new introduced changes do not affect the correctness of the rest of the system, the existing test cases are exercised. This approach is commonly known as *regression testing*.

When the system interacts with any external or third-party system, another testing could be done, known as *system integration testing*. This kind of testing verifies that the system is integrated to any external systems properly.

User or customer testing is a stage in the testing process in which users or customers provide input and advice for system testing. *Acceptance testing* is a type of user testing, but there can also be different types of *user testing*:

- **Alpha testing**: This takes place at developers' sites, working together with the software's consumers, before it is released to external users or customers.
- **Beta testing**: This takes place at customer's sites and involves testing by a group of customers who use the system at their own locations and provide feedback, before the system is released to other customers.
- **Operational testing**: This is performed by the end user in its normal operating environment.

Finally, *release testing* refers to the process of testing a particular release of a system performed by a separate team outside the development team. The primary goal of the release testing process is to convince the supplier of the system that is good enough for use.

Testing frameworks for the JVM

JUnit is a testing framework which allows to create automated tests. The development of JUnit was started by Kent Beck and Erich Gamma in late 1995. Since then, the popularity of the framework has been growing. Nowadays, it is broadly considered as the *de facto* standard for testing Java applications.

JUnit was designed to be a unit-testing framework. Nevertheless, it can be used to implement not just unit tests, but also other kinds of tests. As we will discover in the body of this book, depending on how the test logic exercises the piece of software under test, a test case implemented with JUnit can be considered as an unit, integration, system, and even acceptance test. All in all, we can think of JUnit as a multi-purpose testing framework for Java.

JUnit 3

Since the early versions of JUnit 3, the framework can work with Java 2 and higher. JUnit3 is open source software, released under **Common Public License** (CPL) Version 1.0 and hosted on SourceForge (`https://sourceforge.net/projects/junit/`). The latest version of JUnit 3 was JUnit 3.8.2, released on May 14, 2007. The main requirements introduced by JUnit in the world of testing frameworks were the following:

1. It should be easy to define which tests will run.
2. The framework should be able to run tests independently of all other tests.
3. The framework should detect and report errors test by test.

Standard tests in JUnit 3

In JUnit 3, in order to create test cases, we need to extend the class `junit.framework.TestCase`. This base class includes the framework code that JUnit needs to automatically run the tests. Then, we simply make sure that the method name follows the `testXXX()` pattern. This naming convention makes it clear to the framework that the method is a unit test and that it can be run automatically.

The test life cycle is controlled in the `setup()` and `tearDown()` methods. The `TestCase` calls `setup()` before running each of its tests and then calls `teardown()` when each test is complete. One reason to put more than one test method into the same test case is to share the same test fixture.

Finally, in order to implement the verification stage in the test case, JUnit 3 defines several assert methods in a utility class named `junit.framework.Assert`. The following table summarizes the main assertions provided by this class:

Method	Description
`assertTrue`	Asserts that a condition is true. If it isn't, the method throws an `AssertionFailedError` with the given message (if any).
`assertFalse`	Asserts that a condition is false. If it isn't, the method throws an `AssertionFailedError` with the given message (if any).
`assertEquals`	Asserts that two objects are equal. If they are not, the method throws an `AssertionFailedError` with the given message (if any).
`assertNotNull`	Asserts that an object is not null. If it is, the method throws an `AssertionFailedError` with the message (if any).

assertNull	Asserts that an object is null. If it isn't, the method throws an `AssertionFailedError` with the given message (if any).
assertSame	Asserts that two objects refer to the same object. If they do not, the method throws an `AssertionFailedError` with the given message (if any).
assertNotSame	Asserts that two objects do not refer to the same object. If they do, the method throws an `AssertionFailedError` with the given message (if any).
fail	Fails a test (throwing `AssertionFailedError`) with the given message (if any).

The following class shows a simple test implemented with JUnit 3.8.2. As we can see, this test case contains two tests. Before each test, the method `setUp()` will be invoked by the framework, and after the execution of each test, the method `tearDown()` will be also invoked. This example has been coded so that the first test, named `testSuccess()` finishes correctly, and the second test named `testFailure()` ends with an error (the assertion throws an exception):

```
package io.github.bonigarcia;

import junit.framework.TestCase;

public class TestSimple extends TestCase {

    // Phase 1: Setup (for each test)
    protected void setUp() throws Exception {
        System.out.println("<Setup>");
    }

    // Test 1: This test is going to succeed
    public void testSuccess() {
        // Phase 2: Simulation of exercise
        int expected = 60;
        int real = 60;
        System.out.println("** Test 1 **");

        // Phase 3: Verify
        assertEquals(expected + " should be equals to "
        + real, expected, real);
    }

    // Test 2: This test is going to fail
    public void testFailure() {
        // Phase 2: Simulation of exercise
        int expected = 60;
```

```
    int real = 20;
    System.out.println("** Test 2 **");

    // Phase 3: Verify
    assertEquals(expected + " should be equals to "
     + real, expected, real);
}

// Phase 4: Teardown (for each test)
protected void tearDown() throws Exception {
    System.out.println("</Ending>");
}

}
```

All the code examples explained in this book are available on the GitHub
repository https://github.com/bonigarcia/mastering-junit5.

Test execution in JUnit 3

JUnit 3 allows to run test cases by means of Java applications called test runners. JUnit 3.8.2 provides three different test runners out of the box: two graphical (Swing and AWT based) and one textual that can be used from the command line. The JUnit framework provides separate class loaders for each test, in order to avoid side effects among tests.

It is a common practice that build tools (such as Ant or Maven) and **Integrated Development Environments -IDE-** (such as Eclipse and IntelliJ) implement its own JUnit test runner.

The following image shows what the previous test looks like when we use the JUnit Swing runner, and also when we use Eclipse to run the same test case.

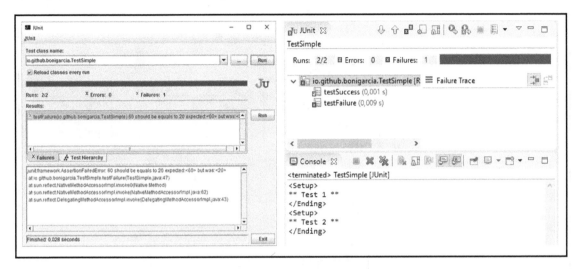

Execution of an JUnit 3 test case using the graphical Swing test runner and also with the Eclipse test runner

When a test is not succeeded in JUnit, it can be for two reasons: a failure or an error. On the one hand, a failure is caused by an assertion (`Assert` class) which is not meet. On the other hand, an error is an unexpected condition not expected by the test, such as a conventional exception in the software under test.

Another important contribution of JUnit 3 is the concept of the test suite, which is a convenient way to group tests that are related. Test suites are implemented by means of the JUnit class `junit.framework.TestSuite`. This class, in the same way as `TestCase`, implements the framework interface `junit.framework.Test`.

A diagram containing the main classes and methods of JUnit 3 is depicted as follows:

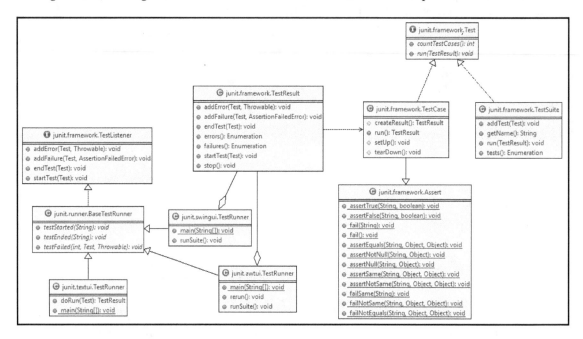

Core JUnit 3 classes

The following snippet shows an example of the use of test suites in JUnit 3. In short, we can create a group of tests simply instantiating a `TestSuite` object, and then add single test cases using the method `addTestSuite()`:

```
package io.github.bonigarcia;

import junit.framework.Test;
import junit.framework.TestSuite;

public class TestAll {

    public static Test suite() {
        TestSuite suite = new TestSuite("All tests");
        suite.addTestSuite(TestSimple.class);
        suite.addTestSuite(TestMinimal.class);
        return suite;
    }
}
```

This test suite can be later executed using a test runner. For example, we could use the command-line test runner (`junit.textui.TestRunner`) and the command line, as follows:

```
D:\junit3>java -cp .;junit-3.8.2.jar junit.textui.TestRunner io.github.bonigarcia.TestAll
.<Setup>
** Test 1 **
</Ending>
.<Setup>
** Test 2 **
</Ending>
F.
Time: 0,005
There was 1 failure:
1) testFailure(io.github.bonigarcia.TestSimple)junit.framework.AssertionFailedError: 60 should be
  equals to 20 expected:<60> but was:<20>
        at io.github.bonigarcia.TestSimple.testFailure(TestSimple.java:47)
        at sun.reflect.NativeMethodAccessorImpl.invoke0(Native Method)
        at sun.reflect.NativeMethodAccessorImpl.invoke(NativeMethodAccessorImpl.java:62)
        at sun.reflect.DelegatingMethodAccessorImpl.invoke(DelegatingMethodAccessorImpl.java:43)

FAILURES!!!
Tests run: 3,  Failures: 1,  Errors: 0
```

Test suite executed using the textual test runner and the command line

JUnit 4

JUnit 4 is still an open source framework, though the license changed with respect to JUnit 3, from CPL to **Eclipse Public License** (**EPL**) Version 1.0. The source code of JUnit 4 is hosted on GitHub (`https://github.com/junit-team/junit4/`).

On February 18, 2006, JUnit 4.0 was released. It follows the same high-level guidelines than JUnit 3, that is, easily define test, the framework run tests independently, and the framework detects and report errors by the test.

One of the main differences of JUnit 4 with respect to JUnit 3 is the way that JUnit 4 allows to define tests. In JUnit 4, Java annotations are used to mark methods as tests. For this reason, JUnit 4 can only be used for Java 5 or later. As the documentation of JUnit 4.0 stated back in 2006:

The architecture of JUnit 4.0 is a substantial departure from that of earlier releases. Instead of tagging test classes by subclassing junit.framework.TestCase and tagging test methods by starting their name with 'test', you now tag test methods with the @Test annotation.

Standard tests in JUnit 4

In JUnit 4, the `@Test` annotation (contained in package `org.junit`) represents a test. Any public method can be annotated with `@Test` to make it a test method.

In order to set up the test fixture, JUnit 4 provides the `@Before` annotation. This annotation can be used in any public method. Similarly, any public method annotated with `@After` gets executed after each test method execution. JUnit 4 provides two more annotations to enhance the test life cycle: `@BeforeClass` and `@AfterClass`. They are executed only once per test class, before and after all tests, respectively. The following picture depicts the life cycle of a JUnit 4 test case:

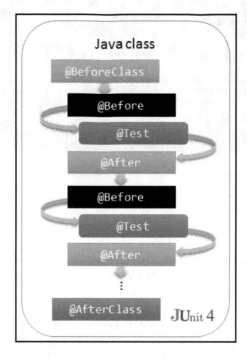

JUnit 4 test life cycle

 `@Before` and `@After` can be applied to any public void methods. `@AfterClass` and `@BeforeClass` can be applied to only public static void methods.

The following table summarizes the main differences between JUnit 3 and JUnit 4 seen so far:

Feature	JUnit 3	JUnit 4
Test definition	`testXXX` pattern	`@Test` annotation
Run before the first test	Not supported	`@BeforeClass` annotation
Run after all the tests	Not supported	`@AfterClass` annotation
Run before each test	Override `setUp()` method	`@Before` annotation
Run after each test	Override `tearDown()` method	`@After` annotation
Ignore tests	Not supported	`@Ignore` annotation

The `org.junit.Assert` class provides static methods to carry out assertions (predicates). The following are the most useful assertion methods:

- `assertTrue`: If the condition becomes false, the assertion fails and `AssertionError` is thrown.
- `assertFalse`: If the condition becomes true, the assertion fails and `AssertionError` is thrown.
- `assertNull`: This checks whether the argument is null, otherwise throws `AssertionError` if the argument is not `null`.
- `assertNotNull`: This checks whether the argument is not null; otherwise, it throws `AssertionError`
- `assertEquals`: This compares two objects or primitive types. Moreover, if the actual value doesn't match the expected value, `AssertionError` is thrown.
- `assertSame`: This supports only objects and checks the object reference using the == operator.
- `assertNotSame`: This is the opposite of `assertSame`.

The following snippets provide a simple example of a JUnit 4 test case. As we can see, it is the equivalent test case as seen in the previous section, this time using the JUnit 4 programming model, that is, using `@Test` annotation to identify tests and other annotations (`@AfterAll`, `@After`, `@BeforeAll`, `@Before`) to implement the test life cycle (setup and teardown test fixture):

```
package io.github.bonigarcia;

import static org.junit.Assert.assertEquals;
```

```java
import org.junit.After;
import org.junit.AfterClass;
import org.junit.Before;
import org.junit.BeforeClass;
import org.junit.Test;

public class TestSimple {

    // Phase 1.1: Setup (for all tests)
    @BeforeClass
    public static void setupAll() {
        System.out.println("<Setup Class>");
    }

    // Phase 1.2: Setup (for each test)
    @Before
    public void setupTest() {
        System.out.println("<Setup Test>");
    }

    // Test 1: This test is going to succeed
    @Test
    public void testSuccess() {
        // Phase 2: Simulation of exercise
        int expected = 60;
        int real = 60;
        System.out.println("** Test 1 **");

        // Phase 3: Verify
        assertEquals(expected + " should be equals to "
          + real, expected, real);
    }

    // Test 2: This test is going to fail
    @Test
    public void testFailure() {
        // Phase 2: Simulation of exercise
        int expected = 60;
        int real = 20;
        System.out.println("** Test 2 **");

        // Phase 3: Verify
        assertEquals(expected + " should be equals to "
          + real, expected, real);
    }

    // Phase 4.1: Teardown (for each test)
    @After
```

```java
public void teardownTest() {
    System.out.println("</Ending Test>");
}

// Phase 4.2: Teardown (for all test)
@AfterClass
public static void teardownClass() {
    System.out.println("</Ending Class>");
}

}
```

Test execution in JUnit 4

The concept of the test runner is also present in JUnit 4, but it was slightly improved with respect to JUnit 3. In JUnit 4, a test runner is a Java class used to manage a test's life cycle: instantiation, calling setup and teardown methods, running the test, handling exceptions, sending notifications, and so on. The default JUnit 4 test runner is called `BlockJUnit4ClassRunner`, and it implements the JUnit 4 standard test case class model.

The test runner to be used in a JUnit 4 test case can be changed simply using the annotation `@RunWith`. JUnit 4 provides a collection of built-in test runners that allows to change the nature of the test class. In this section, we are going to review the most important ones.

- To run a group of tests (that is, a test suite) JUnit 4 provides the `Suite` runner. In addition to the runner, the class `Suite.SuiteClasses` allows to define the individual test classes belonging to the suite. For example:

  ```java
  package io.github.bonigarcia;

  import org.junit.runner.RunWith;
  import org.junit.runners.Suite;

  @RunWith(Suite.class)
  @Suite.SuiteClasses({ TestMinimal1.class, TestMinimal2.class })
  public class MySuite {
  }
  ```

- Parameterized tests are used to specify different input data that is going to be used in the same test logic. To implement this kind of tests, JUnit 4 provides the `Parameterized` runner. To define the data parameters in this type of test, we need to annotate a static method of the class with the annotation `@Parameters`. This method should return a `Collection` of the two-dimensional array providing input parameters for the test. Now, there will be two options to inject the input data into the test:
    1. Using the constructor class.
    2. Annotating class attributes with the annotation `@Parameter`.

The following snippets show an example of the latter:

```java
package io.github.bonigarcia;

import static org.junit.Assert.assertTrue;

import java.util.Arrays;
import java.util.Collection;
import org.junit.Test;
import org.junit.runner.RunWith;
import org.junit.runners.Parameterized;
import org.junit.runners.Parameterized.Parameter;
import org.junit.runners.Parameterized.Parameters;

@RunWith(Parameterized.class)
public class TestParameterized {

    @Parameter(0)
    public int input1;

    @Parameter(1)
    public int input2;

    @Parameter(2)
    public int sum;

    @Parameters(name = "{index}: input1={0} input2={1} sum={2}?")
    public static Collection<Object[]> data() {
        return Arrays.asList(
                new Object[][] { { 1, 1, 2 }, { 2, 2, 4 }, { 3, 3, 9 } });
    }

    @Test
    public void testSum() {
        assertTrue(input1 + "+" + input2 + " is not " + sum,
                input1 + input2 == sum);
```

```
        }

    }
```

The execution of this test on Eclipse would be as follows:

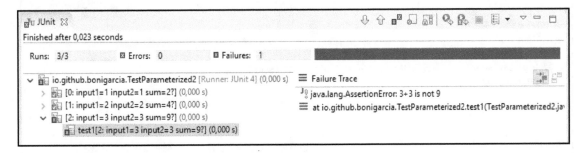

Execution of a Parameterized test in Eclipse

- JUnit theories are an alternative to JUnit's parameterized tests. A JUnit theory is expected to be true for all datasets. Thus, in JUnit theories, we have a method providing data points (that is, the input values to be used for the test). Then, we need to specific a method annotated with @Theory which takes parameters. The theories in a class get executed with every possible combination of data points:

```java
package io.github.bonigarcia;

import static org.junit.Assert.assertTrue;

import org.junit.experimental.theories.DataPoints;
import org.junit.experimental.theories.Theories;
import org.junit.experimental.theories.Theory;
import org.junit.runner.RunWith;

@RunWith(Theories.class)
public class MyTheoryTest {

    @DataPoints
    public static int[] positiveIntegers() {
        return new int[] { 1, 10, 100 };
    }

    @Theory
    public void testSum(int a, int b) {
        System.out.println("Checking " + a + "+" + b);
        assertTrue(a + b > a);
        assertTrue(a + b > b);
```

```
      }
   }
```

Take a look at the execution of this example, again in Eclipse:

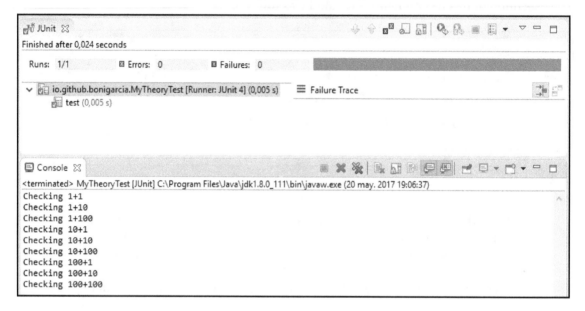

Execution of a JUnit 4 theory in Eclipse

Advanced features of JUnit 4

One of the most significant innovations introduced in JUnit 4 was the use of *rules*. Rules allow flexible addition or redefinition of the behavior of each test method in a test class. A rule should be included in a test case by annotating a class attribute with the annotation @Rule. The type of this attribute should inherit the JUnit interface org.junit.rulesTestRule. The following rules are provided out of the box in JUnit 4:

- ErrorCollector: This rule allows execution of a test to continue after the first problem is found
- ExpectedException: This rule allows to verify that a test throws a specific exception
- ExternalResource: This rule provides a base class for Rules that set up an external resource before a test (a file, socket, server, database connection, and so on) and guarantee to tear it down afterward

- `TestName`: This rule makes the current test name available inside test methods
- `TemporaryFolder`: This rule allows creation of files and folders that should be deleted when the test method finishes
- `Timeout`: This rule applies the same timeout to all test methods in a class
- `TestWatcher`: It is a base class for rules that will keep a log of each passing and failing test

Another advance JUnit 4 features allow to:

- Execute tests is a given order, using the annotation `@FixMethodOrder`.
- Create assumptions using the class Assume. This class offers many static methods, such as `assumeTrue(condition)`, `assumeFalse(condition)`, `assumeNotNull(condition)`, and `assumeThat(condition)`. Before executing a test, JUnit checks the assumptions present in the test. If one of the assumptions fail, the JUnit runner ignores the tests with failing assumptions.
- JUnit provides a timeout value (in milliseconds) in the `@Test` annotation to make sure that if a test runs longer than the specified value, the test fails.
- Categorize tests using the test runner `Categories` and identify the types of test annotating the tests method with the annotation `Category`.

 Meaningful examples for each of one of the earlier mentioned features can be found in the GitHub repository (`https://github.com/bonigarcia/mastering-junit5`).

JUnit ecosystem

JUnit is one of the most popular test frameworks for the JVM, and it is considered one of the most influential frameworks in software engineering. We can find several libraries and frameworks that provide additional functionality on top of JUnit. Some examples of these ecosystem enhancers are:

- Mockito (`http://site.mockito.org/`): This is the mock framework, which can be used in conjunction with JUnit.
- AssertJ (`http://joel-costigliola.github.io/assertj/`): This is the fluent assertions library for Java.
- Hamcrest (`http://hamcrest.org/`): This is the library with matchers that can be combined to create flexible and readable assertions.

- Cucumber (https://cucumber.io/): This is the testing framework that allows to run automated acceptance tests written in a **Behavior-Driven Development (BDD)** style.
- FitNesse (http://www.fitnesse.org/): This is the testing framework designed to support acceptance testing by facilitating detailed readable descriptions of system functions.

While JUnit is the largest testing framework for the JVM, it is not the only one. There are several other testing frameworks available for the JVM. Some examples are:

- TestNG (http://testng.org/): This is the testing framework inspired from JUnit and NUnit.
- Spock (http://spockframework.org/): This is the testing and specification framework for Java and Groovy applications.
- Jtest (https://www.parasoft.com/product/jtest/): This is the automated Java testing and static analysis framework made and distributed by the company Parasoft.
- Scalatest (http://www.scalatest.org/): This is the testing framework for Scala, Scala.js (JavaScript), and Java applications.

Thanks to JUnit, testing has moved to a central part of programming. Consequently, the underlying testing model implemented in JUnit, has been ported to a set of testing frameworks outside the boundary of the JVM, in the so-called xUnit family. In this model, we find the concepts of test case, runner, fixture, suite, test execution, report, and assertion. To name a few, consider the following frameworks. All of them fall into the xUnit family:

- Google Test (https://github.com/google/googletest): Google's C++ testing framework.
- JSUnit (http://www.jsunit.net/): Unit testing framework for JavaScript.
- Mocha (https://mochajs.org/): Unit testing framework running on Node.js.
- NUnit (https://www.nunit.org/): Unit testing framework for Microsoft.NET.
- PHPUnit (https://phpunit.de/): Unit testing framework for PHP.
- SimplyVBUnit (http://simplyvbunit.sourceforge.net/): Unit testing framework for VB.NET.
- Unittest (https://docs.python.org/3/library/unittest.html): Unit testing framework for Python.

Summary

Software quality is a key concept in software engineering, since it determines the degree in which a software system meets its requirements and user expectations. Verification and Validation is the name given to set of activities aimed to assess a software system. The goal of V&V is to ensure the quality of a piece of software while reducing the number of defects. The two core activities in V&V are *software testing* (evaluation of a running piece of software) and *static analysis* (assessment of software artefacts without its execution).

Automated software testing has experienced biggest advances in the last few decades. In this arena, the *JUnit framework* has a remarkable position. JUnit was designed to be a unit framework for the JVM. Nowadays, it is a fact that JUnit is the most popular test frameworks in the Java community, providing a comprehensive programming model to create and execute test cases. In the next section, we will discover the features and capabilities provided by the new version of the framework, JUnit 5.

2

What's New In JUnit 5

Those who can imagine anything, can create the impossible.
- Alan Turing

JUnit is the most important testing framework for the JVM and one of the most influential in software engineering in general. JUnit 5 is the next generation of JUnit, and its first **General Availability (GA)** version (5.0.0) was released on September 10, 2017. As we will discover, JUnit 5 supposes a small revolution with respect to JUnit 4, providing a completely new architecture, programming, and extension model. This chapter covers the following content:

- **Road to JUnit 5**: In the first section, we will discover the motivation to create a new major version of JUnit (that is, the limitations of JUnit 4), the design principles guiding the development of JUnit 5, and finally the details of the JUnit 5 open source community.
- **JUnit 5 architecture**: JUnit 5 is a modular framework composed of three major components, named Platform, Jupiter, and Vintage.
- **Running tests in JUnit 5**: We will discover how to run JUnit 5 tests using popular build tools, such as Maven or Gradle, and also with IDEs such as IntelliJ or Eclipse.
- **The extension model of JUnit 5**: The extension model allows for third-party libraries and frameworks to extend the JUnit 5 programming model with their own additions.

Road to JUnit 5

Software testing has changed a lot since the first release of JUnit 4 in 2006. Since then, not only have Java and the JVM has evolved, but also our testing needs matured. We are not writing just unit tests anymore. Instead, in addition to verifying a single piece of code, software engineers and testers demand other kinds of tests, such as integration and end-to-end tests.

In addition, our expectations about testing frameworks have grown. Nowadays, we demand advanced capabilities for these frameworks, such as extensibility or modularity, to name a few. In this section, we discover the main limitations of JUnit 4, the vision of JUnit 5, and the community supporting its development.

JUnit 5 motivation

According to several studies, JUnit 4 is the most used library for Java projects. For instance, *The Top 100 Java libraries on GitHub* is a well-known report published by OverOps (@overopshq), a software analytics company focused on large-scale Java and Scala code bases.

In its edition of 2017, this report analyzed the import statements of unique Java libraries that are used by the top 1,000 Java projects on GitHub (by stars). In the light of the results, JUnit 4 is the undisputed king of Java Libraries: the imports of the packages `org.junit` and `org.junit.runner` appear in the first and second position, respectively:

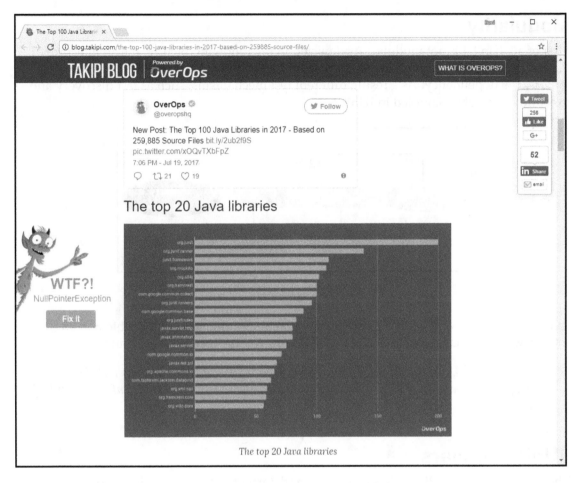

The Top 20 Java libraries on GitHub

Despite this fact, JUnit 4 is a framework created more than a decade ago, and there are important several limitations that impose a complete redesign of the framework.

Modularity

First of all, JUnit 4 is not modular. As depicted in the following picture, the architecture of JUnit 4 is completely monolithic. All the capabilities of JUnit 4 are provided by the `junit.jar` dependency. As a result, different test mechanisms, such as test discovery and execution, are tightly coupled in JUnit 4.

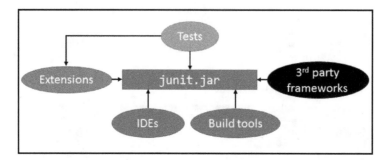

The JUnit 4 Architecture

Johannes Link, one of the JUnit 5 core team members, summarizes this problem in an interview for Jax magazine on August 13, 2015 (during the inception of JUnit 5):

> *The success of JUnit as a platform prevents the development of JUnit as a test tool. The basic problem we want to solve is executing test cases by separating a sufficiently powerful and stable API.*

JUnit 4 runners

The JUnit 4's runner API also has an important deterrent. As described in `chapter 1`, *Retrospective on software quality and Java testing*, in JUnit 4 a runner is a Java class used to manage a test's life cycle. The runner API in JUnit 4 is quite powerful, nevertheless, it has an important drawback: runners are not composable, that is, we can only use a single runner at a time.

For example, a parameterized test cannot be combined with the Spring test support, due to the fact that both tests would use their own runner implementation. Thinking in Java (see the snippets given follow), each test case uses its own unique @RunWith annotation. The first one uses the Parameterized runner:

```
import org.junit.Test;
import org.junit.runner.RunWith;
import org.junit.runners.Parameterized;

@RunWith(Parameterized.class)
public class MyParameterizedTest {

    @Test
    public void myFirstTest() {
        // my test code
    }

}
```

While this second example is using the SpringJUnit4ClassRunner runner, it would not be combined with the previous one due to a limitation on JUnit 4 (runners are not composable):

```
import org.junit.Test;
import org.junit.runner.RunWith;
import org.springframework.test.context.junit4.SpringJUnit4ClassRunner;

@RunWith(SpringJUnit4ClassRunner.class)
public class MySpringTest {

    @Test
    public void yetAnotherTest() {
        // my test code
    }

}
```

JUnit 4 rules

Due to the strict limitation of uniqueness of a JUnit 4 runner within the same test class, version 4.7 of JUnit introduced the concept of method-level rules, which are annotated fields in a test class with `@Rule`. These rules allow for addition or redefinition of test behavior by executing some code before and after the execution of the test. JUnit 4.9 also incorporates the concept of class-level rules, which are rules that are executed before and after all tests within the class. These rules are identified by annotating static fields with `@ClassRule`, as shown in the following example:

```java
import org.junit.ClassRule;
import org.junit.Test;
import org.junit.rules.TemporaryFolder;

public class MyRuleTest {

   @ClassRule
   public static TemporaryFolder temporaryFolder = new TemporaryFolder();
   @Test
   public void anotherTest() {
      // my test code
   }

}
```

While rules are simpler and mostly compostable, they have other drawbacks. The main inconvenience when using JUnit 4 rules for complex tests is that we are not able to use a single rule entity for method-level and class-level. At the end of the day, this imposes limitations to customize the life cycle management (the before/after behavior).

JUnit 5 inception

Even though JUnit 4 was the default testing framework for millions of Java developers worldwide, none of the active JUnit maintainers were paid by their employer to do that work. For that reason, and in order to overcome the drawbacks of JUnit 4, in July 2015 Johannes Link and Marc Philipp started the JUnit Lambda crowdfunding campaign (http:/ /junit.org/junit4/junit-lambda-campaign.html) on Indiegogo (an international crowdfunding website):

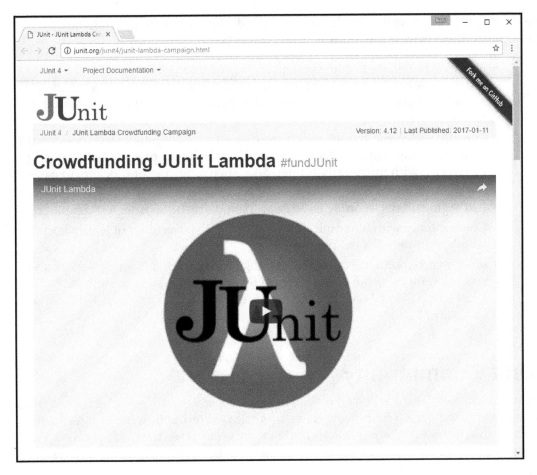

JUnit Lambda Crowdfunding Campaign

JUnit Lambda was the name given to the project, which was the seed of the current JUnit 5 framework. The inclusion of the word lambda in the project name enforces the idea of using Java 8 from the very beginning of the project. Quoting the JUnit Lambda project site:

> *The goal is to create an up-to-date foundation for developer-side testing on the JVM. This includes focusing on Java 8 and above, as well as enabling many different styles of testing.*

The JUnit Lambda Crowdfunding Campaign ran from July to October 2015. It was a success, raising 53,937 euros from 474 individuals and companies worldwide. From this point, the JUnit 5 kick-off team was created, joining people from Eclipse, Gradle, IntelliJ, or Spring.

The JUnit Lambda project became JUnit 5, and the design principles guiding the development process were the follows:

- Modularization: As introduced before, JUnit 4 was not modular, and this causes some problems. From its inception, JUnit 5 architecture is much completely modular, allowing developers to use the specific parts of the framework they require.
- Powerful extension model with focus on composability: Extensibility is a must for modern testing frameworks. Therefore, JUnit 5 should provide seamless integration with third-party frameworks, such as Spring or Mockito, to name a few.
- API segregation: Decouple test discovery and execution from test definition.
- Compatibility with older releases: Supporting the execution of legacy Java 3 and Java 4 in the new JUnit 5 platform.
- Modern programming model for writing tests (Java 8): Nowadays, more and more developers write code with Java 8 new features, such as lambda expressions. JUnit 4 was built on Java 5, but JUnit 5 has been created from scratch using Java 8.

JUnit 5 community

The source code of JUnit 5 is hosted on GitHub (`https://github.com/junit-team/junit5`). All modules of the JUnit 5 framework have been released under the terms of the open source license EPL v1.0. There is one exception to this rule, since the module called `junit-platform-surefire-provider` (described later) has been released using Apache License v2.0.

The roadmap of the JUnit development (`https://github.com/junit-team/junit5/wiki/Roadmap`) and the definition and status of the different releases and milestones (`https://github.com/junit-team/junit5/milestones/`) are public on GitHub. The following table summarizes this roadmap:

Phase	Date	Release
0. Crowdfunding	From July 2015 to October 2015	-
1. Kick off	From October 20 to 22, 2015	-

2. First prototype	From October 23, 2015 to the end of November 2015	-
3. Alpha version	February 1, 2016	5.0 Alpha
4. First milestone	July 9, 2016	5.0 M1: Stable, documented IDE-facing APIs (Launcher API and Engine SPI), dynamic tests
5. Additional milestones	July 23, 2016 (5.0 M2) November 30, 2016 (5.0 M3) April 1, 2017 (5.0 M4) July 5, 2017 (5.0 M5) July 16, 2017 (5.0 M6)	5.0 M2: Bugfix and minor improvement release 5.0 M3: JUnit 4 interoperability, additional discovery selectors 5.0 M4: Test templates, repeated tests, and parameterized tests 5.0 M5: Dynamic containers and minor API changes 5.0 M6: Java 9 compatibility, scenario tests, additional extension APIs for JUnit Jupiter
6. **Release candidate (RC)**	July 30, 2017 July 30, 2017 August 23, 2017	5.0 RC1: Final bug fixes and documentation improvements 5.0 RC2: Fix Gradle consumption of *junit-jupiter-engine* 5.0 RC3: Configuration parameters and bug fixes
7. **General availability (GA)**	September 10, 2017	5.0 GA: First stable release

The JUnit 5 contributors are more than just developers. Contributors are also testers, maintainers, and communicators. At the time of writing, the top JUnit 5 contributors on GitHub are:

- Sam Brannen (`@sam_brannen`): Core Spring Framework and JUnit 5 committer. Enterprise Java Consultant at Swiftmind. Spring & JUnit trainer. Conference speaker.
- Marc Philipp (`@marcphilipp`): Senior Software Engineer on LogMeIn, active contributor to open source projects such as JUnit or Usus. Conference speaker.
- Johannes Link (`@johanneslink`): Programmer and software therapist. JUnit 5 supporter.

• Matthias Merdes: Lead Developer at Heidelberg Mobil GmbH, Germany.

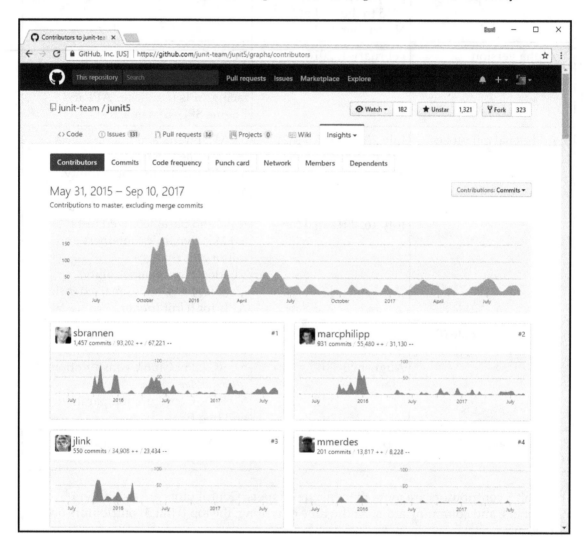

Top JUnit 5 contributors on GitHub

The following list provides a collection of online JUnit 5 resources:

- Official website (`http://junit.org/junit5/`).
- Source code (`https://github.com/junit-team/junit5/`).
- JUnit 5 developer guide (`http://junit.org/junit5/docs/current/user-guide/`). Reference documentation.
- Twitter of the JUnit team (`https://twitter.com/junitteam`). Usually, the tweets about JUnit 5 are tagged with `#JUnit5` (`https://twitter.com/hashtag/JUnit5`).
- Issues (`https://github.com/junit-team/junit5/issues`). Problems or suggestions for additional functionality on GitHub.
- Questions on Stack Overflow (`https://stackoverflow.com/questions/tagged/junit5`). Stack Overflow is a popular question-and-answer website for computer programming. The tag `junit5` should be used to ask questions about JUnit 5.
- JUnit 5 JavaDoc (`http://junit.org/junit5/docs/current/api/`).
- JUnit 5 Gitter (`https://gitter.im/junit-team/junit5`), an instant messaging and chat room system used to discuss directly with the JUnit 5 team members and other practitioners.
- Open Test Alliance for the JVM (`https://github.com/ota4j-team/opentest4j`). It is an initiative started by the JUnit 5 team, and its objective is to provide a minimal common foundation for testing libraries (JUnit, TestNG, Spock, and so on) and third-party assertion libraries (Hamcrest, AssertJ, and so on) on the JVM. The idea is to use a common set of exceptions that IDEs and build tools can support in a consistent manner across all testing scenarios (so far there is no standard for testing on the JVM, and the only common building block is the Java exception `java.lang.AssertionError`).

JUnit 5 architecture

The JUnit 5 framework has been designed to be consumed by different programmatic clients. The first group of clients are Java tests. These tests can be based on JUnit 4 (tests which use the test legacy programming model), JUnit 5 (tests which use the brand new programming model), and even other kinds of Java tests (third party). The second group of clients are build tools (such as Maven or Gradle) and IDEs (such as IntelliJ or Eclipse).

In order to achieve the integration of all these pieces in a loosely coupled manner, JUnit 5 was designed to be modular. As depicted in the following picture, the JUnit 5 framework is composed of three major components, called **Platform**, **Jupiter**, and **Vintage**:

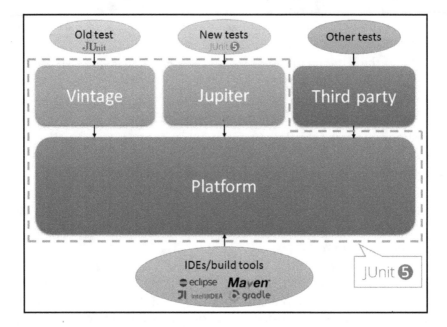

JUnit 5 Architecture: high-level component

The high-level components of the JUnit 5 architecture are enumerated as follows:

- The first high-level component is called *Jupiter*. It provides the brand-new programming and extension model of the JUnit 5 framework.
- In the core of JUnit 5, we find the JUnit *Platform*. This component is aimed to become the foundation for any testing framework executed in the JVM. In other words, it provides mechanisms to run Jupiter tests, legacy JUnit 4, and also third-party tests (for example, Spock, FitNesse, and so on).
- The last high-level component of the JUnit 5 architecture is called *Vintage*. This component allows running legacy JUnit tests on the JUnit Platform out of the box.

Let's take a closer look at the details of each component to find out their internal modules:

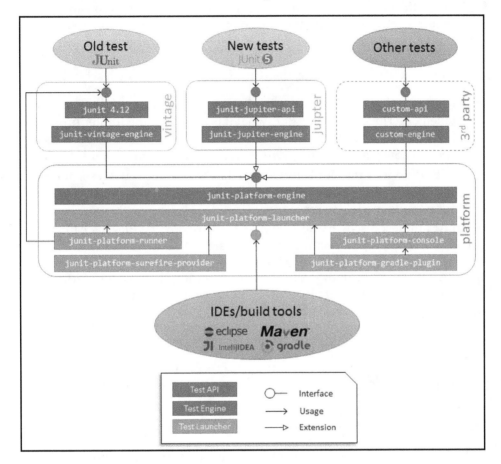

JUnit 5 Architecture: modules

As can be seen in the picture preceding, there are three types of module:

- **Test APIs**: These are the modules facing users (that is, software engineer and testers). These modules provide the programming model for a particular Test Engine (for example, `junit-jupiter-api` for JUnit 5 tests and `junit` for JUnit 4 tests).
- **Test Engines**: These modules allow to execute a kind of test (Jupiter tests, legacy JUnit 4, or other Java tests) within the JUnit Platform. They are created by extending the general *Platform Engine* (`junit-platform-engine`).

- **Test Launcher**: These modules provide the ability of test discovery inside the JUnit platform for external build tools and IDEs. This API is consumed by tools such as Maven, Gradle, IntelliJ, and so on, using the `junit-platform-launcher` module.

As a result of this modular architecture, the JUnit framework exposes a set of interfaces:

- An **API** (**Application Programming Interface**) to write tests, the *Jupiter API*. The detailed description of this API is what it is known as the Jupiter programming model and it is described in detail in `chapters 3`, *JUnit 5 Standard Tests* and `chapter 4`, *Simplifying Testing With Advanced JUnit Features* of this book.
- An **SPI** (**Service Provider Interface**) to discover and execute tests, the *Engine SPI*. This SPI is typically extended by test engines, which in the end provide the programming models to write tests.
- An API for test discovery and execution, the *Launcher API*. This API is typically consumed by programmatic clients, that are IDEs and build tools.

 API and SPI are both a sets of assets (typically classes and interfaces) used by software engineers for a given purpose. The difference is that API is *called* while SPI is *extended*.

Test Engine SPI

The Test Engine SPI allows for creating test executors on top of the JVM. In the JUnit 5 framework, there are two Test Engine implementations out of the box:

- The `junit-vintage-engine`: This allows running JUnit 3 and 4 tests in the JUnit platform.
- The `junit-jupiter-engine`: This allows running JUnit 5 tests in the JUnit platform.

Moreover, third-party test libraries (for example, Spock, TestNG, and so on) can plug into the JUnit Platform by providing a custom Test Engine. To do that, these frameworks should create its own Test Engine by extending the JUnit 5 interface `org.junit.platform.engine.TestEngine`. In order to extend this interface, three mandatory methods must be overridden:

- `getId`: The unique identifier for the test engine.
- `discover`: The logic to find and filter the test(s).

- execute: The logic to run the previously found test(s).

The following example provides the skeleton for a custom Test Engine:

```
package io.github.bonigarcia;

import org.junit.platform.engine.EngineDiscoveryRequest;
import org.junit.platform.engine.ExecutionRequest;
import org.junit.platform.engine.TestDescriptor;
import org.junit.platform.engine.TestEngine;
import org.junit.platform.engine.UniqueId;
import org.junit.platform.engine.support.descriptor.EngineDescriptor;

public class MyCustomEngine implements TestEngine {

    public static final String ENGINE_ID = "my-custom-engine";

    @Override
    public String getId() {
        return ENGINE_ID;
    }

    @Override
    public TestDescriptor discover(EngineDiscoveryRequest discoveryRequest,
            UniqueId uniqueId) {
        // Discover test(s) and return a TestDescriptor object
        TestDescriptor testDescriptor = new EngineDescriptor(uniqueId,
                "My test");
        return testDescriptor;
    }

    @Override
    public void execute(ExecutionRequest request) {
        // Use ExecutionRequest to execute TestDescriptor
        TestDescriptor rootTestDescriptor =
                request.getRootTestDescriptor();
        request.getEngineExecutionListener()
                .executionStarted(rootTestDescriptor);
    }

}
```

 A list of existing Test Engines (for example, Specsy, Spek, and others) is maintained by the community in the wiki located in the GitHub site of the JUnit 5 team: https://github.com/junit-team/junit5/wiki/Third-party-Extensions.

Test Launcher API

One of the goals of JUnit 5 is to make the interface between JUnit and its programmatic clients (build tools and IDEs) more powerful and stable. To that aim, the Test Launcher API has been implemented. This API is used by IDEs and build tools for discovering, filtering, and executing tests.

Looking closer at the details of this API, we find the class `LauncherDiscoveryRequest`, which exposes a fluent API to select the location of tests (for example classes, methods, or packages). This group of tests can be filtered, for example, using a match pattern:

```
import static
org.junit.platform.engine.discovery.ClassNameFilter.includeClassNamePattern
s;
import static
org.junit.platform.engine.discovery.DiscoverySelectors.selectClass;
import static
org.junit.platform.engine.discovery.DiscoverySelectors.selectPackage;

import org.junit.platform.launcher.Launcher;
import org.junit.platform.launcher.LauncherDiscoveryRequest;
import org.junit.platform.launcher.TestPlan;
import org.junit.platform.launcher.core.LauncherDiscoveryRequestBuilder;
import org.junit.platform.launcher.core.LauncherFactory;

// Discover and filter tests
LauncherDiscoveryRequest request = LauncherDiscoveryRequestBuilder
        .request()
        .selectors(selectPackage("io.github.bonigarcia"),
         selectClass(MyTest.class))
        .filters(includeClassNamePatterns(".*Test")).build();
Launcher launcher = LauncherFactory.create();
TestPlan plan = launcher.discover(request);
```

After that, the resulting test suite can be executed using the class `TestExecutionListener`. This class can be also used to get feedback and receive events:

```
import org.junit.platform.launcher.TestExecutionListener;
import org.junit.platform.launcher.listeners.SummaryGeneratingListener;

// Executing tests
TestExecutionListener listener = new SummaryGeneratingListener();
launcher.registerTestExecutionListeners(listener);
launcher.execute(request);
```

Running tests in JUnit 5

At the time of writing, Jupiter tests can be executed in several ways:

- **Using a build tool**: Maven (implemented in the module `junit-plaform-surefire-provider`) or Gradle (implemented in the module `junit-platform-gradle-plugin`).
- **Using the Console Launcher**: A command-line Java application that allows to launch the JUnit Platform from the console.
- **Using an IDE**: IntelliJ (since version 2016.2) and Eclipse (since version 4.7, Oxygen).

As we are going to discover, and due to the modular architecture of JUnit 5, we need to include three dependencies in our projects: one for the Test API (to implement tests), an other for the Test Engine (to run tests), and the last one of the Test Launcher (to discover tests).

Jupiter tests with Maven

In order to run Jupiter tests within a Maven project, we need to configure the `pom.xml` file properly. First of all, we need to include the `junit-jupiter-api` module as a dependency. This is needed to write our test, and typically with test scope:

```
<dependencies>
    <dependency>
        <groupId>org.junit.jupiter</groupId>
        <artifactId>junit-jupiter-api</artifactId>
        <version>${junit.jupiter.version}</version>
        <scope>test</scope>
    </dependency>
</dependencies>
```

In general, it is recommended to use the latest version of the dependencies. In order to check what it that version, we can check it on Maven Central (`http://search.maven.org/`)

Then, the `maven-surefire-plugin` has to be declared. Internally, this plugin needs two dependencies: the Test Launcher (`junit-platform-surefire-provider`) and the Test Engine (`junit-jupiter-engine`):

```
<build>
    <plugins>
        <plugin>
            <artifactId>maven-surefire-plugin</artifactId>
            <version>${maven-surefire-plugin.version}</version>
            <dependencies>
                <dependency>
                    <groupId>org.junit.platform</groupId>
                    <artifactId>junit-platform-surefire-provider</artifactId>
                    <version>${junit.platform.version}</version>
                </dependency>
                <dependency>
                    <groupId>org.junit.jupiter</groupId>
                    <artifactId>junit-jupiter-engine</artifactId>
                    <version>${junit.jupiter.version}</version>
                </dependency>
            </dependencies>
        </plugin>
    </plugins>
</build>
```

 All the source code of this book is publicly available on the GitHub repository at `https://github.com/bonigarcia/mastering-junit5`.

Last but not least, we need to create a Jupiter test case. So far, we have not learned how to implement Jupiter tests (this part is covered in chapter 3, JUnit 5 Standard Tests). Nevertheless, the test we execute here is the simplest test to demonstrate the execution of the JUnit 5 framework. A Jupiter test, in its minimal expression, is just a Java class in which one (or more) of its methods are annotated with `@Test` (package `org.junit.jupiter.api`). The following snippet provides an example:

```
package io.github.bonigarcia;

import static org.junit.jupiter.api.Assertions.assertEquals;

import org.junit.jupiter.api.Test;

class MyFirstJUnit5Test {

    @Test
```

```
void myFirstTest() {
    String message = "1+1 should be equal to 2";
    System.out.println(message);
    assertEquals(2, 1 + 1, message);
}

}
```

 JUnit requires Java 8 (or higher) at runtime. However, we can still test code that has been compiled with previous versions of Java.

As shown in the following picture, this test can be executed using the command `mvn test`:

```
D:\dev\mastering-junit5\junit5-hello-world>mvn test
[INFO] Scanning for projects...
[INFO]
[INFO]
[INFO] ------------------------------------------------------------------------
[INFO] Building junit5-hello-world 1.0.0
[INFO] ------------------------------------------------------------------------
[INFO]
[INFO]
[INFO] --- maven-resources-plugin:2.6:resources (default-resources) @ junit5-hello-world ---
[INFO] Using 'UTF-8' encoding to copy filtered resources.
[INFO] skip non existing resourceDirectory D:\dev\mastering-junit5\junit5-hello-world\src\main\resources
[INFO]
[INFO] --- maven-compiler-plugin:3.1:compile (default-compile) @ junit5-hello-world ---
[INFO] No sources to compile
[INFO]
[INFO] --- maven-resources-plugin:2.6:testResources (default-testResources) @ junit5-hello-world ---
[INFO] Using 'UTF-8' encoding to copy filtered resources.
[INFO] skip non existing resourceDirectory D:\dev\mastering-junit5\junit5-hello-world\src\test\resources
[INFO]
[INFO] --- maven-compiler-plugin:3.1:testCompile (default-testCompile) @ junit5-hello-world ---
[INFO] Nothing to compile - all classes are up to date
[INFO]
[INFO] --- maven-surefire-plugin:2.19.1:test (default-test) @ junit5-hello-world ---

-------------------------------------------------------
 T E S T S
-------------------------------------------------------
Running io.github.bonigarcia.MyFirstJUnit5Test
1+1 should be equal to 2
Tests run: 1, Failures: 0, Errors: 0, Skipped: 0, Time elapsed: 0.109 sec - in io.github.bonigarcia.MyFirstJUnit5Test

Results :

Tests run: 1, Failures: 0, Errors: 0, Skipped: 0

[INFO] ------------------------------------------------------------------------
[INFO] BUILD SUCCESS
[INFO] ------------------------------------------------------------------------
[INFO] Total time: 3.960 s
[INFO] Finished at: 2017-06-07T01:05:26+02:00
[INFO] Final Memory: 13M/309M
[INFO] ------------------------------------------------------------------------

D:\dev\mastering-junit5\junit5-hello-world>
```

Running Jupiter tests with Maven

Jupiter tests with Gradle

Now, we are going to study the same example, but this time executed with Gradle. Therefore, we need to configure the `build.gradle` file. In this file, we need to define:

- The dependency for the Jupiter API (`junit-jupiter-api`).
- The dependency for the Test Engine (`junit-jupiter-engine`).
- The plugin for the Test Launcher (`junit-platform-gradle-plugin`).

The complete source of `build.gradle` is as follows:

```
buildscript {
    repositories {
        mavenCentral()
    }
    dependencies {
        classpath("org.junit.platform:junit-platform-gradle-
plugin:${junitPlatformVersion}")
    }
}
repositories {
    mavenCentral()
}

apply plugin: 'java'
apply plugin: 'eclipse'
apply plugin: 'idea'
apply plugin: 'org.junit.platform.gradle.plugin'

compileTestJava {
    sourceCompatibility = 1.8
    targetCompatibility = 1.8
    options.compilerArgs += '-parameters'
}

dependencies {
    testCompile("org.junit.jupiter:junit-jupiter-
api:${junitJupiterVersion}")
    testRuntime("org.junit.jupiter:junit-jupiter-
engine:${junitJupiterVersion}")
}
```

We use the command `gradle test` to run our Jupiter test from the command line with Gradle:

```
Command Prompt                                          —  □  ×

D:\dev\mastering-junit5\junit5-hello-world>gradle test
:compileJava NO-SOURCE
:processResources NO-SOURCE
:classes UP-TO-DATE
:compileTestJava
:processTestResources NO-SOURCE
:testClasses
:junitPlatformTest
1+1 should be equal to 2

Test run finished after 94 ms
[         2 containers found      ]
[         0 containers skipped    ]
[         2 containers started    ]
[         0 containers aborted    ]
[         2 containers successful ]
[         0 containers failed     ]
[         1 tests found           ]
[         0 tests skipped         ]
[         1 tests started         ]
[         0 tests aborted         ]
[         1 tests successful      ]
[         0 tests failed          ]

:test SKIPPED

BUILD SUCCESSFUL

Total time: 1.826 secs
D:\dev\mastering-junit5\junit5-hello-world>
```

Running Jupiter tests with Gradle

Legacy tests with Maven

The following is the image we want to run the legacy test (JUnit 4 in this case) inside the JUnit Plaform:

```java
package io.github.bonigarcia;

import static org.junit.Assert.assertEquals;

import org.junit.Test;

public class LegacyJUnit4Test {

    @Test
    public void myFirstTest() {
```

```
        String message = "1+1 should be equal to 2";
        System.out.println(message);
        assertEquals(message, 2, 1 + 1);
    }

}
```

To that aim, in Maven, we first need to include the old JUnit 4 dependency in our `pom.xml`, as follows:

```
<dependencies>
    <dependency>
        <groupId>junit</groupId>
        <artifactId>junit</artifactId>
        <version>4.12</version>
        <scope>test</scope>
    </dependency>
</dependencies>
```

Then, we need to include `maven-surefire-plugin`, using the following dependencies for the plugin: the Test Engine (`junit-vintage-engine`) and the Test Launcher (`junit-platform-surefire-provider`):

```
<build>
    <plugins>
        <plugin>
            <artifactId>maven-surefire-plugin</artifactId>
            <version>${maven-surefire-plugin.version}</version>
            <dependencies>
                <dependency>
                    <groupId>org.junit.platform</groupId>
                    <artifactId>junit-platform-surefire-provider</artifactId>
                    <version>${junit.platform.version}</version>
                </dependency>
                <dependency>
                    <groupId>org.junit.vintage</groupId>
                    <artifactId>junit-vintage-engine</artifactId>
                    <version>${junit.vintage.version}</version>
                </dependency>
            </dependencies>
        </plugin>
    </plugins>
</build>
```

The execution from the command line will also be using the command `mvn test`:

```
Command Prompt                                                      —    □    ×

D:\dev\mastering-junit5\junit5-vintage>mvn test
[INFO] Scanning for projects...
[INFO]
[INFO] ------------------------------------------------------------------------
[INFO] Building junit5-vintage 1.0.0
[INFO] ------------------------------------------------------------------------
[INFO]
[INFO] --- maven-resources-plugin:2.6:resources (default-resources) @ junit5-vintage ---
[INFO] Using 'UTF-8' encoding to copy filtered resources.
[INFO] skip non existing resourceDirectory D:\dev\mastering-junit5\junit5-vintage\src\main\resources
[INFO]
[INFO] --- maven-compiler-plugin:3.1:compile (default-compile) @ junit5-vintage ---
[INFO] No sources to compile
[INFO]
[INFO] --- maven-resources-plugin:2.6:testResources (default-testResources) @ junit5-vintage ---
[INFO] Using 'UTF-8' encoding to copy filtered resources.
[INFO] skip non existing resourceDirectory D:\dev\mastering-junit5\junit5-vintage\src\test\resources
[INFO]
[INFO] --- maven-compiler-plugin:3.1:testCompile (default-testCompile) @ junit5-vintage ---
[INFO] Nothing to compile - all classes are up to date
[INFO]
[INFO] --- maven-surefire-plugin:2.19.1:test (default-test) @ junit5-vintage ---

-------------------------------------------------------
 T E S T S
-------------------------------------------------------
Running io.github.bonigarcia.LegacyJUnit4Test
1+1 should be equal to 2
Tests run: 1, Failures: 0, Errors: 0, Skipped: 0, Time elapsed: 0.094 sec - in io.github.bonigarcia.LegacyJUnit4Test

Results :

Tests run: 1, Failures: 0, Errors: 0, Skipped: 0

[INFO] ------------------------------------------------------------------------
[INFO] BUILD SUCCESS
[INFO] ------------------------------------------------------------------------
[INFO] Total time: 3.806 s
[INFO] Finished at: 2017-06-07T01:20:53+02:00
[INFO] Final Memory: 11M/309M
[INFO] ------------------------------------------------------------------------

D:\dev\mastering-junit5\junit5-vintage>
```

Running Legacy tests with Maven

Legacy tests wih Gradle

If we want to execute the same test presented in the example before
(`io.github.bonigarcia.LegacyJUnit4Test`), but this time using Gradle, we need to
include the following in our `build.gradle` file:

- The dependency for JUnit 4.12.
- The dependency for the Test Engine (`junit-vintage-engine`).
- The plugin for the Test Launcher (`junit-platform-gradle-plugin`).

Thus, the complete source of `build.gradle` would be as follows:

```
buildscript {
    repositories {
        mavenCentral()
    }
    dependencies {
        classpath("org.junit.platform:junit-platform-gradle-
plugin:${junitPlatformVersion}")
    }
}

repositories {
    mavenCentral()
}

apply plugin: 'java'
apply plugin: 'eclipse'
apply plugin: 'idea'
apply plugin: 'org.junit.platform.gradle.plugin'

compileTestJava {
    sourceCompatibility = 1.8
    targetCompatibility = 1.8
    options.compilerArgs += '-parameters'
}

dependencies {
    testCompile("junit:junit:${junitLegacy}")
    testRuntime("org.junit.vintage:junit-vintage-
engine:${junitVintageVersion}")
}
```

The execution from the command line would be as follows:

```
Command Prompt                                                    —    □    ×

D:\dev\mastering-junit5\junit5-vintage>gradle test
:compileJava NO-SOURCE
:processResources NO-SOURCE
:classes UP-TO-DATE
:compileTestJava
:processTestResources NO-SOURCE
:testClasses
:junitPlatformTest
1+1 should be equal to 2

Test run finished after 78 ms
[         2 containers found      ]
[         0 containers skipped    ]
[         2 containers started    ]
[         0 containers aborted    ]
[         2 containers successful ]
[         0 containers failed     ]
[         1 tests found           ]
[         0 tests skipped         ]
[         1 tests started         ]
[         0 tests aborted         ]
[         1 tests successful      ]
[         0 tests failed          ]

:test SKIPPED

BUILD SUCCESSFUL

Total time: 1.907 secs
D:\dev\mastering-junit5\junit5-vintage>
```

Running Legacy tests with Gradle

The ConsoleLauncher

The ConsoleLauncher is a command-line Java application that allows launching the JUnit Platform from the console. For example, it can be used to run Vintage and Jupiter tests from the command line.

An executable JAR with all dependencies included is published in the central Maven repository under the junit-platform-console-standalone artifact. The standalone Console Launcher can be executed as follows:

```
java -jar junit-platform-console-standalone-version.jar <Options>
```

The example GitHub repository `junit5-console-launcher` contains a simple example for the use of the Console Launcher. As depicted in the following picture, a run configuration entry has been created in Eclipse, running the main class, `org.junit.platform.console.ConsoleLauncher`. Then, the test class name is passed as an argument using the option `--select-class` and the qualified class name (in this example, `io.github.bonigarcia.EmptyTest`). After that, we can run the application, obtaining the test result in the integrated console of Eclipse:

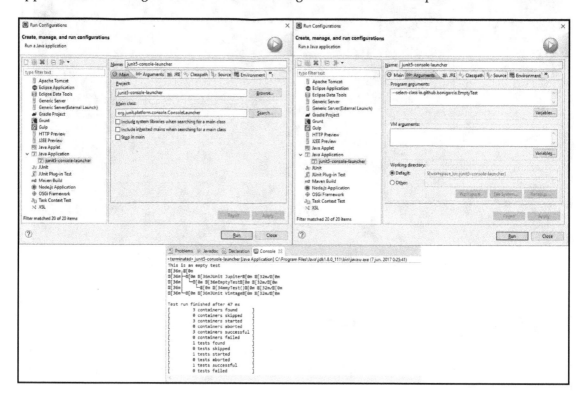

Example of ConsoleLauncher in Eclipse

Jupiter tests in JUnit 4

JUnit 5 has been designed to be forward and backward compatible. On the one hand, the Vintage component supports running legacy code on JUnit 3 and 4. On the other hand, JUnit 5 provides a JUnit 4 runner that allows to run JUnit 5 in IDEs and build systems that support JUnit 4, but does not yet support the new JUnit Platform 5 directly.

Let's see one example. Imagine we want to run a Jupiter test in an IDE does not support JUnit 5, for example, an old version of Eclipse. In this case, we need to annotate our Jupiter test with `@RunWith(JUnitPlatform.class)`. The `JUnitPlatform` runner is a JUnit 4-based runner, which enables to run any test whose programming model is supported on the JUnit Platform in a JUnit 4 environment. Therefore, our test would result as follows:

```java
package io.github.bonigarcia;

import static org.junit.jupiter.api.Assertions.assertEquals;

import org.junit.jupiter.api.Test;
import org.junit.platform.runner.JUnitPlatform;
import org.junit.runner.RunWith;

@RunWith(JUnitPlatform.class)
public class JUnit5CompatibleTest {

    @Test
    void myTest() {
        String message = "1+1 should be equal to 2";
        System.out.println(message);
        assertEquals(2, 1 + 1, message);
    }

}
```

If this test is contained in a Maven project, our `pom.xml` should contain the following dependencies:

```xml
<dependencies>
  <dependency>
     <groupId>org.junit.jupiter</groupId>
     <artifactId>junit-jupiter-api</artifactId>
     <version>${junit.jupiter.version}</version>
     <scope>test</scope>
  </dependency>
  <dependency>
     <groupId>org.junit.jupiter</groupId>
     <artifactId>junit-jupiter-engine</artifactId>
     <version>${junit.jupiter.version}</version>
     <scope>test</scope>
  </dependency>
  <dependency>
     <groupId>org.junit.platform</groupId>
     <artifactId>junit-platform-runner</artifactId>
     <version>${junit.platform.version}</version>
     <scope>test</scope>
```

```
        </dependency>
    </dependencies>
```

On the other hand, for a Gradle project, our `build.gradle` is the following:

```
buildscript {
    repositories {
        mavenCentral()
    }
    dependencies {
        classpath("org.junit.platform:junit-platform-gradle-
plugin:${junitPlatformVersion}")
    }
}

repositories {
    mavenCentral()
}

apply plugin: 'java'
apply plugin: 'eclipse'
apply plugin: 'idea'
apply plugin: 'org.junit.platform.gradle.plugin'

compileTestJava {
    sourceCompatibility = 1.8
    targetCompatibility = 1.8
    options.compilerArgs += '-parameters'
}

dependencies {
    testCompile("org.junit.jupiter:junit-jupiter-
api:${junitJupiterVersion}")
    testRuntime("org.junit.jupiter:junit-jupiter-
engine:${junitJupiterVersion}")
    testCompile("org.junit.platform:junit-platform-
runner:${junitPlatformVersion}")
}
```

IntelliJ

IntelliJ 2016.2+ has been the first IDE which supports the execution of Jupiter tests natively. As shown in the following screenshot, any Jupiter test can be executed using the integrated functions of the IDE:

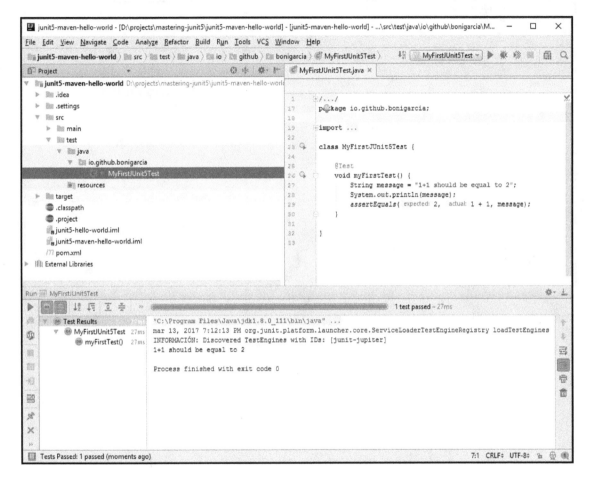

Running a Jupiter test in IntelliJ 2016.2+

Eclipse

Eclipse 4.7 (*Oxygen*) has beta support for JUnit 5. Thanks to this, Eclipse provides the ability of running Jupiter tests directly in Eclipse, as shown in the following screenshot:

Running a Jupiter test in Eclipse 4.7+

Moreover, Eclipse 4.7 (*Oxygen*) provides a wizard to create Jupiter tests in a simple way, as shown in the following pictures:

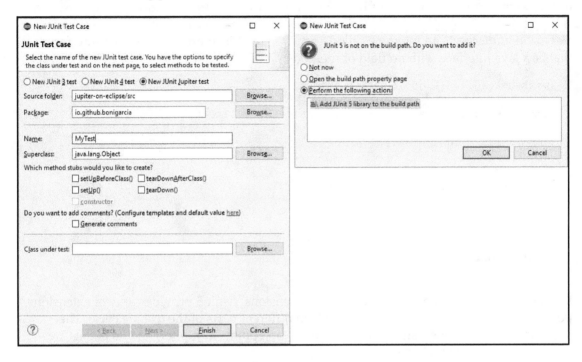

Eclipse wizard to create Jupiter tests

The extension model of JUnit 5

As introduced before, Jupiter is the name given to the new programming model of JUnit 5, described in detail in `chapter 3`, *JUnit 5 standard tests* and `chapter 4`, *Simplifying testing with advanced JUnit features*, together with the extension model. The extension model allows to extend the Jupiter programming model with custom additions. Thanks to this, third-party frameworks (such as Spring or Mockito, to name a few) can achieve interoperability with JUnit 5 in a seamless way. The extensions provided by these frameworks will be studied in `chapter 5`, *Integration of JUnit 5 with external frameworks*. In the current section, we analyze the general performance of the extension model and also the extensions provided out of the box in JUnit 5.

In contrast to former extension points in JUnit 4 (that is, test runners and rules), the JUnit 5 extension model consists of a single, coherent concept: the **Extension API**. This API allows to extend the core functionality of JUnit 5 by any third party (tool vendor, developers, and so on). The first thing we need to understand about extensions in Jupiter is that each new extension implements an interface called `Extension`. This interface is a *marker* interface, that is, a Java interface with no field or methods:

```java
package org.junit.jupiter.api.extension;

import static org.apiguardian.api.API.Status.STABLE;

import org.apiguardian.api.API;

/**
 * Marker interface for all extensions.
 *
 * @since 5.0
 */
@API(status = STABLE, since = "5.0")
public interface Extension {
}
```

In order to make ease the creation of Jupiter extensions, JUnit 5 provides a set of extensions points which allows to execute custom code in different parts of the test life cycle. The following table contains a summary of the extension points in Jupiter, and its details are presented in the next sections:

Extension point	Implemented by extensions which want to...
TestInstancePostProcessor	Provide additional behavior just after the test instantiation
BeforeAllCallback	Provide additional behavior before all tests are invoked in a test container
BeforeEachCallback	Provide additional behavior to tests before each test is invoked
BeforeTestExecutionCallback	Provide additional behavior to tests immediately before each test is executed
TestExecutionExceptionHandler	Handle exceptions thrown during test execution
AfterAllCallback	Provide additional behavior to test containers after all tests have been invoked

AfterEachCallback	Provide additional behavior to tests after each test has been invoked
AfterTestExecutionCallback	Provide additional behavior to tests immediately after each test has been executed
ExecutionCondition	Conditionate the test execution at runtime
ParameterResolver	Resolve parameters at runtime

Once we created an extension, in order to use it, we need to use the annotation `ExtendWith`. This annotation can be used to register one or more extensions. It can be declared on interfaces, classes, methods, fields, and even in other annotations:

```
import org.junit.jupiter.api.Test;
import org.junit.jupiter.api.extension.ExtendWith;

public class MyTest {

    @ExtendWith(MyExtension.class)
    @Test
    public void test() {
        // My test logic
    }

}
```

Test lifecycle

There are a set of extension points aimed at controlling the life cycle of tests. First of all, the `TestInstancePostProcessor` can be used to execute some logic after the test instantiation. After that, there are different extensions which control the pre-test stage:

- The `BeforeAllCallback` defines the logic executed before all tests.
- The `BeforeEachCallback` defines the logic executed before a test method.
- The `BeforeTestExecutionCallback` defines the logic executed immediately before a test method.

Similarly, there are extensions to control the post-test phases:

- The `AfterAllCallback` defines the logic executed after all tests.
- The `AfterEachCallback` defines the logic executed after a test method.
- The `AfterTestExecutionCallback` defines the logic executed immediately after a test method.

In between the `Before*` and `After*` callbacks, there is an extension that provides a way for collecting exceptions: the `TestExecutionExceptionHandler`.

All these callbacks, and their order in the test life cycl are depicted in the following picture:

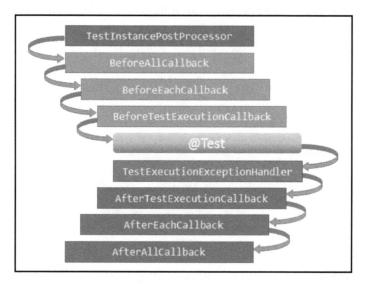

Lifecycle of extension callbacks

Let's see an example. We created an extension called `IgnoreIOExceptionExtension`, which implements `TestExecutionExceptionHandler`. In this example, the extension checks whether or not the exception is `IOException`. If so, the exception is discarded:

```java
package io.github.bonigarcia;

import java.io.IOException;
import org.junit.jupiter.api.extension.ExtensionContext;
import org.junit.jupiter.api.extension.TestExecutionExceptionHandler;

public class IgnoreIOExceptionExtension
    implements TestExecutionExceptionHandler {
    @Override
```

```
   public void handleTestExecutionException(ExtensionContext context,
          Throwable throwable) throws Throwable {
       if (throwable instanceof IOException) {
          return;
       }
       throw throwable;
   }

}
```

Consider the following test class, which contains two tests (@Test). The first one is annotated with @ExtendWith and our custom extension (IgnoreIOExceptionExtension):

```
package io.github.bonigarcia;

import java.io.IOException;
import org.junit.jupiter.api.Test;
import org.junit.jupiter.api.extension.ExtendWith;

public class ExceptionTest {

    @ExtendWith(IgnoreIOExceptionExtension.class)
    @Test
    public void firstTest() throws IOException {
        throw new IOException("IO Exception");
    }

    @Test
    public void secondTest() throws IOException {
        throw new IOException("My IO Exception");
    }

}
```

When executing this test class, the first test is succeeded due to the fact that the IOException has been internally handled by our extension. On the other hand, the second will fail since that exception is not handled.

The execution of this test class in the console can be seen in the next screenshot. Note that we select the test to be executed using the Maven command `mvn test -Dtest=ExceptionTest`:

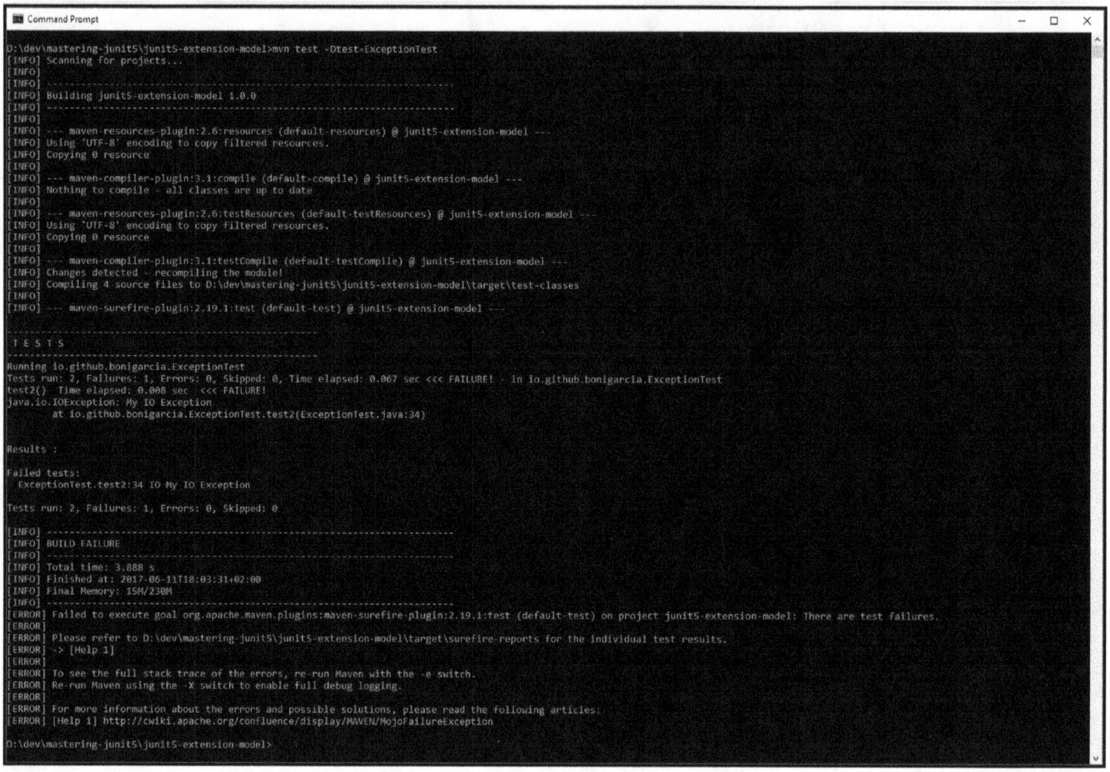

Output of ignore exception example

Conditional extension points

In order to create extensions that activate or deactivate tests depending on a given condition, JUnit 5 provides one conditional extension point callled `ExecutionCondition`. The following snippet shows the declaration of this extension point:

```
package org.junit.jupiter.api.extension;

import static org.apiguardian.api.API.Status.STABLE;

import org.apiguardian.api.API;
```

```
@FunctionalInterface
@API(status = STABLE, since = "5.0")
public interface ExecutionCondition extends Extension {
    ConditionEvaluationResult evaluateExecutionCondition
      ExtensionContext context);

}
```

The extension can be used to deactivate either all tests in a container (likely a class) or individual tests (likely a test method). Examples of this extension are provided in the section *Conditional Test Execution* of chapter 3, *JUnit 5 Standard Tests*.

Dependency injection

The ParameterResolver extension provides dependency injection at method level. In this example, we can see how an argument is injected in the test method with a custom implementation of ParameterResolver called MyParameterResolver. Following the code, we can see that this resolver will simply inject hard-coded String parameters with the value my parameter:

```java
package io.github.bonigarcia;

import org.junit.jupiter.api.extension.ExtensionContext;
import org.junit.jupiter.api.extension.ParameterContext;
import org.junit.jupiter.api.extension.ParameterResolutionException;
import org.junit.jupiter.api.extension.ParameterResolver;

public class MyParameterResolver implements ParameterResolver {

    @Override
    public boolean supportsParameter(ParameterContext parameterContext,
            ExtensionContext extensionContext)
            throws ParameterResolutionException {
        return true;
    }

    @Override
    public Object resolveParameter(ParameterContext parameterContext,
            ExtensionContext extensionContext)
            throws ParameterResolutionException {
        return "my parameter";
    }

}
```

Then, this parameter resolver can be used in a test, declaring it as usual using the annotation @ExtendWith:

```java
package io.github.bonigarcia;

import org.junit.jupiter.api.Test;
import org.junit.jupiter.api.extension.ExtendWith;

public class DependencyInjectionTest {

    @ExtendWith(MyParameterResolver.class)
    @Test
    public void test(Object parameter) {
        System.out.println("My parameter " + parameter);
    }
}
```

Finally, if we execute this test (for example using Maven and the command line), we can see how the injected parameter is logged in the standard output:

Output of dependency injection extension example

Third-party extensions

In the real world, extensions typically implement several of the previously explained extension points. For example, `SpringExtension` (explained in detail in `chapter 5`, *Integration of JUnit 5 with external frameworks*) implements the extensions points `BeforeAllCallback`, `TestInstancePostProcessor`, `ParameterResolver`, among others. The following snippet provides the structure of `SpringExtension`:

```
package org.springframework.test.context.junit.jupiter;

import org.junit.jupiter.api.extension.*;

public class SpringExtension implements BeforeAllCallback,
    AfterAllCallback,
    TestInstancePostProcessor, BeforeEachCallback, AfterEachCallback,
    BeforeTestExecutionCallback, AfterTestExecutionCallback,
    ParameterResolver {

  @Override
  public void afterTestExecution(TestExtensionContext context)
   throws Exception {
     // implementation
  }

  // Rest of methods
}
```

> A list of existing JUnit 5 extensions (for example, Spring, Selenium, Docker, and others) is maintained by the community in the wiki located in the GitHub site of the JUnit 5 team: `https://github.com/junit-team/junit5/wiki/Third-party-Extensions`. Some of them are also detailed in `chapter 5`, *Integration of JUnit 5 with external frameworks*.

Summary

This chapter provides an overview of the JUnit 5 testing framework. Due to the limitations of JUnit 4 (monolithic architecture, impossibility of compose test runners, and limitations of test rules), a new major version of the framework was needed. In order to carry out the implementations, the JUnit Lambda project started a crowdfunding campaign in 2015. As a result, the JUnit 5 development team was born, and the GA release of the framework was released on September 10, 2017.

JUnit 5 was designed to be modern (that is, using Java 8 and Java 9 compliant from the very beginning) and modular. The three major components within JUnit 5 are: Jupiter (new programming an extension model), Platform (foundation for any testing framework executed in the JVM), and Vintage (integration with legacy JUnit 3 and 4 tests). At the time of this writing, JUnit 5 tests can be executed using build tools (Maven or Gradle) and also with IDEs (IntelliJ 2016.2+ or Eclipse 4.7+).

The extension model of JUnit 5 allows to extend the core functionality of JUnit 5 by any third party. In order to create JUnit 5 extensions, we need to implement one or several JUnit extension points (such as `BeforeAllCallback`, `ParameterResolver`, or `ExecutionCondition`, among others), and then register the extension in our tests using the annotation `@ExtendWith`.

In the next `chapter 3`, *JUnit 5 Standard Tests*, we are going to learn the basics of the Jupiter programming model. In other words, we are going to learn how to create standard JUnit 5 tests.

3
JUnit 5 Standard Tests

Talk is cheap. Show me the code.
- Linus Torvalds

JUnit 5 provides a brand-new programming model called Jupiter. We can see this programming model as an API for software engineers and testers which allow to create JUnit 5 tests. These tests are later executed on the JUnit Platform. As we will discover, the Jupiter programming model allows to create many different types of tests. This chapter tackles the basics of Jupiter. To that aim, this chapter is structured as follows:

- **Test lifecycle**: In this section, we analyze the structure of the Jupiter tests, describing the annotations involved in the management of the test life cycle in the JUnit 5 programming model. Then, we discover how to skip tests, and also how to annotate tests with a custom display name.

- **Assertions**: In this section, first we present a brief overview of the verification assets, called assertions (also known as predicates). Second, we study how the assertions have been implemented in Jupiter. Finally, we present several third-party libraries about assertions, providing some examples for Hamcrest.

- **Tagging and filtering tests**: In this section, first we will learn how to label Jupiter tests, that is, how to create tags in JUnit 5. Then, we will learn how to filter our tests using Maven and Gradle. Finally, we are going to analyze how to create meta-annotations using Jupiter.

- **Conditional test execution**: In this section, we will learn how to disable tests based on a given condition. After that, we make a review of the so-called assumptions in Jupiter, which are a mechanism provided out of the box by Jupiter to run tests only if certain conditions are as expected.

- **Nested tests**: This section presents how Jupiter allows to express the relationship among a group of tests, called nested tests.

- **Repeated tests**: This section reviews how Jupiter provides the ability to repeat a test a specified number of times.
- **Migration from JUnit 4 to JUnit 5**: This section provides a set of hints about the main differences between JUnit 5 and its immediate antecessor, that is, JUnit 4. Then, this section presents the support for several JUnit 4 rules within Jupiter tests.

Test lifecycle

As we saw in `Chapter 1`, *Retrospective on software quality and Java testing*, a unit test case is composed of four stages:

1. **Setup** (optional): First, the test initializes the test fixture (before the picture of the SUT).
2. **Exercise**: Second, the test interacts with the SUT, getting some outcome from it as a result.
3. **Verify**: Third, the outcome from the system under test is compared to the expected value using one or several assertions (also known as predicates). As a result, a test verdict is created.
4. **Teardown** (optional): Finally, the test releases the test fixture to put the SUT back into the initial state.

In JUnit 4, there were different annotations to control these test phases. JUnit 5 follows the same approach, that is, Java annotations are used to identify different methods within Java classes, implementing the test life cycle. In Jupiter, all these annotations are contained in the package `org.junit.jupiter.api`.

The most basic JUnit annotation is `@Test`, which identifies the methods that have to be executed as tests. Therefore, a Java method annotated with `org.junit.jupiter.api.Test` will be treated as a test. The difference of this annotation with respect to JUnit 4's `@Test` is two folded. On the one hand, the Jupiter `@Test` annotation does not declare any attributes. In JUnit 4, `@Test` can declare the test timeout (as long attribute with the timeout in milliseconds), on the other hand, in JUnit 5, neither test classes nor test methods need to be public (this was a requirement in JUnit 4).

Take a look at the following Java class. Possibly, it is the simplest test case we can create with Jupiter. It has simply a method with the `@Test` annotation. The test logic (that is the exercise and verify stages as described before) would be contained inside the method `myTest`.

```java
package io.github.bonigarcia;

import org.junit.jupiter.api.Test;

class SimpleJUnit5Test {

    @Test
    void mySimpleTest() {
        // My test logic here
    }

}
```

The Jupiter annotations (also located in the package `org.junit.jupiter.api`) aimed to control the setup and tear down stages in JUnit 5 tests are described in the following table:

JUnit 5 annotation	Description	JUnit 4's equivalence
`@BeforeEach`	Method executed before each `@Test` in the current class	`@Before`
`@AfterEach`	Method executed after each `@Test` in the current class	`@After`
`@BeforeAll`	Method executed before all `@Test` in the current class	`@BeforeClass`
`@AfterAll`	Method executed after all `@Test` in the current class	`@AfterClass`

 Methods annotated with these annotations (`@BeforeEach`, `@AfterEach`, `@AfterAll`, and `@BeforeAll`) are always inherited.

The following picture depicts the order of execution of these annotations in a Java class:

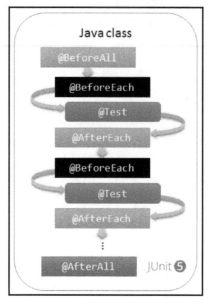

Jupiter annotations to control the test lyfecycle

Let's go back to the generic structure for tests we saw at the beginning of this section. Now, we are able to map the Jupiter annotations to control the test lifecycle with the different parts of a test case. As illustrated in the following picture, we carry out the setup stage by annotating methods with @BeforeAll and @BeforeEach. Then, we carry out the exercise and verify stages in methods annotated with @Test. Finally, we carry out the tear down process in the methods with @AfterEach and @AfterAll.

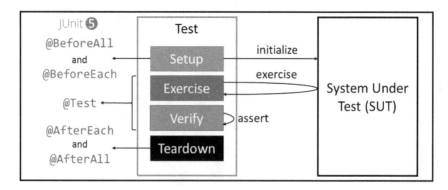

Relationship among the unit test cases stages and the Jupiter annotations

Let's see a simple example, which uses all these annotations in a single Java class. This example defines two tests (that is, two methods annotated with @Test), and we define additional methods for the rest of the test life cycle with the annotations @BeforeAll, @BeforeEach, @AfterEach, and @AfterAll:

```java
package io.github.bonigarcia;

import org.junit.jupiter.api.AfterAll;
import org.junit.jupiter.api.AfterEach;
import org.junit.jupiter.api.BeforeAll;
import org.junit.jupiter.api.BeforeEach;
import org.junit.jupiter.api.Test;

class LifecycleJUnit5Test {

    @BeforeAll
    static void setupAll() {
        System.out.println("Setup ALL TESTS in the class");
    }

    @BeforeEach
    void setup() {
        System.out.println("Setup EACH TEST in the class");
    }

    @Test
    void testOne() {
        System.out.println("TEST 1");
    }

    @Test
    void testTwo() {
        System.out.println("TEST 2");
    }

    @AfterEach
    void teardown() {
        System.out.println("Teardown EACH TEST in the class");
    }

    @AfterAll
    static void teardownAll() {
        System.out.println("Teardown ALL TESTS in the class");
    }

}
```

If we run this test class, first @BeforeAll will be executed. Then, the two test methods will be executed sequentially, that is, the first one and then the other. In each execution, the setup method annotated with @BeforeEach will be executed before the test, and then the @AfterEach method. The following screenshot shows an execution of the tests using Maven and the command line:

```
-------------------------------------------------------
 T E S T S
-------------------------------------------------------
Running io.github.bonigarcia.LifecycleJUnit5Test
Setup ALL TESTS in the class
Setup EACH TEST in the class
TEST 1
Teardown EACH TEST in the class
Setup EACH TEST in the class
TEST 2
Teardown EACH TEST in the class
Teardown ALL TESTS in the class
Tests run: 2, Failures: 0, Errors: 0, Skipped: 0, Time elapsed: 0.168 sec
- in io.github.bonigarcia.LifecycleJUnit5Test

Results :

Tests run: 2, Failures: 0, Errors: 0, Skipped: 0
```

Execution of a Jupiter test which controls its lifecycle

Test instance lifecycle

In order to provide execution in isolation, the JUnit 5 framework creates a new test instance before executing the actual test (that is, the method annotated with @Test). This *per-method* test instance life cycle is the behavior in the Jupiter test and also in its antecessors (JUnit 3 and 4). As a novelty, this default behavior can be changed in JUnit 5, simply by annotating a test class with @TestInstance(Lifecycle.PER_CLASS). Using this mode, the test instance will be created once per class, instead of once per test method.

This *per-class* behavior implies that it is possible to declare the `@BeforeAll` and `@AfterAll` methods as non-static. This is beneficial to be used in conjunction with some advanced capabilities, such as nested test or default test interfaces (explained in the next chapter).

All in all, and taking into account the extension callback (as explained in the *The extension model of JUnit 5* section of Chapter 2, *What's new in JUnit 5*), the relative execution order of user code and extensions is depicted in the following picture:

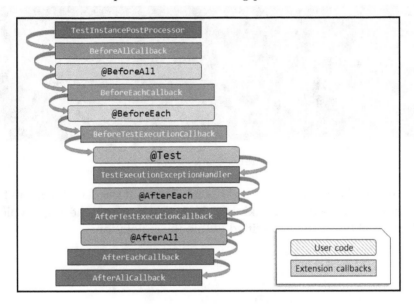

Relative execution order of user code and extensions

Skipping tests

The Jupiter annotation `@Disabled` (located in the package `org.junit.jupiter.api`) can be used to skip tests. It can be used at class level or method level. The following example uses the annotation `@Disabled` at method level and therefore it forces to skip the test:

```
package io.github.bonigarcia;

import org.junit.jupiter.api.Disabled;
import org.junit.jupiter.api.Test;

class DisabledTest {

    @Disabled
    @Test
```

```
    void skippedTest() {
    }

  }
```

As shown in the following screenshot, when we execute this example, the test will be counted as skipped:

```
------------------------------------------------------
 T E S T S
------------------------------------------------------
Running io.github.bonigarcia.DisabledTest
Tests run: 1, Failures: 0, Errors: 0, Skipped: 1, Time elapsed: 0.142 sec
 - in io.github.bonigarcia.DisabledTest

Results :

Tests run: 1, Failures: 0, Errors: 0, Skipped: 1
```

Disabled test method console output

In this other example, the annotation @Disabled is placed at the class level and therefore all the tests contained in the class will be skipped. Note that a custom message, typically with the reason of the disabling, can be specified within the annotation:

```java
package io.github.bonigarcia;

import org.junit.jupiter.api.Disabled;
import org.junit.jupiter.api.Test;

@Disabled("All test in this class will be skipped")
class AllDisabledTest {

    @Test
    void skippedTestOne() {
    }

    @Test
    void skippedTestTwo() {
    }

}
```

The following screenshot shows how the test case is skipped when it is executed (in this example using Maven and the command line):

```
----------------------------------------------------
 T E S T S
----------------------------------------------------
Running io.github.bonigarcia.AllDisabledTest
Tests run: 1, Failures: 0, Errors: 0, Skipped: 1, Time elapsed: 0.102 sec
- in io.github.bonigarcia.AllDisabledTest

Results :

Tests run: 1, Failures: 0, Errors: 0, Skipped: 1
```

Disabled test class console output

Display names

JUnit 4 identified tests basically with the name of the method annotated with @Test. This imposes a limitation on name tests, since these names are constrained by the way of declaring methods in Java.

To overcome this problem, Jupiter provides the ability of declaring a custom display name (different to the test name) for tests. This is done with the annotation @DisplayName. This annotation declares a custom display name for a test class or a test method. This name will be displayed by test runners and reporting tools, and it can contain spaces, special characters, and even emojis.

Take a look at the following example. We are annotating the test class, and also the three test methods declared inside the class with a custom test name using @DisplayName:

```java
package io.github.bonigarcia;

import org.junit.jupiter.api.DisplayName;
import org.junit.jupiter.api.Test;

@DisplayName("A special test case")
class DisplayNameTest {

    @Test
    @DisplayName("Custom test name containing spaces")
    void testWithDisplayNameContainingSpaces() {
    }

    @Test
    @DisplayName("(╯°Д°)╯")
```

```
    void testWithDisplayNameContainingSpecialCharacters() {
    }

    @Test
    @DisplayName("😱")
    void testWithDisplayNameContainingEmoji() {
    }

}
```

As a result, we see these labels when executing this test in a JUnit 5 compliant IDE. The following picture shows the execution of the example on IntelliJ 2016.2+:

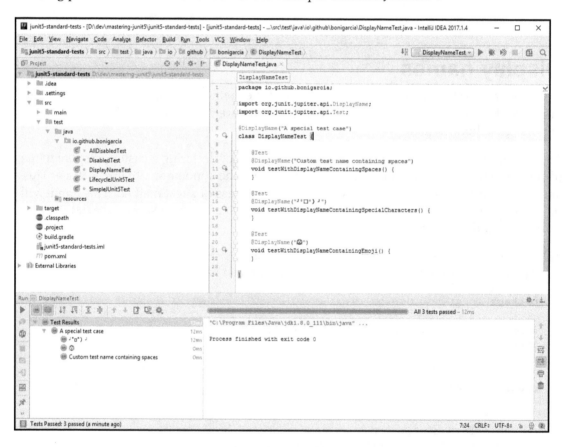

Execution of a test case using *@DisplayName* in IntelliJ

On the other hand, the display name can be also seen in Eclipse 4.7 (Oxygen) or newer:

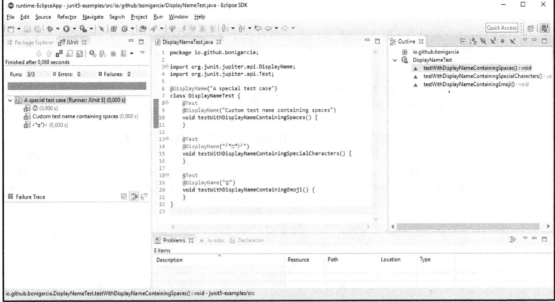

Execution of a test case using *@DisplayName* in Eclipse

Assertions

As we know, the general structure of a test case is composed of four stages: setup, exercise, verify, and tear down. The actual test happens during the second and third stage, when the test logic interacts with the system under test, getting some kind of outcome from it. This outcome is compared with the expected result in the verify stage. In this stage, we find what we call assertions. In this section, we take a closer look at them.

An assertion (also known as a predicate) is a `boolean` statement typically used to reason about software correctness. From a technical point of view, an assertion is composed of three parts (see the image after the list):

1. First, we find the expected value, which comes from what we call test oracles. A test oracle is a reliable source of expected outputs, for example, the system specification.
2. Second, we find the real outcome, which comes from the exercise stage made by the test against the SUT.

3. Finally, these two values are compared using some logic comparator. This comparison can be done in many different ways, for example, we can compare the object identity (equals or not), the magnitude (higher or lower value), and so on. As a result, we obtain a test verdict, which, in the end, is going to define if the test has succeeded or failed.

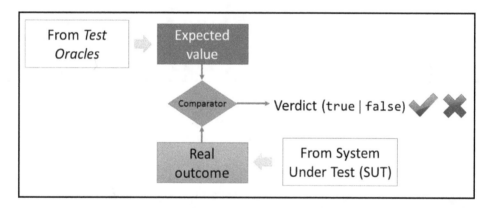

Schematic view of an assertion

Jupiter assertions

Let's move on to the JUnit 5 programming model. Jupiter comes with many of the assertion methods such as the ones in JUnit 4, and also adds several that can be used with Java 8 lambdas. All JUnit Jupiter assertions are static methods in the `Assertions` class located in `org.junit.jupiter` package.

The following picture shows the complete list of these methods:

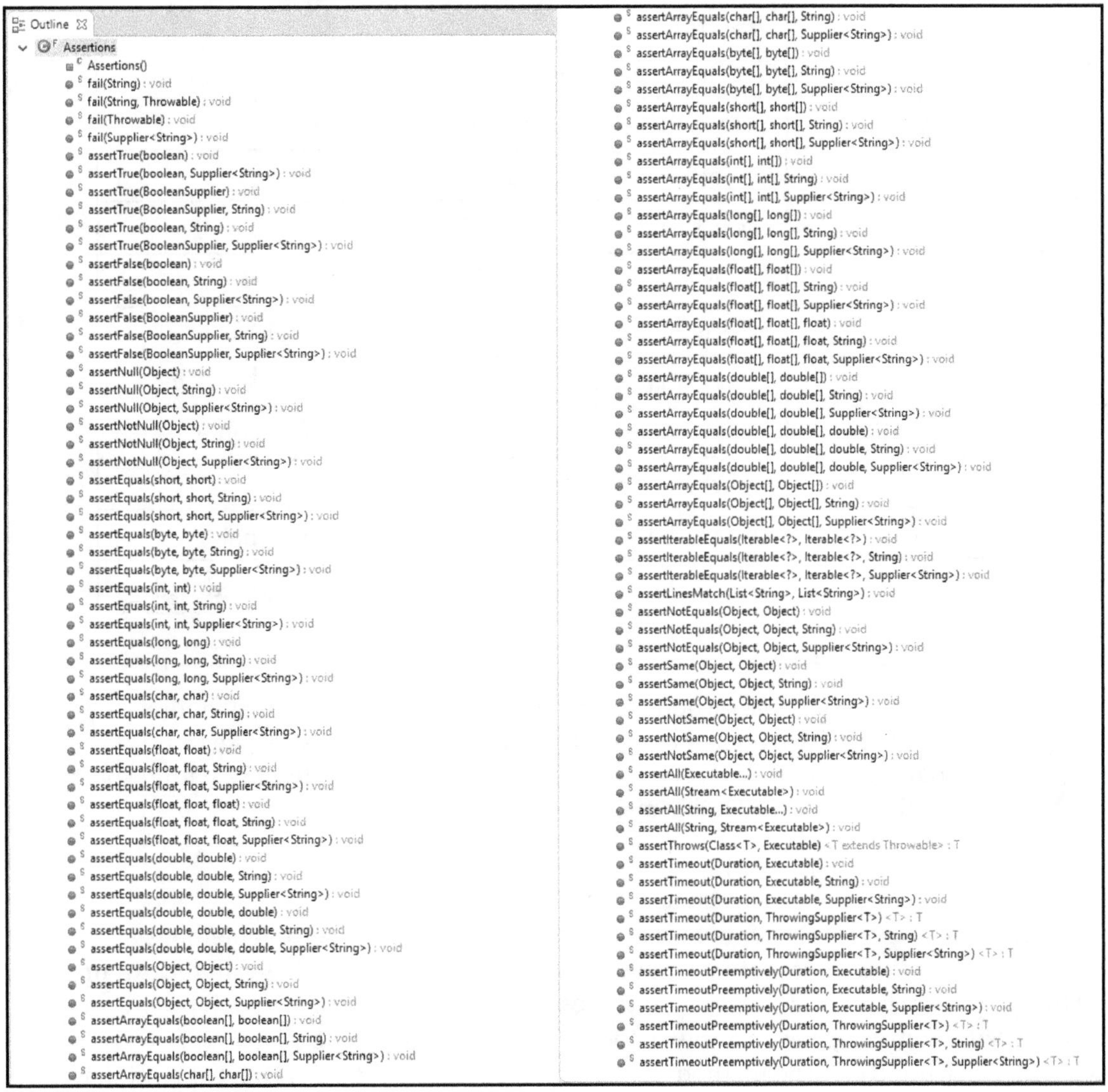

Complete list of Jupiter assertions (class *org.junit.jupiter.Assertions*)

The following table reviews the different types of basic assertions in Jupiter:

Assertion	Description
`fail`	Fails a test with a given message and/or exception
`assertTrue`	Asserts that a supplied condition is true
`assertFalse`	Asserts that a supplied condition is false
`assertNull`	Asserts that a supplied object is `null`
`assertNotNull`	Asserts that a supplied object is not `null`
`assertEquals`	Asserts that two supplied objects are equal
`assertArrayEquals`	Asserts that two supplied arrays are equal
`assertIterableEquals`	Asserts that two iterable objects are deeply equal
`assertLinesMatch`	Asserts that two lists of Strings are equals
`assertNotEquals`	Asserts that two supplied objects are not equal
`assertSame`	Asserts that two objects are the same, compared with `==`
`assertNotSame`	Asserts that two objects are different, compared with `!=`

For each of the assertions contained in the table, an optional failure message (String) can be provided. This message is always the last parameter in the assertion method. This is a small difference with respect to JUnit 4, in which this message was the first parameter in the method invocation.

The following example shows a test using the `assertEquals`, `assertTrue`, and `assertFalse` assertion. Note that we are importing the static assertion methods at the beginning of the class in order to improve the readability of the test logic. In the example, we find the `assertEquals` method, in this case comparing two primitive types (it could also be used for objects). Second, the method `assertTrue` evaluates if a `boolean` expression is true. Third, the method `assertFalse` evaluates if a Boolean expression is false. In this case, notice that the message is created as a Lamdba expression. This way, assertion messages are lazily evaluated to avoid constructing complex messages unnecessarily:

```
package io.github.bonigarcia;

import static org.junit.jupiter.api.Assertions.assertEquals;
import static org.junit.jupiter.api.Assertions.assertFalse;
```

```
import static org.junit.jupiter.api.Assertions.assertTrue;

import org.junit.jupiter.api.Test;

class StandardAssertionsTest {

    @Test
    void standardAssertions() {
        assertEquals(2, 2);
        assertTrue(true,
        "The optional assertion message is now the last parameter");
        assertFalse(false, () -> "Really " + "expensive " + "message"
            + ".");
    }

}
```

The following parts of this section review the advance assertions provided by Jupiter: `assertAll`, `assertThrows`, `assertTimeout`, and `assertTimeoutPreemptively`.

Group of assertions

An important Jupiter assertion is `assertAll`. This method allows to group different assertions at the same time. In a grouped assertion, all assertions are always executed, and any failures will be reported together.

The method `assertAll` accepts a vargargs of lambda expressions (`Executable...`) or a stream of those (`Stream<Executable>`). Optionally, the first parameter of `assertAll` can be a String message aimed to label the assertion group.

Let's see an example. In the following test, we are grouping a couple of `assertEquals` using lambda expressions:

```
package io.github.bonigarcia;

import static org.junit.jupiter.api.Assertions.assertAll;
import static org.junit.jupiter.api.Assertions.assertEquals;

import org.junit.jupiter.api.Test;

class GroupedAssertionsTest {

    @Test
    void groupedAssertions() {
        Address address = new Address("John", "Smith");
        // In a grouped assertion all assertions are executed, and any
```

```
        // failures will be reported together.
        assertAll("address", () -> assertEquals("John",
        address.getFirstName()),
            () -> assertEquals("User", address.getLastName()));
    }

}
```

When executing this test, all assertions of the group will be evaluated. Since the second assertion fails (`lastname` does not match), one failure is reported in the final verdict, as can be seen in the following screenshot:

```
----------------------------------------------------------
 T E S T S
----------------------------------------------------------
Running io.github.bonigarcia.GroupedAssertionsTest
Tests run: 1, Failures: 1, Errors: 0, Skipped: 0, Time elapsed: 0.173 sec <<< FAILURE!
- in io.github.bonigarcia.GroupedAssertionsTest
groupedAssertions()  Time elapsed: 0.037 sec  <<< FAILURE!
org.opentest4j.MultipleFailuresError:
address (1 failure)
        expected: <User> but was: <Smith>
        at io.github.bonigarcia.GroupedAssertionsTest.groupedAssertions(GroupedAssertio
nsTest.java:32)


Results :

Failed tests:
  GroupedAssertionsTest.groupedAssertions:32 address (1 failure)
        expected: <User> but was: <Smith>

Tests run: 1, Failures: 1, Errors: 0, Skipped: 0
```

Console output of grouped assertions example

Asserting exceptions

Another important Jupiter assertion is `assertThrows`. This assertion allows to verify if a given exception is raised in a piece of code. To that aim, the method `assertThrows` accepts two arguments. First, the exception class expected, and second, an executable object (lambda expression), in which the exception is supposed to happen:

```
package io.github.bonigarcia;

import static org.junit.jupiter.api.Assertions.assertEquals;
import static org.junit.jupiter.api.Assertions.assertThrows;
```

```java
import org.junit.jupiter.api.Test;

class ExceptionTest {

    @Test
    void exceptionTesting() {
        Throwable exception =
            assertThrows(IllegalArgumentException.class,
            () -> {
                throw new IllegalArgumentException("a message");});
            assertEquals("a message", exception.getMessage());
    }


}
```

The is expecting `IllegalArgumentException` to be thrown, and this is actually happening inside this lambda expression. The following screenshot shows that the test actually succeeds:

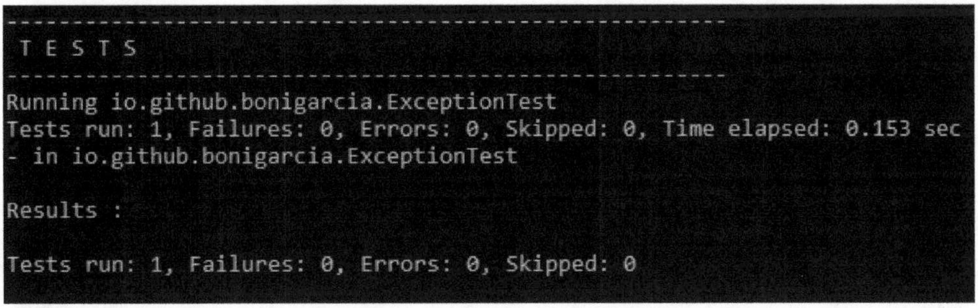

```
-------------------------------------------------------
 T E S T S
-------------------------------------------------------
Running io.github.bonigarcia.ExceptionTest
Tests run: 1, Failures: 0, Errors: 0, Skipped: 0, Time elapsed: 0.153 sec
- in io.github.bonigarcia.ExceptionTest

Results :

Tests run: 1, Failures: 0, Errors: 0, Skipped: 0
```

Console output of *assertThrows* example

Asserting timeouts

To assess timeouts in JUnit 5 tests, Jupiter provides two assertions: `assertTimeout` and `assertTimeoutPreemptively`. On the one hand, `assertTimeout`, allows us to verify the timeout of a given operation. In this assertion, the expected time is defined using the class `Duration` of the standard Java package `java.time`.

We are going to see several running examples to clarify the use of this assertion method. In the following class, we find two tests using `assertTimeout`. The first test is designed to be succeeded, due to the fact that we are expecting that a given operation takes less than 2 minutes, and we are doing nothing there. On the other side, the second test will fail, since we are expecting that a given operation takes a maximum of 10 milliseconds, and we are forcing it to last 100 milliseconds.

```java
package io.github.bonigarcia;

import static java.time.Duration.ofMillis;
import static java.time.Duration.ofMinutes;
import static org.junit.jupiter.api.Assertions.assertTimeout;

import org.junit.jupiter.api.Test;

class TimeoutExceededTest {

    @Test
    void timeoutNotExceeded() {
        assertTimeout(ofMinutes(2), () -> {
            // Perform task that takes less than 2 minutes
        });
    }

    @Test
    void timeoutExceeded() {
        assertTimeout(ofMillis(10), () -> {
            Thread.sleep(100);
        });
    }
}
```

When we execute this test, the second test is declared as failed because the timeout has been exceeded in 90 milliseconds:

```
-------------------------------------------------------
 T E S T S
-------------------------------------------------------
Running io.github.bonigarcia.TimeoutExceededTest
Tests run: 2, Failures: 1, Errors: 0, Skipped: 0, Time elapsed: 0.177 sec <<< FAILURE!
- in io.github.bonigarcia.TimeoutExceededTest
timeoutExceeded()  Time elapsed: 0.13 sec  <<< FAILURE!
org.opentest4j.AssertionFailedError: execution exceeded timeout of 10 ms by 90 ms
        at io.github.bonigarcia.TimeoutExceededTest.timeoutExceeded(TimeoutExceededTes
t.java:36)


Results :

Failed tests:
  TimeoutExceededTest.timeoutExceeded:36 execution exceeded timeout of 10 ms by 90 ms

Tests run: 2, Failures: 1, Errors: 0, Skipped: 0
```

Console output of *assertTimeout* first example

Let's see a couple more tests using `assertTimeout`. In the first test, `assertTimeout` evaluates a piece of code as a lambda expression in a given timeout, obtaining its result. In the second test, `assertTimeout` evaluates a method in a given timeout, obtaining its result:

```java
package io.github.bonigarcia;

import static java.time.Duration.ofMinutes;
import static org.junit.jupiter.api.Assertions.assertEquals;
import static org.junit.jupiter.api.Assertions.assertTimeout;

import org.junit.jupiter.api.Test;

class TimeoutWithResultOrMethodTest {

    @Test
    void timeoutNotExceededWithResult() {
        String actualResult = assertTimeout(ofMinutes(1), () -> {
            return "hi there";
        });
        assertEquals("hi there", actualResult);
    }

    @Test
    void timeoutNotExceededWithMethod() {
```

```
          String actualGreeting = assertTimeout(ofMinutes(1),
              TimeoutWithResultOrMethodTest::greeting);
          assertEquals("hello world!", actualGreeting);
    }

    private static String greeting() {
        return "hello world!";
    }

}
```

In both cases, the tests take less time than expected and therefore both of them are succeeded:

```
------------------------------------------------------------
 T E S T S
------------------------------------------------------------
Running io.github.bonigarcia.TimeoutWithResultOrMethodTest
Tests run: 2, Failures: 0, Errors: 0, Skipped: 0, Time elapsed: 0.12 sec
- in io.github.bonigarcia.TimeoutWithResultOrMethodTest

Results :

Tests run: 2, Failures: 0, Errors: 0, Skipped: 0
```

Console output of *assertTimeout* second example

The other Jupiter assertion for timeouts is called `assertTimeoutPreemptively`. The difference with `assertTimeoutPreemptively` with respect to `assertTimeout` is that `assertTimeoutPreemptively` does not wait until the end of the operation, and the execution is aborted when the expected timeout is exceeded.

In this example, the test will fail since we are simulating an operation which lasts 100 milliseconds, and we have defined a timeout of 10 milliseconds:

```
package io.github.bonigarcia;

import static java.time.Duration.ofMillis;
import static org.junit.jupiter.api.Assertions.assertTimeoutPreemptively;

import org.junit.jupiter.api.Test;

class TimeoutWithPreemptiveTerminationTest {

    @Test
```

```
void timeoutExceededWithPreemptiveTermination() {
    assertTimeoutPreemptively(ofMillis(10), () -> {
        Thread.sleep(100);
    });
}

}
```

In this example, when the timeout of 10 ms is reached, instantly the test is declared as a failure:

```
----------------------------------------------------
 T E S T S
----------------------------------------------------
Running io.github.bonigarcia.TimeoutWithPreemptiveTerminationTest
Tests run: 1, Failures: 1, Errors: 0, Skipped: 0, Time elapsed: 0.174 sec <<< FAILURE!
- in io.github.bonigarcia.TimeoutWithPreemptiveTerminationTest
timeoutExceededWithPreemptiveTermination()  Time elapsed: 0.051 sec  <<< FAILURE!
org.opentest4j.AssertionFailedError: execution timed out after 10 ms
        at io.github.bonigarcia.TimeoutWithPreemptiveTerminationTest.timeoutExceededWit
hPreemptiveTermination(TimeoutWithPreemptiveTerminationTest.java:28)


Results :

Failed tests:
  TimeoutWithPreemptiveTerminationTest.timeoutExceededWithPreemptiveTermination:28 exec
ution timed out after 10 ms

Tests run: 1, Failures: 1, Errors: 0, Skipped: 0
```

Console output of *assertTimeoutPreemptively* example

Third-party assertion libraries

As we have seen, the built-in assertions provided out of the box for Jupiter are sufficient for many testing scenarios. Nevertheless, there are times when more additional functionality, such as matchers, can be desired or required. In such situations, the JUnit team recommends the use of the following third-party assertion libraries:

- Hamcrest (http://hamcrest.org/): an assertion framework to write matcher objects allowing rules to be defined declaratively.

- AssertJ (http://joel-costigliola.github.io/assertj/): fluent assertions for Java.
- Truth (https://google.github.io/truth/): an assertions Java library designed to make test assertions and failure messages more readable.

In this section, we are going to make a brief review of Hamcrest. This library provided the assertion assertThat, which allows to create readable highly configurable assertions. The method assertThat accepts two arguments: first the actual object, and second a Matcher object. This matcher implements the interface org.hamcrest.Matcher, and enables a partial or an exact match for an expectation. Hamcrest provides different matcher utilities, such as is, either, or, not, and hasItem. The Matcher methods use the builder pattern, allowing to combine one or more matchers to build a matcher chain.

In order to use Hamcrest, first we need to import the dependency in our project. In a Maven project, this means that we have to include the following dependency in our pom.xml file:

```
<dependency>
        <groupId>org.hamcrest</groupId>
        <artifactId>hamcrest-core</artifactId>
        <version>${hamcrest.version}</version>
        <scope>test</scope>
</dependency>
```

If we are using Gradle, we need to add the equivalent configuration within the build.gradle file:

```
dependencies {
        testCompile("org.hamcrest:hamcrest-core:${hamcrest}")
}
```

As usual, it is recommended using the latest version of Hamcrest. We can check it on the Maven central web (http://search.maven.org/).

The following example demonstrates how to use Hamcrest inside a Jupiter test. Concretely, this test uses the assertion assertThat together with the matchers containsString, equalTo, and notNullValue:

```
package io.github.bonigarcia;

import static org.hamcrest.CoreMatchers.containsString;
import static org.hamcrest.CoreMatchers.equalTo;
import static org.hamcrest.CoreMatchers.notNullValue;
```

```java
import static org.hamcrest.MatcherAssert.assertThat;

import org.junit.jupiter.api.Test;

class HamcrestTest {

    @Test
    void assertWithHamcrestMatcher() {
        assertThat(2 + 1, equalTo(3));
        assertThat("Foo", notNullValue());
        assertThat("Hello world", containsString("world"));
    }

}
```

As shown in the following screenshot, this test is executed with no failure:

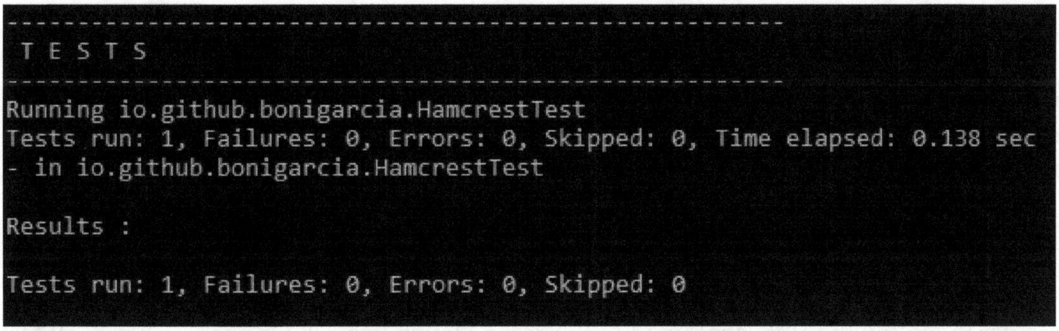

```
-------------------------------------------------
 T E S T S
-------------------------------------------------
Running io.github.bonigarcia.HamcrestTest
Tests run: 1, Failures: 0, Errors: 0, Skipped: 0, Time elapsed: 0.138 sec
- in io.github.bonigarcia.HamcrestTest

Results :

Tests run: 1, Failures: 0, Errors: 0, Skipped: 0
```

Console output of example using the Hamcrest assertion library

Tagging and filtering tests

Test classes and methods can be tagged in the JUnit 5 programming model by means of the annotation @Tag (package org.junit.jupiter.api). Those tags can later be used to filter test discovery and execution. In the following example, we see the use of @Tag at class level and also at method level:

```java
package io.github.bonigarcia;

import org.junit.jupiter.api.Tag;
import org.junit.jupiter.api.Test;

@Tag("simple")
class SimpleTaggingTest {
```

```
    @Test
    @Tag("taxes")
    void testingTaxCalculation() {
    }

}
```

As of JUnit 5 M6, the label for tagging tests should meet the following syntax rules:

- A tag must not be null or blank.
- A trimmed tag (that is, tags in which leading and trailing whitespace have been removed) must not contain a white space.
- A trimmed tag must not contain ISO control characters nor the following reserved characters: `,`, `(`, `)`, `&`, `|`, and `!`.

Filtering tests with Maven

As we already know, we need to use `maven-surefire-plugin` in a Maven project to execute Jupiter test. Moreover, this plugin allows us to filter the test execution in several ways: filtering by JUnit 5 tags and also using the regular inclusion/exclusion support of `maven-surefire-plugin`.

In order to filter by tags, the properties `includeTags` and `excludeTags` of the `maven-surefire-plugin` configuration should be used. Let's see an example to demonstrate how. Consider the following tests contained in the same Maven project. On the one hand, all tests in this class are tagged with the `functional` word.

```java
package io.github.bonigarcia;

import org.junit.jupiter.api.Tag;
import org.junit.jupiter.api.Test;

@Tag("functional")
class FunctionalTest {

    @Test
    void testOne() {
        System.out.println("Functional Test 1");
    }

    @Test
    void testTwo() {
        System.out.println("Functional Test 2");
    }
```

```
}
```

On the other hand, all tests in the second class are tagged as `non-functional` and each individual test is also labeled with more tags (`performance`, `security`, `usability`, and so on):

```java
package io.github.bonigarcia;

import org.junit.jupiter.api.Tag;
import org.junit.jupiter.api.Test;

@Tag("non-functional")
class NonFunctionalTest {

    @Test
    @Tag("performance")
    @Tag("load")
    void testOne() {
        System.out.println("Non-Functional Test 1 (Performance/Load)");
    }

    @Test
    @Tag("performance")
    @Tag("stress")
    void testTwo() {
        System.out.println("Non-Functional Test 2 (Performance/Stress)");
    }

    @Test
    @Tag("security")
    void testThree() {
        System.out.println("Non-Functional Test 3 (Security)");
    }

    @Test
    @Tag("usability")
    void testFour() {
        System.out.println("Non-Functional Test 4 (Usability)");
    }

}
```

As described before, we use the configuration keywords `includeTags` and `excludeTags` in the Maven `pom.xml` file. In this example, we include the test with the tag `functional` and exclude `non-functional`:

```
<build>
    <plugins>
        <plugin>
            <artifactId>maven-surefire-plugin</artifactId>
            <version>${maven-surefire-plugin.version}</version>
            <configuration>
                <properties>
                    <includeTags>functional</includeTags>
                    <excludeTags>non-functional</excludeTags>
                </properties>
            </configuration>
            <dependencies>
                <dependency>
                    <groupId>org.junit.platform</groupId>
                    <artifactId>junit-platform-surefire-
provider</artifactId>
                    <version>${junit.platform.version}</version>
                </dependency>
                <dependency>
                    <groupId>org.junit.jupiter</groupId>
                    <artifactId>junit-jupiter-engine</artifactId>
                    <version>${junit.jupiter.version}</version>
                </dependency>
            </dependencies>
        </plugin>
    </plugins>
</build>
```

As a result, when we try to execute all the tests within the project, only two will be executed (those with the tag `functional`), and the rest are not recognized as tests:

```
--------------------------------------------------------
T E S T S
--------------------------------------------------------
Running io.github.bonigarcia.FunctionalTest
Functional Test 1
Functional Test 2
Tests run: 2, Failures: 0, Errors: 0, Skipped: 0, Time elapsed: 0.09 sec
- in io.github.bonigarcia.FunctionalTest

Results :

Tests run: 2, Failures: 0, Errors: 0, Skipped: 0
```

Maven execution of test filtering by tags

Maven regular support

The regular inclusion/exclusion support of the Maven plugin can still be used to select which tests are going to be executed by `maven-surefire-plugin`. To that aim, we use the keywords `includes` and `excludes` to configure the test name pattern used to filter the execution by the plugin. Notice that for both inclusions and exclusions, regular expressions can be used to specify a pattern of the test filenames:

```
<configuration>
    <includes>
        <include>**/Test*.java</include>
        <include>**/*Test.java</include>
        <include>**/*TestCase.java</include>
    </includes>
</configuration>
<configuration>
    <excludes>
        <exclude>**/TestCircle.java</exclude>
        <exclude>**/TestSquare.java</exclude>
    </excludes>
</configuration>
```

 These three patterns, that is, the Java files containing the word *Test* or ending with *TestCase*, are included by default by a *maven-surefire plugin*.

Filtering tests with Gradle

Let's move now to Gradle. As we already know, we can also use Gradle to run JUnit 5 tests. Regarding the filtering process, we can select the test to be executed based on:

- The test engine: Using the keyword engines we can include or exclude the test engine to be used (that is `junit-jupiter` or `junit-vintage`).
- The Jupiter tags: Using the keyword `tags`.
- The Java packages: Using the keyword `packages`.
- The class name patterns: Using the keyword `includeClassNamePattern`.

By default, all engines and tags are included in the test plan. Only the classname containing the word `Tests` is applied. Let's see a working example. We reuse the same tests presented in the former Maven project, but this time in a Gradle project:

```
junitPlatform {
    filters {
        engines {
            include 'junit-jupiter'
            exclude 'junit-vintage'
        }
        tags {
            include 'non-functional'
            exclude 'functional'
        }
        packages {
            include 'io.github.bonigarcia'
            exclude 'com.others', 'org.others'
        }
        includeClassNamePattern '.*Spec'
        includeClassNamePatterns '.*Test', '.*Tests'
    }
}
```

Notice that we are including the tags `non-functional` and excluding `functional`, and therefore we execute four tests:

```
D:\dev\mastering-junit5\junit5-tagging-filtering>gradle test
:compileJava NO-SOURCE
:processResources NO-SOURCE
:classes UP-TO-DATE
:compileTestJava
:processTestResources NO-SOURCE
:testClasses
:junitPlatformTest
Non-Functional Test 1 (Performance/Load)
Non-Functional Test 2 (Performance/Stress)
Non-Functional Test 3 (Security)
Non-Functional Test 4 (Usability)

Test run finished after 81 ms
[         2 containers found      ]
[         0 containers skipped    ]
[         2 containers started    ]
[         0 containers aborted    ]
[         2 containers successful ]
[         0 containers failed     ]
[         4 tests found           ]
[         0 tests skipped         ]
[         4 tests started         ]
[         0 tests aborted         ]
[         4 tests successful      ]
[         0 tests failed          ]

:test SKIPPED

BUILD SUCCESSFUL
```

Gradle execution of test filtering by tags

Meta-annotations

The final part of this section is about the definition of meta-annotations. The JUnit Jupiter annotations can be used in the definition of other annotations (that is, can be used as meta-annotations). That means that we can define our own composed annotation that will automatically inherit the semantics of its meta-annotations. This feature is very convenient to create our custom test taxonomy by reusing the JUnit 5 annotation `@Tag`.

Let's see an example. Consider the following classification for test cases, in which we classify all tests as functional and non-functional, and then we make another level under the non-functional tests:

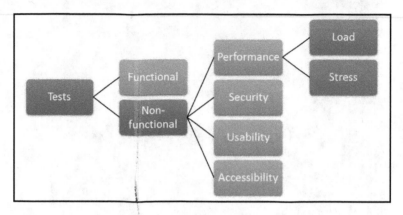

Example taxonomy for tests (functional and non-functional)

With that scheme in mind, we are going to create our custom meta-annotations for leaves of that tree structure: @Functional, @Security, @Usability, @Accessiblity, @Load, and @Stress. Notice that in each annotation we are using one or more @Tag annotations, depending on the structure previously defined. First, we can see the declaration of @Functional:

```java
package io.github.bonigarcia;

import java.lang.annotation.ElementType;
import java.lang.annotation.Retention;
import java.lang.annotation.RetentionPolicy;
import java.lang.annotation.Target;
import org.junit.jupiter.api.Tag;

@Target({ ElementType.TYPE, ElementType.METHOD })
@Retention(RetentionPolicy.RUNTIME)
@Tag("functional")
public @interface Functional {
}
```

Then, we define the annotation `@Security` with tags `non-functional` and `security`:

```java
package io.github.bonigarcia;

import java.lang.annotation.ElementType;
import java.lang.annotation.Retention;
import java.lang.annotation.RetentionPolicy;
import java.lang.annotation.Target;
import org.junit.jupiter.api.Tag;

@Target({ ElementType.TYPE, ElementType.METHOD })
@Retention(RetentionPolicy.RUNTIME)
@Tag("non-functional")
@Tag("security")
public @interface Security {
}
```

Similarly, we define the annotation `@Load`, but this time tagging with `non-functional`, `performance`, and `load`:

```java
package io.github.bonigarcia;

import java.lang.annotation.ElementType;
import java.lang.annotation.Retention;
import java.lang.annotation.RetentionPolicy;
import java.lang.annotation.Target;
import org.junit.jupiter.api.Tag;

@Target({ ElementType.TYPE, ElementType.METHOD })
@Retention(RetentionPolicy.RUNTIME)
@Tag("non-functional")
@Tag("performance")
@Tag("load")
public @interface Load {
}
```

Finally we create the annotation `@Stress` (with tags `non-functional`, `performance`, and `stress`):

```java
package io.github.bonigarcia;

import java.lang.annotation.ElementType;
import java.lang.annotation.Retention;
import java.lang.annotation.RetentionPolicy;
import java.lang.annotation.Target;
import org.junit.jupiter.api.Tag;

@Target({ ElementType.TYPE, ElementType.METHOD })
```

```
@Retention(RetentionPolicy.RUNTIME)
@Tag("non-functional")
@Tag("performance")
@Tag("stress")
public @interface Stress {
}
```

Now, we can use our annotations to tag (and later filter) tests. For instance, in the following example we are using the annotation @Functional at class level:

```
package io.github.bonigarcia;

import org.junit.jupiter.api.Test;

@Functional
class FunctionalTest {

    @Test
    void testOne() {
        System.out.println("Test 1");
    }

    @Test
    void testTwo() {
        System.out.println("Test 2");
    }

}
```

We can also out annotations at method level. In the following test, we annotate the different tests (methods) with different annotations (@Load, @Stress, @Security, and @Accessibility):

```
package io.github.bonigarcia;

import org.junit.jupiter.api.Test;

class NonFunctionalTest {

    @Test
    @Load
    void testOne() {
        System.out.println("Test 1");
    }

    @Test
    @Stress
    void testTwo() {
```

```
        System.out.println("Test 2");
    }

    @Test
    @Security
    void testThree() {
        System.out.println("Test 3");
    }

    @Test
    @Usability
    void testFour() {
        System.out.println("Test 4");
    }

}
```

All in all, we can filter the test by simply changing the included tags. On the one hand, we can filter by the tag `functional`. Notice that in this case, only two tests are executed. The following snippet shows the output of this kind of filtering using Maven:

```
-------------------------------------------------------------
 T E S T S
-------------------------------------------------------------
Running io.github.bonigarcia.FunctionalTest
Functional Test 1
Functional Test 2
Tests run: 2, Failures: 0, Errors: 0, Skipped: 0, Time elapsed: 0.153 sec
  - in io.github.bonigarcia.FunctionalTest

Results :

Tests run: 2, Failures: 0, Errors: 0, Skipped: 0
```

Filtering test by tags (functional) using Maven and the command line

On the other hand, we can also filter with different tags, such as `non-functional`. The following picture shows an example of this type of filtering, this time using Gradle. As usual, we can play with these examples by forking the GitHub repository (`https://github.com/bonigarcia/mastering-junit5`):

```
D:\dev\mastering-junit5\junit5-meta-annotations>gradle test
:compileJava
:processResources NO-SOURCE
:classes
:compileTestJava
:processTestResources NO-SOURCE
:testClasses
:junitPlatformTest
Non-Functional Test 1 (Performance/Load)
Non-Functional Test 2 (Performance/Stress)
Non-Functional Test 2 (Security)
Non-Functional Test 2 (Usability)

Test run finished after 97 ms
[         2 containers found      ]
[         0 containers skipped    ]
[         2 containers started    ]
[         0 containers aborted    ]
[         2 containers successful ]
[         0 containers failed     ]
[         4 tests found           ]
[         0 tests skipped         ]
[         4 tests started         ]
[         0 tests aborted         ]
[         4 tests successful      ]
[         0 tests failed          ]

:test SKIPPED

BUILD SUCCESSFUL

Total time: 2.073 secs
>
```

Filtering test by tags (non-functional) using Gradle and the command line

Conditional test execution

In order to establish custom conditions for test execution, we need to use the JUnit 5 extension model (introduced in `Chapter 2`, *What's new in JUnit 5*, in the section *The extension model of JUnit 5*). Concretely, we need to use the conditional extension point called `ExecutionCondition`. This extension can be used to deactivate either all tests in a class or individual tests.

We are going to see a working example in which we create a custom annotation to disable tests based on the operative system. First of all, we create a custom utility enumeration to select one operative system (WINDOWS, MAC, LINUX, and OTHER):

```
package io.github.bonigarcia;

public enum Os {
    WINDOWS, MAC, LINUX, OTHER;

    public static Os determine() {
        Os out = OTHER;
        String myOs = System.getProperty("os.name").toLowerCase();
        if (myOs.contains("win")) {
            out = WINDOWS;
        }
        else if (myOs.contains("mac")) {
            out = MAC;
        }
        else if (myOs.contains("nux")) {
            out = LINUX;
        }
        return out;
    }
}
```

Then, we create an extension of ExecutionCondition. In this example, the evaluation is done by checking whether or not the custom annotation @DisabledOnOs is present. When the annotation @DisabledOnOs is present, the value of the operative system is compared with the current platform. Depending on the result of that condition, the test is disabled or enabled.

```
package io.github.bonigarcia;

import java.lang.reflect.AnnotatedElement;
import java.util.Arrays;
import java.util.Optional;
import org.junit.jupiter.api.extension.ConditionEvaluationResult;
import org.junit.jupiter.api.extension.ExecutionCondition;
import org.junit.jupiter.api.extension.ExtensionContext;
import org.junit.platform.commons.util.AnnotationUtils;

public class OsCondition implements ExecutionCondition {

    @Override
    public ConditionEvaluationResult evaluateExecutionCondition(
            ExtensionContext context) {
        Optional<AnnotatedElement> element = context.getElement();
```

```
        ConditionEvaluationResult out = ConditionEvaluationResult
            .enabled("@DisabledOnOs is not present");
        Optional<DisabledOnOs> disabledOnOs = AnnotationUtils
            .findAnnotation(element, DisabledOnOs.class);
    if (disabledOnOs.isPresent()) {
        Os myOs = Os.determine();
        if(Arrays.asList(disabledOnOs.get().value())
            .contains(myOs)) {
        out = ConditionEvaluationResult
          .disabled("Test is disabled on " + myOs);
        }
        else {
          out = ConditionEvaluationResult
            .enabled("Test is not disabled on " + myOs);
        }
    }
        System.out.println("--> " + out.getReason().get());
        return out;
    }

}
```

Moreover, we need to create our custom annotation @DisabledOnOs, which is also
annotated with @ExtendWith pointing to our extension point.

```
package io.github.bonigarcia;

import java.lang.annotation.ElementType;
import java.lang.annotation.Retention;
import java.lang.annotation.RetentionPolicy;
import java.lang.annotation.Target;
import org.junit.jupiter.api.extension.ExtendWith;

@Target({ ElementType.TYPE, ElementType.METHOD })
@Retention(RetentionPolicy.RUNTIME)
@ExtendWith(OsCondition.class)
public @interface DisabledOnOs {
    Os[] value();
}
```

Finally, we use our annotation @DisabledOnOs in a Jupiter test.

```java
import org.junit.jupiter.api.Test;

import static io.github.bonigarcia.Os.MAC;
import static io.github.bonigarcia.Os.LINUX;

class DisabledOnOsTest {

    @DisabledOnOs({ MAC, LINUX })
    @Test
    void conditionalTest() {
        System.out.println("This test will be disabled on MAC and LINUX");
    }

}
```

If we execute this test in a Windows machine, the test is not skipped, as we can see in this snapshot:

```
-------------------------------------------------------
 T E S T S
-------------------------------------------------------
Running io.github.bonigarcia.DisabledOnOsTest
--> Test is not disabled on WINDOWS
This test will be disabled on MAC and LINUX
Tests run: 1, Failures: 0, Errors: 0, Skipped: 0, Time elapsed: 0.145 sec
- in io.github.bonigarcia.DisabledOnOsTest

Results :

Tests run: 1, Failures: 0, Errors: 0, Skipped: 0
```

Execution of conditional test example

Assumptions

In this part of this section is about the so-called assumptions. Assumptions allow us to only run tests if certain conditions are as expected. All JUnit Jupiter assumptions are static methods in the class `Assumptions`, located inside the `org.junit.jupiter` package. The following screenshot shows all the methods of this class:

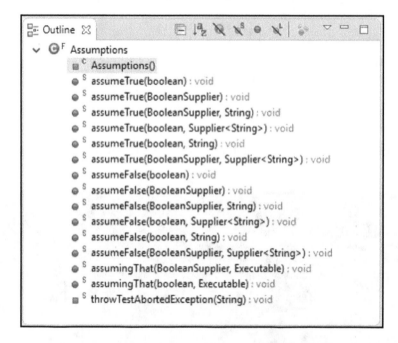

Methods of the class *org.junit.jupiter.Assumptions*

On the one hand, the methods `assumeTrue` and `assumeFalse` can be used to skip tests whose preconditions are not met. On the other hand, the method `assumingThat` is used to condition the execution of a part in a test:

```
package io.github.bonigarcia;

import static org.junit.jupiter.api.Assertions.fail;
import static org.junit.jupiter.api.Assumptions.assumeFalse;
import static org.junit.jupiter.api.Assumptions.assumeTrue;
import static org.junit.jupiter.api.Assumptions.assumingThat;

import org.junit.jupiter.api.Test;

class AssumptionsTest {
```

```
@Test
void assumeTrueTest() {
    assumeTrue(false);
    fail("Test 1 failed");
}

@Test
void assumeFalseTest() {
    assumeFalse(this::getTrue);
    fail("Test 2 failed");
}

private boolean getTrue() {
    return true;
}

@Test
void assummingThatTest() {
    assumingThat(false, () -> fail("Test 3 failed"));
}

}
```

Notice that in this example, the two first tests (assumeTrueTest and assumeFalseTest)
are skipped since the assumptions are not met. Nevertheless, in the
assummingThatTest test, only this part of the test (a lambda expression in this case) is not
executed, but the whole test is not skipped:

```
-------------------------------------------------------------
 T E S T S
-------------------------------------------------------------
Running io.github.bonigarcia.AssumptionsTest
Tests run: 3, Failures: 0, Errors: 0, Skipped: 2, Time elapsed: 0.183 sec
- in io.github.bonigarcia.AssumptionsTest

Results :

Tests run: 3, Failures: 0, Errors: 0, Skipped: 2
```

Execution of assumptions test example

Nested tests

Nested tests give the test writer more capabilities to express the relationship and order in a group of tests. JUnit 5 makes it effortless to nest test classes. We simply need to annotate inner classes with @Nested and all test methods in there will be executed as well, going from the regular tests (defined in the top-level class) to the tests defined in each of the inner classes.

The first thing we need to take into account is that only non-static nested classes (that is inner classes) can serve as @Nested tests. Nesting can be arbitrarily deep, and the setup and tear down for each test (that is, @BeforeEach and @AfterEach methods) are inherited in the nested tests. Nevertheless, inner classes cannot define the @BeforeAll and @AfterAll methods, due to the fact that Java does not allow static members in inner classes. However, this restriction can be avoided using the annotation @TestInstance(Lifecycle.PER_CLASS) in the test class. As described in the section *Test instance lifecycle* in this chapter, this annotation force to instance a test instance per class, instead of a test instance per method (default behavior). This way, the methods @BeforeAll and @AfterAll do not need to be static and therefore it can be used in nested tests.

Let's see a simple example composed by a Java class with two levels of inner classes, that is, the class contains two nested inner classes annotated with @Nested. As we can see, there are tests in the three levels of the class. Notice that the top class defined a setup method (@BeforeEach), and also the first nested class (called InnerClass1 in the example). In the top-level class, we define a single test (called topTest), and in each nested class we find another test (called innerTest1 and innerTest2, respectively):

```
package io.github.bonigarcia;

import org.junit.jupiter.api.BeforeEach;
import org.junit.jupiter.api.Nested;
import org.junit.jupiter.api.Test;

class NestTest {

    @BeforeEach
    void setup1() {
        System.out.println("Setup 1");
    }

    @Test
    void topTest() {
        System.out.println("Test 1");
    }
```

```java
@Nested
class InnerClass1 {

    @BeforeEach
    void setup2() {
        System.out.println("Setup 2");
    }

    @Test
    void innerTest1() {
        System.out.println("Test 2");
    }

    @Nested
    class InnerClass2 {

        @Test
        void innerTest2() {
            System.out.println("Test 3");
        }
    }
}
}
```

If we execute this example, we can trace the execution of the nested tests by simply looking to the console traces. Note that the top @BeforeEach method (called setup1) is always executed before each test. Therefore, the trace Setup 1 is always present in the console before the actual test execution. Each test also writes a line the console. As we can see, the first test logs Test 1. After that, the tests defined in the inner classes are executed. The first inner class executes the test innerTest1, but after that, the setup method of the top-level class and the first inner class are executed (logging Setup 1 and Setup 2, respectively).

Finally, the test defined in the last inner class (`innerTest2`) is executed, but as usual, the cascade of setup methods is executed before the test:

```
--------------------------------------------------
T E S T S
--------------------------------------------------
Running io.github.bonigarcia.NestTest
Setup 1
Test 1
Setup 1
Setup 2
Test 2
Setup 1
Setup 2
Test 3
Tests run: 3, Failures: 0, Errors: 0, Skipped: 0, Time elapsed: 0.263 sec
- in io.github.bonigarcia.NestTest
Running io.github.bonigarcia.StackTest
Tests run: 7, Failures: 0, Errors: 0, Skipped: 0, Time elapsed: 0.001 sec
- in io.github.bonigarcia.StackTest

Results :

Tests run: 10, Failures: 0, Errors: 0, Skipped: 0
```

Console output of the execution of the nested test example

Nested tests can be used in conjunction with the display name (that is, the annotation `@DisplayName`) to help to produce a nicely readable test output. The following example demonstrates how. This class contains the structure to test the implementation of a stack, that is, a *last-in-first-out* (LIFO) collection. The class is designed to first test the stack when it is just instantiated (the method `isInstantiatedWithNew`). After that, the first inner class (`WhenNew`) is supposed to test the stack as an empty collection (methods `isEmpty`, `throwsExceptionWhenPopped` and `throwsExceptionWhenPeeked`). Finally, the second inner class is supposed to test when the stack is not empty (methods `isNotEmpty`, `returnElementWhenPopped`, and `returnElementWhenPeeked`):

```java
package io.github.bonigarcia;

import org.junit.jupiter.api.DisplayName;
import org.junit.jupiter.api.Nested;
import org.junit.jupiter.api.Test;

@DisplayName("A stack test")

 class StackTest {
```

```
@Test
@DisplayName("is instantiated")
void isInstantiated() {
}

@Nested
@DisplayName("when empty")
class WhenNew {

    @Test
    @DisplayName("is empty")
    void isEmpty() {
    }

    @Test
    @DisplayName("throws Exception when popped")
    void throwsExceptionWhenPopped() {
    }

    @Test
    @DisplayName("throws Exception when peeked")
    void throwsExceptionWhenPeeked() {
    }

    @Nested
    @DisplayName("after pushing an element")
    class AfterPushing {

        @Test
        @DisplayName("it is no longer empty")
        void isNotEmpty() {
        }

        @Test
        @DisplayName("returns the element when popped")
        void returnElementWhenPopped() {
        }

        @Test
        @DisplayName("returns the element when peeked")
        void returnElementWhenPeeked() {
        }

    }
}
}
```

The objective of this type of test is two folded. On the one hand, the class structure provides an order for the execution of the tests. On the other hand, the use of @DisplayName improves the readability of the test execution. We can see that when the test is executed in an IDE, concretely in IntelliJ IDEA.

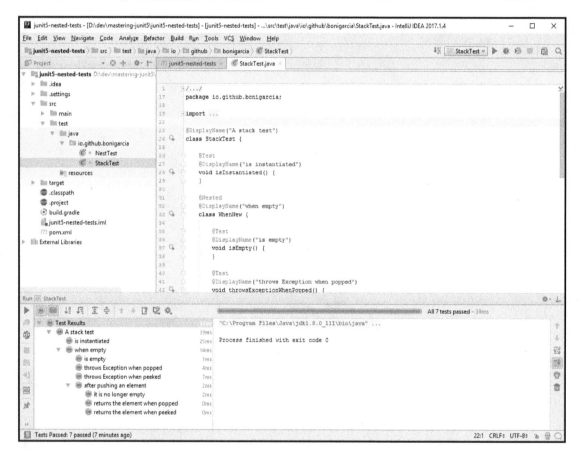

Execution of nested test using *@DisplayName* on Intellij IDEA

Repeated tests

JUnit Jupiter provides for the ability to repeat a test a specified number of times simply by annotating a method with `@RepeatedTest`, specifying the total number of repetitions desired. Each repeated test behaves exactly as a regular `@Test` method. Moreover, each repeated test preserves the same lifecycle callbacks (`@BeforeEach`, `@AfterEach`, and so on).

The following Java class contains a test that is going to be repeated five times:

```java
package io.github.bonigarcia;

import org.junit.jupiter.api.RepeatedTest;

class SimpleRepeatedTest {

    @RepeatedTest(5)
    void test() {
        System.out.println("Repeated test");
    }

}
```

Due to the fact that this test only writes a line (`Repeated test`) in the standard output, when executing this test in the console, we will see that trace five times:

```
-------------------------------------------------
 T E S T S
-------------------------------------------------
Running io.github.bonigarcia.SimpleRepeatedTest
Repeated test
Repeated test
Repeated test
Repeated test
Repeated test
Tests run: 5, Failures: 0, Errors: 0, Skipped: 0, Time elapsed: 0.195 sec
- in io.github.bonigarcia.SimpleRepeatedTest

Results :

Tests run: 5, Failures: 0, Errors: 0, Skipped: 0
```

Execution of repeated test in the console

In addition to specifying the number of repetitions, a custom display name can be configured for each repetition via the name attribute of the `@RepeatedTest` annotation. The display name can be a pattern composed of a combination of static text and dynamic placeholders. The following are currently supported:

- `{displayName}`: This is the name of the `@RepeatedTest` method.
- `{currentRepetition}`: This is the current repetition count.
- `{totalRepetitions}`: This is the total number of repetitions.

The following example shows a class with three repeated tests in which the display name is configured with the property name of `@RepeatedTest`:

```
package io.github.bonigarcia;

import org.junit.jupiter.api.DisplayName;
import org.junit.jupiter.api.RepeatedTest;
import org.junit.jupiter.api.TestInfo;

class TunningDisplayInRepeatedTest {

    @RepeatedTest(value = 2, name = "{displayName}
    {currentRepetition}/{totalRepetitions}")
    @DisplayName("Repeat!")
    void customDisplayName(TestInfo testInfo) {
        System.out.println(testInfo.getDisplayName());
    }

    @RepeatedTest(value = 2, name = RepeatedTest.LONG_DISPLAY_NAME)
    @DisplayName("Test using long display name")
    void customDisplayNameWithLongPattern(TestInfo testInfo) {
        System.out.println(testInfo.getDisplayName());
    }

    @RepeatedTest(value = 2, name = RepeatedTest.SHORT_DISPLAY_NAME)
    @DisplayName("Test using short display name")
    void customDisplayNameWithShortPattern(TestInfo testInfo) {
        System.out.println(testInfo.getDisplayName());
    }

}
```

In this test, the display name for these repeated tests will be as follows:

- For the test `customDisplayName`, the display name will follow the long display format:
  - Repeat 1 out of 2.
  - Repeat 2 out of 2.
- For the test `customDisplayNameWithLongPattern`, the display name will follow the long display format:
  - Repeat! 1/2.
  - Repeat! 2/2.
- For the test `customDisplayNameWithShortPattern`, the display name in this test will follow the short display format:
  - Test using long display name :: repetition 1 of 2.
  - Test using long display name :: repetition 2 of 2.

```
------------------------------------------------------
 T E S T S
------------------------------------------------------
Running io.github.bonigarcia.TunningDisplayInRepeatedTest
repetition 1 of 2
repetition 2 of 2
Test using long display name :: repetition 1 of 2
Test using long display name :: repetition 2 of 2
Repeat! 1/2
Repeat! 2/2
Tests run: 6, Failures: 0, Errors: 0, Skipped: 0, Time elapsed: 0.192 sec
- in io.github.bonigarcia.TunningDisplayInRepeatedTest

Results :

Tests run: 6, Failures: 0, Errors: 0, Skipped: 0
```

Execution of repeated test example in conjunction with *@DisplayName*

Migration from JUnit 4 to JUnit 5

JUnit 5 does not support JUnit 4 features, such as Rules and Runners, natively. Nevertheless, JUnit 5 provides a gentle migration path via the JUnit Vintage test engine, which allows us to execute legacy test cases (including JUnit 4 but also JUnit 3) on the top of the JUnit Platform.

The following table can be used to summarize the main differences between JUnit 4 and 5:

Feature	JUnit 4	JUnit 5
Annotations package	`org.junit`	`org.junit.jupiter.api`
Declaring a test	`@Test`	`@Test`
Setup for all tests	`@BeforeClass`	`@BeforeAll`
Setup per test	`@Before`	`@BeforeEach`
Tear down per test	`@After`	`@AfterEach`
Tear down for all tests	`@AfterClass`	`@AfterAll`
Tagging and filtering	`@Category`	`@Tag`
Disable a test method or class	`@Ignore`	`@Disabled`
Nested tests	NA	`@Nested`
Repeated test	Using custom rule	`@Repeated`
Dynamic tests	NA	`@TestFactory`
Test templates	NA	`@TestTemaplate`
Runners	`@RunWith`	This feature is superseded by the extension model (`@ExtendWith`)
Rules	`@Rule` and `@ClassRule`	This feature is superseded by the extension model (`@ExtendWith`)

Rule support in Jupiter

As described before, Jupiter does not support JUnit 4 rules natively. Nevertheless, the JUnit 5 team realized that JUnit 4 rules are widely adopted in many test codebases nowadays. In order to provide a seamless migration from JUnit 4 to JUnit 5, the JUnit 5 team implemented the `junit-jupiter-migrationsupport` module. If this module is going to be used in a project, the module dependency should be imported. Examples for Maven are shown here:

```
<dependency>
    <groupId>org.junit.jupiter</groupId>
    <artifactId>junit-jupiter-migrationsupport</artifactId>
    <version>${junit.jupiter.version}</version>
    <scope>test</scope>
```

```
</dependency>
```

The Gradle declaration for this dependency is like this:

```
dependencies {
        testCompile("org.junit.jupiter:junit-jupiter-
        migrationsupport:${junitJupiterVersion}")
}
```

The rule support in JUnit 5 is limited to those rules semantically compatible with the Jupiter extension model, including the following rules:

- `junit.rules.ExternalResource` (including `org.junit.rules.TemporaryFolder`).
- `junit.rules.Verifier` (including `org.junit.rules.ErrorCollector`).
- `junit.rules.ExpectedException`.

In order to enable these rules in Jupiter tests, the test class should be annotated with the class-level annotation `@EnableRuleMigrationSupport` (located in the package `org.junit.jupiter.migrationsupport.rules`). Let us see several examples. First, the following test case defines and uses a `TemporaryFolder` JUnit 4 rule within a Jupiter test:

```
package io.github.bonigarcia;

import java.io.IOException;
import org.junit.Rule;
import org.junit.jupiter.api.AfterEach;
import org.junit.jupiter.api.BeforeEach;
import org.junit.jupiter.api.Test;
import org.junit.jupiter.migrationsupport.rules.EnableRuleMigrationSupport;
import org.junit.rules.TemporaryFolder;

@EnableRuleMigrationSupport
class TemporaryFolderRuleTest {

    @Rule
    TemporaryFolder temporaryFolder = new TemporaryFolder();

    @BeforeEach
    void setup() throws IOException {
        temporaryFolder.create();
    }

    @Test
    void test() {
        System.out.println("Temporary folder: " +
```

```
                temporaryFolder.getRoot());
    }

    @AfterEach
    void teardown() {
        temporaryFolder.delete();
    }

}
```

When executing this test, the path of the temporary folder will be logged on the standard output:

```
------------------------------------------------
 T E S T S
------------------------------------------------
Running io.github.bonigarcia.TemporaryFolderRuleTest
Temporary folder: C:\Users\boni\AppData\Local\Temp\junit3324174191725360154

Tests run: 1, Failures: 0, Errors: 0, Skipped: 0, Time elapsed: 0.445 sec -
  in io.github.bonigarcia.TemporaryFolderRuleTest

Results :

Tests run: 1, Failures: 0, Errors: 0, Skipped: 0
```

Execution of Jupiter test using a JUnit 4 *TemporaryFolder* rule

The following test demonstrates the use of the `ErrorCollector` rule in a Jupiter test. Notice that the collector rule allows the execution of a test to continue after one or more problems are found:

```
package io.github.bonigarcia;

import static org.hamcrest.CoreMatchers.equalTo;

import org.junit.Rule;
import org.junit.jupiter.api.Test;
import org.junit.jupiter.migrationsupport.rules.EnableRuleMigrationSupport;
import org.junit.rules.ErrorCollector;

@EnableRuleMigrationSupport
class ErrorCollectorRuleTest {

    @Rule
    public ErrorCollector collector = new ErrorCollector();
```

```
@Test
void test() {
    collector.checkThat("a", equalTo("b"));
    collector.checkThat(1, equalTo(2));
    collector.checkThat("c", equalTo("c"));
}

}
```

These problems are reported together at the end of the test:

```
------------------------------------------------
 T E S T S
------------------------------------------------
Running io.github.bonigarcia.ErrorCollectorRuleTest
Tests run: 1, Failures: 0, Errors: 1, Skipped: 0, Time elapsed: 0.237 sec
<<< FAILURE! - in io.github.bonigarcia.ErrorCollectorRuleTest
  test()  Time elapsed: 0.04 sec  <<< ERROR!
org.junit.internal.runners.model.MultipleFailureException:
There were 2 errors:
  java.lang.AssertionError(
Expected: "b"
    but: was "a")
  java.lang.AssertionError(
 Expected: <2>
    but: was <1>)


Results :

Tests in error:
  ErrorCollectorRuleTest.test » MultipleFailure There were 2 errors:
    java.lang...

Tests run: 1, Failures: 0, Errors: 1, Skipped: 0
```

Execution of Jupiter test using a JUnit 4 *ErrorCollector* rule

Finally, the `ExpectedException` rule allows us to configure a test to anticipate a given exception to be thrown within the test logic:

```
package io.github.bonigarcia;

import org.junit.Rule;
import org.junit.jupiter.api.Test;
import org.junit.jupiter.migrationsupport.rules.EnableRuleMigrationSupport;
import org.junit.rules.ExpectedException;
```

```
@EnableRuleMigrationSupport
class ExpectedExceptionRuleTest {

    @Rule
    ExpectedException thrown = ExpectedException.none();

    @Test
    void throwsNothing() {
    }

    @Test
    void throwsNullPointerException() {
        thrown.expect(NullPointerException.class);
        throw new NullPointerException();
    }

}
```

In this example, even when the second test raises a `NullPointerException`, the test will be marked as having succeeded since that exception was expected.

```
 ---------------------------------------------------------------
 T E S T S
 ---------------------------------------------------------------
 Running io.github.bonigarcia.ExpectedExceptionRuleTest
 Tests run: 2, Failures: 0, Errors: 0, Skipped: 0, Time elapsed: 0.216 sec
 - in io.github.bonigarcia.ExpectedExceptionRuleTest

 Results :

 Tests run: 2, Failures: 0, Errors: 0, Skipped: 0
```

Execution of Jupiter test using a JUnit 4 *ExpectedException* rule

Summary

In this chapter, we introduced the basics of the brand-new programming model of the JUnit 5 framework, known as Jupiter. This programming model provides a rich API that can be used by practitioners to create test cases. The most basic element of Jupiter is the annotation `@Test`, which identifies the methods in Java classes treated as tests (that is logic which exercises and verifies a SUT). Moreover, there are different annotations that can be used to control the test life cycle, namely, `@BeforeAll`, `@BeforeEach`, `@AfterEach`, and `@AfterAll`. Other useful Jupiter annotations are `@Disabled` (to skip tests), `@DisplayName` (to provide a test name), `@Tag` (to label and filter tests).

Jupiter provides a rich set of assertions, which are static methods in the class `Assertions` used to verify if the outcome obtained from the SUT corresponds with some expected value. We can impose conditions for the test execution in several ways. On the one hand, we can use `Assumptions` to only run tests (or a part of those) if certain conditions are as expected.

We have learned how nested tests can be created simple annotating inner Java classes with `@Nested`. This can be used to create test executions following an order given the nested classes relationship. We have also studied how easy is to created repeated test using the JUnit 5 programming model. The annotation `@RepeatedTest` is used to that aim, providing the ability to repeat a test a specified number of times. Finally, we have seen how Jupiter provides support for several legacy JUnit 4 test rules, including `ExternalResource`, `Verifier`, and `ExpectedException`.

In the chapter 4, *Simplifying Testing With Advanced JUnit Features*, we continue discovering the JUnit programming model. Concretely, we review the advance features of JUnit 5, namely, dependency injection, dynamic tests, test interfaces, test templates, parameterized tests, compatibility of JUnit 5 and Java 9. Finally, we review some of the planned features in the backlog for JUnit 5.1, not implemented yet at the time of this writing.

4

Simplifying Testing With Advanced JUnit Features

So far, we have discovered the basics of Jupiter, the brand-new programming model provided by the JUnit 5 framework. Moreover, Jupiter provides a rich range of possibilities which allows to create different types of test cases. In this chapter, we review these advanced features. To that aim, this chapter is structured as follows:

- **Dependency injection**: This section first takes a look at dependency injection for constructors and methods in test classes. Then, it reviews the three parameter resolvers provided out of the box in Jupiter. These resolvers allow to inject objects of `TestInfo`, `RepetitionInfo`, and `TestReporter` inside tests.

- **Dynamic tests**: This section discusses how dynamic tests are implemented in JUnit 5, using the methods `dynamicTest` and `stream`.

- **Test interfaces**: The section reviews the Jupiter annotations that can be declared on test interfaces and default methods.

- **Test templates**: JUnit 5 introduces the concept of a template for tests cases. These templates will be invoked multiple times, depending on the invocation contexts.

- **Parameterized tests**: In the same way as JUnit 4, JUnit 5 provides capabilities to create tests driven by different input data, that is, a parametrized test. We will discover that the support for this kind of test has been significantly enhanced in the Jupiter programming model.

- **Java 9**: On September 21, 2017, Java 9 released. As we will discover, JUnit 5 has been implemented to be compatible with Java 9, with special emphasis on the modularity feature of Java 9.

Dependency injection

In former JUnit versions, test constructors and methods were not allowed to have parameters. One of the major changes in JUnit 5 is that both test constructors and methods are now allowed to include parameters. This feature enables the dependency injection for constructors and methods.

As introduced in `Chapter 2`, *What's New In JUnit 5* of this book, the extension model has an extension that provides dependency injections for Jupiter tests, called `ParameterResolver`, which defines an API for test extensions that wish to dynamically resolve parameters at runtime.

If a test constructor or a method annotated with `@Test`, `@TestFactory`, `@BeforeEach`, `@AfterEach`, `@BeforeAll`, or `@AfterAll` accepts a parameter, that parameter is resolved at runtime by a resolver (object with parent class `ParameterResolver`). There are three built-in resolvers registered automatically in JUnit 5: `TestInfoParameterResolver`, and `RepetitionInfoParameterResolver`, `TestReporterParameterResolver`. We review each one of these resolvers in this section.

TestInfoParameterResolver

Given a test class, if a method parameter is of type `TestInfo`, the JUnit 5 resolver `TestInfoParameterResolver` supplies an instance of `TestInfo` corresponding to the current test as the value for the declared parameter. The `TestInfo` object is used to retrieve information about the current test, such as the test display name, the test class, the test method, or associated tags.

`TestInfo` acts as a drop-in replacement for the `TestName` rule from JUnit 4.

The class `TestInfo` is placed in the package `org.junit.jupiter.api` and offers the following API:

- `String getDisplayName()` : This returns the display name of the test or container.
- `Set<String> getTags()` : This gets the set of all tags for the current test or container.
- `Optional<Class<?>> getTestClass()` : This gets the class associated with the current test or container, if available.
- `Optional<Method> getTestMethod()` : This gets the method associated with the current test, if available.

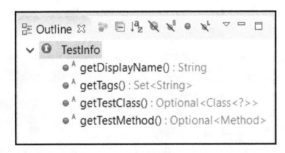

TestInfo API

Let's see an example. Notice that in the following class, both the methods annotated with `@BeforeEach` and `@Test` accepts a parameter of `TestInfo`. This parameter is injected by `TestInfoParameterResolver`:

```
package io.github.bonigarcia;

import org.junit.jupiter.api.BeforeEach;
import org.junit.jupiter.api.DisplayName;
import org.junit.jupiter.api.Tag;
import org.junit.jupiter.api.Test;
import org.junit.jupiter.api.TestInfo;

class TestInfoTest {

    @BeforeEach
    void init(TestInfo testInfo) {
        String displayName = testInfo.getDisplayName();
        System.out.printf("@BeforeEach %s %n", displayName);
    }

    @Test
    @DisplayName("My test")
```

```
        @Tag("my-tag")
        void testOne(TestInfo testInfo) {
            System.out.println(testInfo.getDisplayName());
            System.out.println(testInfo.getTags());
            System.out.println(testInfo.getTestClass());
            System.out.println(testInfo.getTestMethod());
        }

        @Test
        void testTwo() {
        }

    }
```

Therefore, in the body of each method, we are able to use the `TestInfo` API to get the test information at runtime, as the following screenshot demonstrates:

```
------------------------------------------------------------
 T E S T S
------------------------------------------------------------
Running io.github.bonigarcia.TestInfoTest
@BeforeEach My test
My test
[my-tag]
Optional[class io.github.bonigarcia.TestInfoTest]
Optional[void io.github.bonigarcia.TestInfoTest.test1(org.junit.jupiter.api.
TestInfo)]
@BeforeEach test2()
Tests run: 2, Failures: 0, Errors: 0, Skipped: 0, Time elapsed: 0.423 sec -
in io.github.bonigarcia.TestInfoTest

Results :

Tests run: 2, Failures: 0, Errors: 0, Skipped: 0
```

Console output of dependency injection of *TestInfo* objects

RepetitionInfoParameterResolver

The second resolver provided out of the box in JUnit 5 is called
`RepetitionInfoParameterResolver`. Given a test class, if a method parameter in a
`@RepeatedTest`, `@BeforeEach`, or `@AfterEach` method is of type `RepetitionInfo`, the
`RepetitionInfoParameterResolver` will supply an instance of `RepetitionInfo`.

`RepetitionInfo` can be used to retrieve information about the current repetition and the
total number of repetitions for the corresponding `@RepeatedTest`. The API of
`RepetitionInfo` offers two methods, as shown in the screenshot after the list:

- `int getCurrentRepetition()`: Gets the current repetition of the
  corresponding `@RepeatedTest` method
- `int getTotalRepetitions()`: Gets the total number of repetitions of the
  corresponding `@RepeatedTest` method

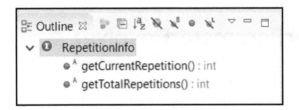

RepetitionInfo API

The class here contains a simple example for the use of `RepetitionInfo`:

```
package io.github.bonigarcia;

import org.junit.jupiter.api.RepeatedTest;
import org.junit.jupiter.api.RepetitionInfo;

class RepetitionInfoTest {

    @RepeatedTest(2)
    void test(RepetitionInfo repetitionInfo) {
        System.out.println("** Test " +
            repetitionInfo.getCurrentRepetition()
            + "/" + repetitionInfo.getTotalRepetitions());
    }

}
```

As can be seen in the test output, we are able to read the information about the repeated test at runtime:

```
-------------------------------------------------------------
 T E S T S
-------------------------------------------------------------
Running io.github.bonigarcia.RepetitionInfoTest
** Test 1/2
** Test 2/2
Tests run: 2, Failures: 0, Errors: 0, Skipped: 0, Time elapsed: 0.125 sec -
in io.github.bonigarcia.RepetitionInfoTest

Results :

Tests run: 2, Failures: 0, Errors: 0, Skipped: 0
```

The console output of dependency injection of *RepetitionInfo* objects.

TestReporterParameterResolver

The last built-in resolver in JUnit 5 is `TestReporterParameterResolver`. Again, given a test class, if a method parameter is of type `TestReporter`, the `TestReporterParameterResolver` supplies an instance of `TestReporter`.

`TestReporter` is used to publish additional data about the test execution. The data can be consumed through the method `reportingEntryPublished`, and then, it can be requested by IDEs or included in test reports. Each `TestReporter` object stores information as a map, that is, a key-value collection:

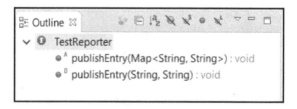

TestReporter API

This test provides a simple example of `TestReporter`. As we can see, we use the injected `testReporter` object to add custom information using key-value pairs:

```
package io.github.bonigarcia;

import java.util.HashMap;
import org.junit.jupiter.api.Test;
import org.junit.jupiter.api.TestReporter;

class TestReporterTest {

    @Test
    void reportSingleValue(TestReporter testReporter) {
        testReporter.publishEntry("key", "value");
    }

    @Test
    void reportSeveralValues(TestReporter testReporter) {
        HashMap<String, String> values = new HashMap<>();
        values.put("name", "john");
        values.put("surname", "doe");
        testReporter.publishEntry(values);
    }

}
```

Dynamic tests

As we know, in JUnit 3, we identified tests by parsing method names and checking whether they started with the word test. Then, in JUnit 4, we identified tests by collecting methods annotated with `@Test`. Both of these techniques share the same approach: tests are defined at compile time. This concept is what we call static testing.

Static tests are considered a limited approach, especially for the common scenario in which the same test is supposed to be executed for a variety of input data. In JUnit 4, this limitation was addressed in several ways. A very simple solution to the problem is to loop the input test data and exercising the same test logic (JUnit 4 example here). Following this approach, one test is executed until the first assertion fails:

```
package io.github.bonigarcia;

import org.junit.Test;

public class MyTest {
```

```
@Test
public void test() {
    String[] input = { "A", "B", "C" };
    for (String s : input) {
        exercise(s);
    }
}

private void exercise(String s) {
    System.out.println(s);
}

}
```

A more elaborate solution is to use the JUnit 4 support for parameterized tests, using the parameterized runner. This approach does not create tests at runtime either, it simply repeats the same test several times depending on the parameters:

```
package io.github.bonigarcia;

import java.util.Arrays;
import java.util.Collection;
import org.junit.Test;
import org.junit.runner.RunWith;
import org.junit.runners.Parameterized;
import org.junit.runners.Parameterized.Parameter;
import org.junit.runners.Parameterized.Parameters;

@RunWith(Parameterized.class)
public class ParameterizedTest {

    @Parameter(0)
    public Integer input1;

    @Parameter(1)
    public String input2;

    @Parameters(name = "My test #{index} -- input data: {0} and {1}")
    public static Collection<Object[]> data() {
        return Arrays
            .asList(new Object[][] { { 1, "hello" }, { 2, "goodbye" } });
    }

    @Test
    public void test() {
        System.out.println(input1 + " " + input2);
    }
}
```

We can see the execution of the preceding example in the Eclipse IDE:

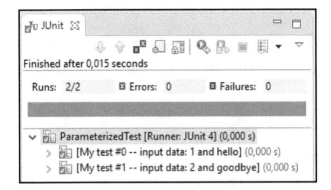

Execution of JUnit 4's parameterized test in Eclipse

On the other hand, JUnit 5 allows to generate test at runtime by a factory method that is annotated with @TestFactory. In contrast to @Test, a @TestFactory method is not a test but a factory. A @TestFactory method must return a Stream, Collection, Iterable, or Iterator of DynamicTest instances. These DynamicTest instances are executed lazily, enabling dynamic generation of test cases.

In order to create a dynamic test, we can use the static method dynamicTest of the class DynamicTest located in the org.junit.jupiter.api package. If we inspect the source code of this class, we can see that a DynamicTest is composed of a display name in form of the String and one executable object, which can be provided as lambda expressions or as method references.

Let's see several examples of dynamic tests. In the following example, the first dynamic test will fail, due to the fact we are not returning the expected collection of DynamicTests. The next three methods are very simple examples that demonstrate the generation of Collection, Iterable, and Iterator of DynamicTest instances:

```
package io.github.bonigarcia;

import static org.junit.jupiter.api.Assertions.assertEquals;
import static org.junit.jupiter.api.Assertions.assertTrue;
import static org.junit.jupiter.api.DynamicTest.dynamicTest;

import java.util.Arrays;
import java.util.Collection;
import java.util.Iterator;
import java.util.List;
import org.junit.jupiter.api.DynamicTest;
```

```java
import org.junit.jupiter.api.TestFactory;

class CollectionTest {

    // Warning: this test will raise an exception
    @TestFactory
    List<String> dynamicTestsWithInvalidReturnType() {
        return Arrays.asList("Hello");
    }

    @TestFactory
    Collection<DynamicTest> dynamicTestsFromCollection() {
        return Arrays.asList(
                dynamicTest("1st dynamic test", () ->
                    assertTrue(true)),
                dynamicTest("2nd dynamic test", () -> assertEquals(4, 2
                    * 2)));
    }

    @TestFactory
    Iterable<DynamicTest> dynamicTestsFromIterable() {
        return Arrays.asList(
                dynamicTest("3rd dynamic test", () ->
                    assertTrue(true)),
                dynamicTest("4th dynamic test", () -> assertEquals(4, 2
                    * 2)));
    }

    @TestFactory
    Iterator<DynamicTest> dynamicTestsFromIterator() {
        return Arrays.asList(
                dynamicTest("5th dynamic test", () ->
                    assertTrue(true)),
                dynamicTest("6th dynamic test", () -> assertEquals(4, 2
                    * 2))).iterator();
    }

}
```

These examples do not really exhibit dynamic behavior, but merely demonstrate the supported return types. Note that the first test is going to fail due to `JUnitException`:

```
--------------------------------------------------┴--
T E S T S
--------------------------------------------------
Running io.github.bonigarcia.CollectionTest
Tests run: 7, Failures: 0, Errors: 1, Skipped: 0, Time elapsed: 0.31 sec <<<
 FAILURE! - in io.github.bonigarcia.CollectionTest
dynamicTestsWithInvalidReturnType()  Time elapsed: 0.052 sec  <<< ERROR!
org.junit.platform.commons.JUnitException: @TestFactory method [java.util.Li
st<java.lang.String> io.github.bonigarcia.CollectionTest.dynamicTestsWithInv
alidReturnType()] must return a Stream, Collection, Iterable, or Iterator of
 org.junit.jupiter.api.DynamicNode.
Caused by: java.lang.ClassCastException: java.lang.String cannot be cast to
org.junit.jupiter.api.DynamicNode


Results :

Tests in error:
  CollectionTest.dynamicTestsWithInvalidReturnType » JUnit @TestFactory meth
od [...

Tests run: 7, Failures: 0, Errors: 1, Skipped: 0
```

Console output of the first example for dynamic test execution

The following example demonstrates how easy it is to generate dynamic tests for a given set of input data:

```java
package io.github.bonigarcia;

import static org.junit.jupiter.api.DynamicTest.dynamicTest;

import java.util.stream.Stream;
import org.junit.jupiter.api.DynamicTest;
import org.junit.jupiter.api.TestFactory;

class DynamicExampleTest {

    @TestFactory
    Stream<DynamicTest> dynamicTestsFromStream() {
        Stream<String> inputStream = Stream.of("A", "B", "C");
        return inputStream.map(
                input -> dynamicTest("Display name for input " + input,
                () -> {
```

```
                    System.out.println("Testing " + input);
            }));
      }


   }
```

Notice that, in the end, three tests were executed, and these three tests were created at runtime by JUnit 5:

```
--------------------------------------------------
 T E S T S
--------------------------------------------------
Running io.github.bonigarcia.DynamicExampleTest
Testing A
Testing B
Testing C
Tests run: 3, Failures: 0, Errors: 0, Skipped: 0, Time elapsed: 0.086 sec -
in io.github.bonigarcia.DynamicExampleTest

Results :

Tests run: 3, Failures: 0, Errors: 0, Skipped: 0
```

Console output of the second example for dynamic test execution

There is another possibility to create dynamic tests in JUnit 5, using the static method `stream` of the class `DynamicTest`. This method needs an input generator, a function that generates a display name based on an input value, and a test executor.

Let's see another example. We create a test factory, providing the input data as an `Iterator`, a display name function using a lambda expression, and finally, a test executor implemented with another lambda expression. In this example, the test executor basically asserts whether or not the input integer is even or odd:

```java
package io.github.bonigarcia;

import static org.junit.jupiter.api.Assertions.assertTrue;
import static org.junit.jupiter.api.DynamicTest.stream;

import java.util.Arrays;
import java.util.Iterator;
import java.util.function.Function;
import java.util.stream.Stream;
import org.junit.jupiter.api.DynamicTest;
import org.junit.jupiter.api.TestFactory;
import org.junit.jupiter.api.function.ThrowingConsumer;

class StreamExampleTest {
```

```
@TestFactory
Stream<DynamicTest> streamTest() {
    // Input data
    Integer array[] = { 1, 2, 3 };
    Iterator<Integer> inputGenerator = Arrays.asList(array).iterator();

    // Display names
    Function<Integer, String> displayNameGenerator = (
            input) -> "Data input:" + input;

    // Test executor
    ThrowingConsumer<Integer> testExecutor = (input) -> {
        System.out.println(input);
        assertTrue(input % 2 == 0);
    };

    // Returns a stream of dynamic tests
    return stream(inputGenerator, displayNameGenerator,
        testExecutor);
}

}
```

The test will fail for odd inputs. As we can see, two out of three tests will fail:

```
-------------------------------------------------
 T E S T S
-------------------------------------------------
Running io.github.bonigarcia.StreamExampleTest
1
2
3
Tests run: 3, Failures: 2, Errors: 0, Skipped: 0, Time elapsed: 0.319 sec <<< FAILURE!
- in io.github.bonigarcia.StreamExampleTest
Data input:1  Time elapsed: 0.068 sec  <<< FAILURE!
org.opentest4j.AssertionFailedError:
        at io.github.bonigarcia.StreamExampleTest.lambda$1(StreamExampleTest.java:46)

Data input:3  Time elapsed: 0.042 sec  <<< FAILURE!
org.opentest4j.AssertionFailedError:
        at io.github.bonigarcia.StreamExampleTest.lambda$1(StreamExampleTest.java:46)


Results :

Failed tests:
  StreamExampleTest.lambda$1:46
  StreamExampleTest.lambda$1:46

Tests run: 3, Failures: 2, Errors: 0, Skipped: 0
```

Console output of dynamic test execution (example three)

Test interfaces

In JUnit 5, there are different rules relative to the use of annotations in Java interfaces. First of all, we need to be aware that `@Test`, `@TestFactory`, `@BeforeEach`, and `@AfterEach` can be declared on interface default methods.

Default methods is a feature of Java introduced in version 8. These methods (declared using the reserve keyword `default`) allows to define a default implementation for a given method within a Java interface. This capability can be useful for backward compatibility with existing interfaces.

The second rule regarding JUnit 5 and interfaces is that `@BeforeAll` and `@AfterAll` can be declared on `static` methods in a test interface. Moreover, if the test class, which implements a given interface, is annotated with `@TestInstance(Lifecycle.PER_CLASS)`, the methods `@BeforeAll` and `@AfterAll` declared on the interface do not need to be `static`, but `default` methods.

The third and final rule concerning interfaces in JUnit 5 is `@ExtendWith` and `@Tag` can be declared on test interfaces to configure extensions and tags.

Let's see some simple examples. In the following class, we are creating an interface, not a class. In this interface, we use the annotations `@BeforeAll`, `@AfterAll`, `@BeforeEach`, and `@AfterEach`. On the one hand, we define `@BeforeAll`, `@AfterAll` as static methods. On the other hand, we are defining `@BeforeEach` and `@AfterEach` as Java 8 default methods:

```
package io.github.bonigarcia;

import org.junit.jupiter.api.AfterAll;
import org.junit.jupiter.api.AfterEach;
import org.junit.jupiter.api.BeforeAll;
import org.junit.jupiter.api.BeforeEach;
import org.junit.jupiter.api.TestInfo;
import org.slf4j.Logger;
import org.slf4j.LoggerFactory;

public interface TestLifecycleLogger {

    static final Logger log = LoggerFactory
            .getLogger(TestLifecycleLogger.class.getName());

    @BeforeAll
    static void beforeAllTests() {
        log.info("beforeAllTests");
    }
```

```java
@AfterAll
static void afterAllTests() {
    log.info("afterAllTests");
}

@BeforeEach
default void beforeEachTest(TestInfo testInfo) {
    log.info("About to execute {}", testInfo.getDisplayName());
}

@AfterEach
default void afterEachTest(TestInfo testInfo) {
    log.info("Finished executing {}", testInfo.getDisplayName());
}

}
```

We are using the library Simple Logging Facade for Java (SLF4J) in this example. Take a look at the code on GitHub (`https://github.com/bonigarcia/mastering-junit5`) for details on the declaration of dependencies.

In this example, we are using the annotation `TestFactory` to define a default method in a Java interface:

```java
package io.github.bonigarcia;

import static org.junit.jupiter.api.Assertions.assertTrue;
import static org.junit.jupiter.api.DynamicTest.dynamicTest;

import java.util.Arrays;
import java.util.Collection;
import org.junit.jupiter.api.DynamicTest;
import org.junit.jupiter.api.TestFactory;

interface TestInterfaceDynamicTestsDemo {

    @TestFactory
    default Collection<DynamicTest> dynamicTestsFromCollection() {
        return Arrays.asList(
                dynamicTest("1st dynamic test in test interface",
                        () -> assertTrue(true)),
                dynamicTest("2nd dynamic test in test interface",
                        () -> assertTrue(true)));
    }

}
```

Finally, we use the annotation @Tag and @ExtendWith in another interface:

```
package io.github.bonigarcia;

import org.junit.jupiter.api.Tag;
import org.junit.jupiter.api.extension.ExtendWith;

@Tag("timed")
@ExtendWith(TimingExtension.class)
public interface TimeExecutionLogger {
}
```

All in all, we can use these interfaces in our Jupiter tests:

```
package io.github.bonigarcia;

import static org.junit.jupiter.api.Assertions.assertEquals;

import org.junit.jupiter.api.Test;

class TestInterfaceTest implements TestLifecycleLogger,
        TimeExecutionLogger,
        TestInterfaceDynamicTestsDemo {

    @Test
    void isEqualValue() {
        assertEquals(1, 1);
    }

}
```

In this test, the fact of implementing all the previously defined interfaces will provide the logging capabilities implemented in the default methods:

```
----------------------------------------------------
 T E S T S
----------------------------------------------------
Running io.github.bonigarcia.TestInterfaceTest
[2017-07-05 08:26:55:714] [main] INFO TestLifecycleLogger - beforeAllTests
[2017-07-05 08:26:55:728] [main] INFO TestLifecycleLogger - About to execute dynamicTestsFromCollection()
[2017-07-05 08:26:55:789] [main] INFO TimingExtension - Method dynamicTestsFromCollection took 57 ms
[2017-07-05 08:26:55:791] [main] INFO TestLifecycleLogger - Finished executing dynamicTestsFromCollection()
[2017-07-05 08:26:55:795] [main] INFO TestLifecycleLogger - About to execute isEqualValue()
[2017-07-05 08:26:55:797] [main] INFO TimingExtension - Method isEqualValue took 2 ms
[2017-07-05 08:26:55:798] [main] INFO TestLifecycleLogger - Finished executing isEqualValue()
[2017-07-05 08:26:55:801] [main] INFO TestLifecycleLogger - afterAllTests
Tests run: 3, Failures: 0, Errors: 0, Skipped: 0, Time elapsed: 0.235 sec - in io.github.bonigarcia.TestInterfaceTest

Results :

Tests run: 3, Failures: 0, Errors: 0, Skipped: 0
```

Console output of test implementing several interfaces

Test templates

A `@TestTemplate` method is not a regular test case but a template for test cases. Method annotated like this will be invoked multiple times, depending on the invocation context returned by the registered providers. Thus, test templates are used together with a registered `TestTemplateInvocationContextProvider` extension.

Let see a simple example of a test template. In the following snippet, we can see a method annotated with `@TestTemplate`, and also declaring an extension of the type `MyTestTemplateInvocationContextProvider`:

```
package io.github.bonigarcia;

import org.junit.jupiter.api.TestTemplate;
import org.junit.jupiter.api.extension.ExtendWith;

class TemplateTest {

    @TestTemplate
    @ExtendWith(MyTestTemplateInvocationContextProvider.class)
    void testTemplate(String parameter) {
        System.out.println(parameter);
    }

}
```

The required provided implements the Jupiter interface `TestTemplateInvocationContextProvider`. Inspecting the code of this class, we can see how two `String` parameters are provided to the test template (in this case, the value for these parameters are `parameter-1` and `parameter-2`):

```
package io.github.bonigarcia;

import java.util.Collections;
import java.util.List;
import java.util.stream.Stream;
import org.junit.jupiter.api.extension.Extension;
import org.junit.jupiter.api.extension.ExtensionContext;
import org.junit.jupiter.api.extension.ParameterContext;
import org.junit.jupiter.api.extension.ParameterResolver;
import org.junit.jupiter.api.extension.TestTemplateInvocationContext;
import
org.junit.jupiter.api.extension.TestTemplateInvocationContextProvider;

public class MyTestTemplateInvocationContextProvider
        implements TestTemplateInvocationContextProvider {
```

```java
    @Override
    public boolean supportsTestTemplate(ExtensionContext context) {
        return true;
    }

    @Override
    public Stream<TestTemplateInvocationContext>
        provideTestTemplateInvocationContexts(
      ExtensionContext context) {
        return Stream.of(invocationContext("parameter-1"),
                invocationContext("parameter-2"));
    }

    private TestTemplateInvocationContext invocationContext(String
parameter) {
        return new TestTemplateInvocationContext() {
            @Override
            public String getDisplayName(int invocationIndex) {
                return parameter;
            }

            @Override
            public List<Extension> getAdditionalExtensions() {
                return Collections.singletonList(new ParameterResolver() {
                    @Override
                    public boolean supportsParameter(
                            ParameterContext parameterContext,
                            ExtensionContext extensionContext) {
                        return parameterContext.getParameter().getType()
                            .equals(String.class);
                    }

                    @Override
                    public Object resolveParameter(
                            ParameterContext parameterContext,
                            ExtensionContext extensionContext) {
                        return parameter;
                    }
                });
            }
        };
    }

}
```

When the test is executed, each invocation of the test template behaves like a regular `@Test`. In this example, the test is only writing the parameter in the standard output.

```
-------------------------------------------------
 T E S T S
-------------------------------------------------
Running io.github.bonigarcia.TemplateTest
parameter-1
parameter-2
Tests run: 2, Failures: 0, Errors: 0, Skipped: 0, Time elapsed: 0.411 sec -
in io.github.bonigarcia.TemplateTest

Results :

Tests run: 2, Failures: 0, Errors: 0, Skipped: 0
```

Console output of test template example

Parameterized tests

Parameterized tests are a special kinds of tests in which the data input is injected in the test in order to reuse the same test logic. This concept was already addressed in JUnit 4, as explained in Chapter 1, *Retrospective On Software Quality And Java Testing*. As we would expect, parameterized tests are also implemented in JUnit 5.

First of all, in order to implement a parameterized test in Jupiter, we need to add the `junit-jupiter-params` to our project. When using Maven, that means adding the following dependency:

```xml
<dependency>
    <groupId>org.junit.jupiter</groupId>
    <artifactId>junit-jupiter-params</artifactId>
    <version>${junit.jupiter.version}</version>
    <scope>test</scope>
</dependency>
```

As usual, as a general rule, it is recommended to use the latest version of the artifacts. To find out that, we can check out the Maven central repository (http://search.maven.org/).

When using Gradle, the `junit-jupiter-params` dependency can be declared as follows:

```
dependencies {
        testCompile("org.junit.jupiter:junit-jupiter-
        params:${junitJupiterVersion}")
    }
```

Then, we need to use the annotation `@ParameterizedTest` (located in the package `org.junit.jupiter.params`) to declare a method within a Java class as a parameterized test. This type of test behaves exactly the same as a regular `@Test`, meaning that all the life cycle callbacks (`@BeforeEach`, `@AfterEach`, and so on) and extensions continue working in the same way.

Nevertheless, the use of `@ParameterizedTest` is not enough to implement a parameterized test. Together with `@ParameterizedTest`, we need to specify at least one argument provider. As we will discover in this section, JUnit 5 implements different annotations to provide data input (that is, parameters for tests) from different sources. These argument providers (implemented as annotations in JUnit 5) are summarized in the following table (each of these annotations are located in the package `org.junit.jupiter.params.provider`):

Arguments provider annotation	Description
`@ValueSource`	Used to specify an array of literal values of `String`, `int`, `long`, or `double`
`@EnumSource`	Argument source for constants of a specified enumeration (`java.lang.Enum`)
`@MethodSource`	Provides access to values returned by static methods of the class in which this annotation is declared
`@CsvSource`	Argument source which reads comma-separated values (CSV) from its attribute
`@CsvFileSource`	Argument source which is used to load CSV files from one or more classpath resources
`@ArgumentsSource`	Used to specify a custom argument provider (that is, a Java class that implements the interface) `org.junit.jupiter.params.provider.ArgumentsProvider`)

@ValueSource

The annotation @ValueSource is used in conjunction with @ParameterizedTest to specify a parameterized test in which the argument source is an array of literal values of String, int, long, or double. These values are specified inside the annotation, using the elements strings, ints, longs, or doubles. Consider the following example:

```
package io.github.bonigarcia;

import static org.junit.jupiter.api.Assertions.assertNotNull;

import org.junit.jupiter.params.ParameterizedTest;
import org.junit.jupiter.params.provider.ValueSource;

class ValueSourceStringsParameterizedTest {

    @ParameterizedTest
    @ValueSource(strings = { "Hello", "World" })
    void testWithStrings(String argument) {
      System.out.println("Parameterized test with (String) parameter:  "
        + argument);
      assertNotNull(argument);
    }
}
```

The method of this class (testWithStrings) defines a parameterized test in which an array of String is specified. Due to the fact that two String arguments are specified in the annotation @ValueSource (in this example "Hello" and "World"), the test logic will be exercised twice, once per value. This data is injected in the test method using the argument of the method, in this case through the String variable named argument. All in all, when executing this test class, the output will be as follows:

```
-------------------------------------------------
 T E S T S
-------------------------------------------------
Running io.github.bonigarcia.ValueSourceStringsParameterizedTest
Parameterized test with (String) parameter: Hello
Parameterized test with (String) parameter: World
Tests run: 2, Failures: 0, Errors: 0, Skipped: 0, Time elapsed: 0.141 sec - in
io.github.bonigarcia.ValueSourceStringsParameterizedTest

Results :

Tests run: 2, Failures: 0, Errors: 0, Skipped: 0
```

Execution of a parameterized test using *@ValueSource* and String argument provider

We can also use integer primitive types (int, long, and double) within the @ValueSource annotation. The following example demonstrates how. The methods of this example class (named testWithInts, testWithLongs, and testWithDoubles) use the annotation @ValueSource to define the arguments in the form of integer values, using the primitive types int, long, and double, respectively. To that aim, the elements ints, longs, and doubles of @ValueSource need to be specified:

```java
package io.github.bonigarcia;

import static org.junit.jupiter.api.Assertions.assertNotNull;

import org.junit.jupiter.params.ParameterizedTest;
import org.junit.jupiter.params.provider.ValueSource;

class ValueSourcePrimitiveTypesParameterizedTest {

    @ParameterizedTest
    @ValueSource(ints = { 0, 1 })
    void testWithInts(int argument) {
        System.out.println("Parameterized test with (int) argument: " +
                argument);
        assertNotNull(argument);
    }

    @ParameterizedTest
    @ValueSource(longs = { 2L, 3L })
    void testWithLongs(long argument) {
        System.out.println(
        "Parameterized test with (long)
                argument: " + argument);
        assertNotNull(argument);
    }

    @ParameterizedTest
    @ValueSource(doubles = { 4d, 5d })
    void testWithDoubles(double argument) {
        System.out.println("Parameterized test with (double)
                argument: " + argument);
        assertNotNull(argument);
    }

}
```

As can be seen in the picture here, each test is executed twice, since in each @ValueSource annotation we specify two different input parameters (type int, long, and double, respectively).

```
--------------------------------------------------------
 T E S T S
--------------------------------------------------------
Running io.github.bonigarcia.ValueSourcePrimitiveTypesParameterizedTest
Parameterized test with (int) argument: 0
Parameterized test with (int) argument: 1
Parameterized test with (long) argument: 2
Parameterized test with (long) argument: 3
Parameterized test with (double) argument: 4.0
Parameterized test with (double) argument: 5.0
Tests run: 6, Failures: 0, Errors: 0, Skipped: 0, Time elapsed: 0.134 sec - in
io.github.bonigarcia.ValueSourcePrimitiveTypesParameterizedTest

Results :

Tests run: 6, Failures: 0, Errors: 0, Skipped: 0
```

Execution of a parameterized test using *@ValueSource* and primitive types

@EnumSource

The annotation `@EnumSource` allows to specify a parameterized test in which the argument source is a Java enumeration class. By default, each value of the enumeration will be used to feed the parameterized test, one at a time.

For example, in the following test class, the method `testWithEnum` is annotated with `@ParameterizedTest` in conjunction with `@EnumSource`. As we can see, the value of this annotation is `TimeUnit.class`, which is a standard Java annotation (package java.util.concurrent) used to represent time duration. The possible values defined in this enumeration are `NANOSECONDS`, `MICROSECONDS`, `MILLISECONDS`, `SECONDS`, `MINUTES`, `HOURS`, and `DAYS`:

```
package io.github.bonigarcia;

import static org.junit.jupiter.api.Assertions.assertNotNull;

import java.util.concurrent.TimeUnit;
import org.junit.jupiter.params.ParameterizedTest;
import org.junit.jupiter.params.provider.EnumSource;

class EnumSourceParameterizedTest {

    @ParameterizedTest
    @EnumSource(TimeUnit.class)
    void testWithEnum(TimeUnit argument) {
```

```
        System.out.println("Parameterized test with (TimeUnit)
            argument: " + argument);
        assertNotNull(argument);
    }

}
```

Therefore, the execution of this test will be carried out seven times, that is, one per `TimeUnit` enumeration value. We can check this in the trace of the output console when executing the test:

```
-------------------------------------------------------------
 T E S T S
-------------------------------------------------------
Running io.github.bonigarcia.EnumSourceParameterizedTest
Parameterized test with (TimeUnit) argument: NANOSECONDS
Parameterized test with (TimeUnit) argument: MICROSECONDS
Parameterized test with (TimeUnit) argument: MILLISECONDS
Parameterized test with (TimeUnit) argument: SECONDS
Parameterized test with (TimeUnit) argument: MINUTES
Parameterized test with (TimeUnit) argument: HOURS
Parameterized test with (TimeUnit) argument: DAYS
Tests run: 7, Failures: 0, Errors: 0, Skipped: 0, Time elapsed: 0.31 sec - in
io.github.bonigarcia.EnumSourceParameterizedTest

Results :

Tests run: 7, Failures: 0, Errors: 0, Skipped: 0
```

Execution of parameterized test using *@EnumSource* and *TimeUnit.class*

Moreover, the `@EnumSource` annotation allows to filter the members of the enumeration in several ways. To implement this selection, the following elements can be specified within a `@EnumSource` annotation:

- `mode`: Constant value which determines the type of filtering. This is defined as an enumeration in the inner class `org.junit.jupiter.params.provider.EnumSource.Mode`, and the possible values are:
  - `INCLUDE`: Used to select those values whose names are supplied via the `names` element. This is the default option.
  - `EXCLUDE`: Used to select all values except those supplied with the `names` element.
  - `MATCH_ALL`: Used to select those values whose names match the patterns in `names` element.

- MATCH_ANY: Used to select those values whose names match any pattern in the names element.
- names: The array of string which allows to select a group of enum constants. The criteria for inclusion/exclusion is directly linked to the value of mode. In addition, this element also allows to define regular expressions to select the names of enum constants to be matched.

Consider the following example. In this class, there are three parameterized tests. First one, named testWithFilteredEnum, uses the class TimeUnit to feed the @EnumSource argument provider. Moreover, the enum constant set is filtered using the element names. As we can see, only the constant "DAYS" and "HOURS" will be used to feed this test (take into account that the default mode is INCLUDE):

```
package io.github.bonigarcia;

import static org.junit.jupiter.api.Assertions.assertNotNull;
import static org.junit.jupiter.params.provider.EnumSource.Mode.EXCLUDE;
import static org.junit.jupiter.params.provider.EnumSource.Mode.MATCH_ALL;

import java.util.concurrent.TimeUnit;
import org.junit.jupiter.params.ParameterizedTest;
import org.junit.jupiter.params.provider.EnumSource;

class EnumSourceFilteringParameterizedTest {

    @ParameterizedTest
    @EnumSource(value = TimeUnit.class, names = { "DAYS", "HOURS" })
    void testWithFilteredEnum(TimeUnit argument) {
        System.out.println("Parameterized test with some (TimeUnit)
            argument: "+ argument);
        assertNotNull(argument);
    }

    @ParameterizedTest
    @EnumSource(value = TimeUnit.class, mode = EXCLUDE, names = {
    "DAYS", "HOURS" })
    void testWithExcludeEnum(TimeUnit argument) {
        System.out.println("Parameterized test with excluded (TimeUnit)
            argument: " + argument);
        assertNotNull(argument);
    }

    @ParameterizedTest
    @EnumSource(value = TimeUnit.class, mode = MATCH_ALL, names =
    "^(M|N).+SECONDS$")
    void testWithRegexEnum(TimeUnit argument) {
```

```
        System.out.println("Parameterized test with regex filtered
            (TimeUnit) argument: " + argument);
        assertNotNull(argument);
    }

}
```

Thus, when executing this class in the console, the output we obtain is the following. Regarding the first test, we can see that only traces for "DAYS" and "HOURS" are present:

```
------------------------------------------------
 T E S T S
------------------------------------------------
Running io.github.bonigarcia.EnumSourceFilteringParameterizedTest
Parameterized test with regex filtered (TimeUnit) argument: NANOSECONDS
Parameterized test with regex filtered (TimeUnit) argument: MICROSECONDS
Parameterized test with regex filtered (TimeUnit) argument: MILLISECONDS
Parameterized test with excluded (TimeUnit) argument: NANOSECONDS
Parameterized test with excluded (TimeUnit) argument: MICROSECONDS
Parameterized test with excluded (TimeUnit) argument: MILLISECONDS
Parameterized test with excluded (TimeUnit) argument: SECONDS
Parameterized test with excluded (TimeUnit) argument: MINUTES
Parameterized test with some (TimeUnit) argument: HOURS
Parameterized test with some (TimeUnit) argument: DAYS
Tests run: 10, Failures: 0, Errors: 0, Skipped: 0, Time elapsed: 0.12 sec - in
  io.github.bonigarcia.EnumSourceFilteringParameterizedTest

Results :

Tests run: 10, Failures: 0, Errors: 0, Skipped: 0
```

Execution of parameterized test using *@EnumSource* using filtering capabilities

Consider now the second test method, named testWithExcludeEnum. This test is exactly the same as before with a difference: the mode here is EXCLUSION (instead of INCLUSION, chosen by default in the previous test). All in all, in the execution (see screenshot before) when can see that this test is executed five times, per one of the enum constant different to DAYS and HOURS. To check that, track the traces with the sentence "Parameterized test with excluded (TimeUnit) argument".

The third and last method of this class (called testWithRegexEnum) defines an inclusion mode, MATCH_ALL, using a regular expression to filter the enumeration (in this case, it is also TimeUnit). The concrete regular expression used in this example is ^(M|N).+SECONDS$, which means that only will be included in those enum constants starting with M or N and ending with SECONDS. As can be checked in the execution screenshot, there are three TimeUnit constants matching these conditions: NANOSECONDS, MICROSECONDS, and MILISECONDS.

@MethodSource

The annotation @MethodSource allows to define the name of the static method in which the arguments for the test are provided as a Java 8 Stream. For instance, in the following example, we can see a parameterized test in which the argument provider is a static method called stringProvider. In this example, this method returns a Stream of String's and therefore the argument of the test method (callled testWithStringProvider) accepts one String argument:

```
package io.github.bonigarcia;

import static org.junit.jupiter.api.Assertions.assertNotNull;

import java.util.stream.Stream;
import org.junit.jupiter.params.ParameterizedTest;
import org.junit.jupiter.params.provider.MethodSource;

class MethodSourceStringsParameterizedTest {

    static Stream<String> stringProvider() {
        return Stream.of("hello", "world");
    }

    @ParameterizedTest
    @MethodSource("stringProvider")
    void testWithStringProvider(String argument) {
        System.out.println("Parameterized test with (String) argument: "
            + argument);
        assertNotNull(argument);
    }

}
```

When running the example, we can see how the test is execute twice, once per `String` contained in the `Stream`.

```
--------------------------------------------------
 T E S T S
--------------------------------------------------
Running io.github.bonigarcia.MethodSourceStringsParameterizedTest
Parameterized test with (String) argument: hello
Parameterized test with (String) argument: world
Tests run: 2, Failures: 0, Errors: 0, Skipped: 0, Time elapsed: 0.297 sec - in
io.github.bonigarcia.MethodSourceStringsParameterizedTest

Results :

Tests run: 2, Failures: 0, Errors: 0, Skipped: 0
```

Execution of a parameterized test using *@MethodSource* and String argument provider

The type of the objects contained in the `Stream` is not required to be `String`. In fact, this type can be anything. Let's consider another example, in which `@MethodSource` is linked to a static method, which returns as `Stream` of custom objects. In this example, this type is named `Person`, and here it is implemented as an inner class with two properties (`name` and `surname`).

```java
package io.github.bonigarcia;

import static org.junit.jupiter.api.Assertions.assertNotNull;

import java.util.stream.Stream;
import org.junit.jupiter.params.ParameterizedTest;
import org.junit.jupiter.params.provider.MethodSource;

class MethodSourceObjectsParameterizedTest {

    static Stream<Person> personProvider() {
        Person john = new Person("John", "Doe");
        Person jane = new Person("Jane", "Roe");
        return Stream.of(john, jane);
    }

    @ParameterizedTest
    @MethodSource("personProvider")
    void testWithPersonProvider(Person argument) {
        System.out.println("Parameterized test with (Person) argument: " +
                argument);
        assertNotNull(argument);
```

```
    }

    static class Person {
        String name;
        String surname;

        public Person(String name, String surname) {
            this.name = name;
            this.surname = surname;
        }

        public String getName() {
            return name;
        }

        public void setName(String name) {
            this.name = name;
        }

        public String getSurname() {
            return surname;
        }

        public void setSurname(String surname) {
            this.surname = surname;
        }

        @Override
        public String toString() {
            return "Person [name=" + name + ", surname=" + surname + "]";
        }

    }

}
```

As the following screenshot shows, when executing this example, the parameterized test is exercise twice, once per `Person` objects contained in the `Stream` ("`John Doe`" and "`Jane Roe`").

```
-------------------------------------------------------------
T E S T S
-------------------------------------------------------------
Running io.github.bonigarcia.MethodSourceObjectsParameterizedTest
Parameterized test with (Person) argument: Person [name=John, surname=Doe]
Parameterized test with (Person) argument: Person [name=Jane, surname=Roe]
Tests run: 2, Failures: 0, Errors: 0, Skipped: 0, Time elapsed: 0.156 sec - in
io.github.bonigarcia.MethodSourceObjectsParameterizedTest

Results :

Tests run: 2, Failures: 0, Errors: 0, Skipped: 0
```

Execution of parameterized test using *@MethodSource* and custom object argument provider

We can also use `@MethodSource` to specify argument providers which contain integer primitive types, concretely of `int`, `double`, and `long`. The following class contains an example. We can see three parameterized tests. The first one (named `testWithIntProvider`) uses the annotation `@MethodSource` to link with the static method `intProvider`. In the body of this method, we use the standard Java class `IntStream` to return an Stream of `int` values. The second and third test (called `testWithDoubleProvider` and `testWithLongProvider`) are quite similar, but using a `Stream` of `double` and `long` values, respectively:

```
package io.github.bonigarcia;

import static org.junit.jupiter.api.Assertions.assertNotNull;

import java.util.stream.DoubleStream;
import java.util.stream.IntStream;
import java.util.stream.LongStream;
import org.junit.jupiter.params.ParameterizedTest;
import org.junit.jupiter.params.provider.MethodSource;

class MethodSourcePrimitiveTypesParameterizedTest {

    static IntStream intProvider() {
        return IntStream.of(0, 1);
    }

    @ParameterizedTest
    @MethodSource("intProvider")
```

```
void testWithIntProvider(int argument) {
    System.out.println("Parameterized test with (int) argument: " +
        argument);
    assertNotNull(argument);
}

static DoubleStream doubleProvider() {
    return DoubleStream.of(2d, 3d);
}

@ParameterizedTest
@MethodSource("doubleProvider")
void testWithDoubleProvider(double argument) {
    System.out.println(
        "Parameterized test with (double) argument: " + argument);
    assertNotNull(argument);
}

static LongStream longProvider() {
    return LongStream.of(4L, 5L);
}

@ParameterizedTest
@MethodSource("longProvider")
void testWithLongProvider(long argument) {
    System.out.println(
        "Parameterized test with (long) argument: " + argument);
    assertNotNull(argument);
}

}
```

Thus, when executing this class, there will be six tests executed (three parameterized tests with two arguments each).

In the following screenshot, we can check this by following the traces written by each test to the standard output:

```
-------------------------------------------------------
 T E S T S
-------------------------------------------------------
Running io.github.bonigarcia.MethodSourcePrimitiveTypesParameterizedTest
Parameterized test with (long) argument: 4
Parameterized test with (long) argument: 5
Parameterized test with (int) argument: 0
Parameterized test with (int) argument: 1
Parameterized test with (double) argument: 2.0
Parameterized test with (double) argument: 3.0
Tests run: 6, Failures: 0, Errors: 0, Skipped: 0, Time elapsed: 0.228 sec - in
io.github.bonigarcia.MethodSourcePrimitiveTypesParameterizedTest

Results :

Tests run: 6, Failures: 0, Errors: 0, Skipped: 0
```

Execution of parameterized test using *@MethodSource* and primitive types argument provider

Finally, with regards to `@MethodSource` parameterized tests, it is worth it to know that the method providers are allowed to return a Stream of different types (objects or primitive types). This is very convenient for real-world test cases. For example, the following class implements a parameterized test in which the argument provider is a method returning arguments of mixed types: `String` and `int`. These parameters are injected in the test as method arguments (called first and second in the example).

```java
package io.github.bonigarcia;

import static org.junit.jupiter.api.Assertions.assertNotEquals;
import static org.junit.jupiter.api.Assertions.assertNotNull;

import java.util.stream.Stream;
import org.junit.jupiter.params.ParameterizedTest;
import org.junit.jupiter.params.provider.Arguments;
import org.junit.jupiter.params.provider.MethodSource;

class MethodSourceMixedTypesParameterizedTest {

    static Stream<Arguments> stringAndIntProvider() {
        return Stream.of(Arguments.of("Mastering", 10),
            Arguments.of("JUnit 5", 20));
    }

    @ParameterizedTest
    @MethodSource("stringAndIntProvider")
```

```
    void testWithMultiArgMethodSource(String first, int second) {
        System.out.println("Parameterized test with two arguments:
            (String) " + first + " and (int) " + second);
        assertNotNull(first);
        assertNotEquals(0, second);
    }
}
```

As usual, there will be test executions as entries contained in the Stream. In this case, there are two: "Mastertering" and 10, and then "JUnit 5" and 20.

```
------------------------------------------------
 T E S T S
------------------------------------------------
Running io.github.bonigarcia.MethodSourceMixedTypesParameterizedTest
Parameterized test with two arguments: (String) Mastering and (int) 10
Parameterized test with two arguments: (String) JUnit 5 and (int) 20
Tests run: 2, Failures: 0, Errors: 0, Skipped: 0, Time elapsed: 0.188 sec - in
io.github.bonigarcia.MethodSourceMixedTypesParameterizedTest

Results :

Tests run: 2, Failures: 0, Errors: 0, Skipped: 0
```

Execution of parameterized test using *@MethodSource* with different types of arguments

@CsvSource and @CsvFileSource

Another way to specify the source of arguments for parameterized tests is using comma-separated values (CSV). This can be done using the annotation @CsvSource, which allows to embed CSV content as String in the value of the annotation.

Consider the following example. It contains a Jupiter parameterized test (named testWithCsvSource), which is using the annotation @CsvSource. This annotation contains an array of Strings. In each element of the array, we can see there is a different value separated by commas.

 The content of the CSV is automatically converted to String and int. To find out more about the implicit type conversion made in parameters by JUnit 5, take a look to the section *Argument conversion* in this chapter.

```
package io.github.bonigarcia;

import static org.junit.jupiter.api.Assertions.assertNotEquals;
import static org.junit.jupiter.api.Assertions.assertNotNull;

import org.junit.jupiter.params.ParameterizedTest;
import org.junit.jupiter.params.provider.CsvSource;

class CsvSourceParameterizedTest {

    @ParameterizedTest
    @CsvSource({ "hello, 1", "world, 2", "'happy, testing', 3" })
    void testWithCsvSource(String first, int second) {
        System.out.println("Parameterized test with (String) " + first
            + " and (int) " + second);
        assertNotNull(first);
        assertNotEquals(0, second);
    }

}
```

All in all, when executing this test class, there will be three single tests, each per entry in the array. Each execution will be invoked, passing two arguments to the test. The first one is named `first` and its type is `String`, and second one is called `second` and its type is `int`.

```
-------------------------------------------------------
T E S T S
-------------------------------------------------------
Running io.github.bonigarcia.CsvSourceParameterizedTest
Parameterized test with (String) hello and (int) 1
Parameterized test with (String) world and (int) 2
Parameterized test with (String) happy, testing and (int) 3
Tests run: 3, Failures: 0, Errors: 0, Skipped: 0, Time elapsed: 0.121 sec - in
io.github.bonigarcia.CsvSourceParameterizedTest

Results :

Tests run: 3, Failures: 0, Errors: 0, Skipped: 0
```

Execution of parameterized test using *@CsvSource*

If the amount of CSV data is big, it might be more convenient using the annotation `@CsvFileSource` instead. This annotation allows to feed the parameterized test with a CSV file located in the classpath of the project. In the following example, we use the file `input.csv`:

```java
package io.github.bonigarcia;

import static org.junit.jupiter.api.Assertions.assertNotEquals;
import static org.junit.jupiter.api.Assertions.assertNotNull;

import org.junit.jupiter.params.ParameterizedTest;
import org.junit.jupiter.params.provider.CsvFileSource;

class CsvFileSourceParameterizedTest {

    @ParameterizedTest
    @CsvFileSource(resources = "/input.csv")
    void testWithCsvFileSource(String first, int second) {
        System.out.println("Yet another parameterized test with "
            + "(String) " + first + " and (int) " + second);
        assertNotNull(first);
        assertNotEquals(0, second);
    }

}
```

Internally, the annotation `@CsvFileSource` locates the file using the method `getResourceAsStream()` of the standard Java class `java.lang.Class`. Therefore, the path of the file is interpreted as a path local to the package class we are calling it from. Since our resource is located in the root of the classpath (in the example it is located in the folder `src/test/resources`), we need to locate it as `/input.csv`.

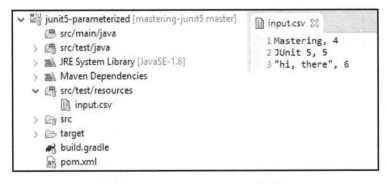

Location and content of input.csv in the example with *@CsvFileSource*

The following screenshot shows the output of the test when it is executed with Maven. Since the CSV has three rows of data, there are three test executions, each one with two parameters (first one as `String` and second one as `int`):

```
------------------------------------------------------------
 T E S T S
------------------------------------------------------------
Running io.github.bonigarcia.CsvFileSourceParameterizedTest
Yet another parameterized test with (String) Mastering and (int) 4
Yet another parameterized test with (String) JUnit 5 and (int) 5
Yet another parameterized test with (String) hi, there and (int) 6
Tests run: 3, Failures: 0, Errors: 0, Skipped: 0, Time elapsed: 0.235 sec - in
io.github.bonigarcia.CsvFileSourceParameterizedTest

Results :

Tests run: 3, Failures: 0, Errors: 0, Skipped: 0
```

Execution of parameterized test using *@CsvFileSource*

@ArgumentsSource

The last annotation aimed to specify the source of arguments for parameterized tests in JUnit 5 is `@ArgumentsSource`. With this annotation, we can specify a custom (and reusable in different tests) class, which will contain the parameters for the test. This class must implement the interface `org.junit.jupiter.params.provider.ArgumentsProvider`.

Let's see an example. The following class implements a Jupiter parameterized test, in which the arguments source will be defined in the class `CustomArgumentsProvider1`:

```java
package io.github.bonigarcia;

import static org.junit.jupiter.api.Assertions.assertNotNull;
import static org.junit.jupiter.api.Assertions.assertTrue;

import org.junit.jupiter.params.ParameterizedTest;
import org.junit.jupiter.params.provider.ArgumentsSource;

class ArgumentSourceParameterizedTest {

    @ParameterizedTest
    @ArgumentsSource(CustomArgumentsProvider1.class)
    void testWithArgumentsSource(String first, int second) {
        System.out.println("Parameterized test with (String) " + first
            + " and (int) " + second);
```

```
            assertNotNull(first);
            assertTrue(second > 0);
    }

}
```

This class (named `CustomArgumentsProvider1`) has been implemented on our side, and due to the fact that it implements the interface `ArgumentsProvider`, must override the method `provideArguments`, in which the actual definition of parameters for the test is implemented. Looking at the code of the example, we can see that this method returns a `Stream` of `Arguments`. In this example, we are returning a couple of entries in the `Stream`, each one with two arguments (`String` and `int`, respectively):

```java
package io.github.bonigarcia;

import java.util.stream.Stream;
import org.junit.jupiter.api.extension.ExtensionContext;
import org.junit.jupiter.params.provider.Arguments;
import org.junit.jupiter.params.provider.ArgumentsProvider;

public class CustomArgumentsProvider1 implements ArgumentsProvider {

    @Override
    public Stream<? extends Arguments> provideArguments(
            ExtensionContext context) {
        System.out.println("Arguments provider to test "
            + context.getTestMethod().get().getName());
        return Stream.of(Arguments.of("hello", 1),
            Arguments.of("world", 2));
    }

}
```

Notice also that this argument has an argument of type `ExtensionContext` (package `org.junit.jupiter.api.extension`). This argument is very useful to know the context in which the test is executed. As illustrated in the screenshot here, ExtensionContext API offers different methods to find out different attributes of the test instance (test method name, display name, tags, and so on).

In our example (`CustomArgumentsProvider1`), the context is used to write the test method name in the standard output:

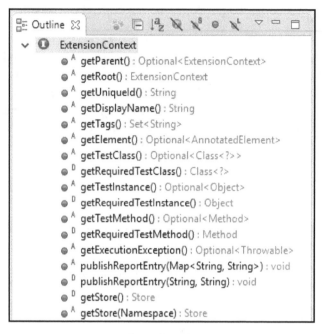

ExtensionContext API

Thus, when executing this example, we can see two tests being executed. Moreover, we can check the log trace with the test method, thanks to the `ExtensionContext` object inside, out `ArgumentsProvider` instance:

```
--------------------------------------------------
 T E S T S
--------------------------------------------------
Running io.github.bonigarcia.ArgumentSourceParameterizedTest
Arguments provider to test testWithArgumentsSource
Parameterized test with (String) hello and (int) 1
Parameterized test with (String) world and (int) 2
Tests run: 2, Failures: 0, Errors: 0, Skipped: 0, Time elapsed: 0.287 sec - in
io.github.bonigarcia.ArgumentSourceParameterizedTest

Results :

Tests run: 2, Failures: 0, Errors: 0, Skipped: 0
```

Execution of parameterized test using *@ArgumentsSource*

Several argument sources can be applied to the same parameterized test. In fact, this can be done in two different ways in the Jupiter programming model:

- Using several annotation of @ArgumentsSource together with the same @ParameterizedTest. This can be done since @ArgumentsSource is a java.lang.annotation.Repeatable annotation.
- Using the annotation @ArgumentsSources (notice the source is plural here). This annotation is simply a container for one or more @ArgumentsSource. The following class shows a simple example:

```java
package io.github.bonigarcia;

import static org.junit.jupiter.api.Assertions.assertNotNull;
import static org.junit.jupiter.api.Assertions.assertTrue;

import org.junit.jupiter.params.ParameterizedTest;
import org.junit.jupiter.params.provider.ArgumentsSource;
import org.junit.jupiter.params.provider.ArgumentsSources;

class ArgumentSourcesParameterizedTest {

    @ParameterizedTest
    @ArgumentsSources({
    @ArgumentsSource(CustomArgumentsProvider1.class),
    @ArgumentsSource(CustomArgumentsProvider2.class) })
    void testWithArgumentsSource(String first, int second) {
        System.out.println("Parameterized test with (String) " + first
            + " and (int) " + second);
        assertNotNull(first);
        assertTrue(second > 0);
    }

}
```

Supposing that the second argument provider (`CustomArgumentsProvider2.class`) specifies two or more sets of argument, when executing the test class there will be four test executions:

```
 T E S T S
 -------------------------------------------------
 Running io.github.bonigarcia.ArgumentSourcesParameterizedTest
 Arguments provider [1] to test testWithArgumentsSource
 Parameterized test with (String) hello and (int) 1
 Parameterized test with (String) world and (int) 2
 Arguments provider [2] to test testWithArgumentsSource
 Parameterized test with (String) more and (int) 3
 Parameterized test with (String) arguments and (int) 4
 Tests run: 4, Failures: 0, Errors: 0, Skipped: 0, Time elapsed: 0.212 sec - in
 io.github.bonigarcia.ArgumentSourcesParameterizedTest

 Results :

 Tests run: 4, Failures: 0, Errors: 0, Skipped: 0
```

Execution of parameterized test using *@ArgumentsSources*

Argument conversion

To support use cases such as `@CsvSource` and `@CsvFileSource`, Jupiter provides a number of built-in implicit converters. Moreover, these converters can be implemented based on specific needs by means of explicit converters. This section covers both types of conversions.

Implicit conversion

Internally, JUnit 5 handles a set of rules for the conversion of parameters from `String` to the actual argument type. For example, if `@ParameterizedTests` declares a parameter of type `TimeUnit`, but the declared source is a `String`, internally this `String` will be converted to `TimeUnit`. The following table summarizes the rules of implicit conversions in JUnit 5 for parameterized test arguments:

Target Type	Example
`boolean/Boolean`	`"false" -> false`
`byte/Byte`	`"1" -> (byte) 1`
`char/Character`	`"a" -> 'a'`

short/Short	"2" -> (short) 2
int/Integer	"3" -> 3
long/Long	"4" -> 4L
float/Float	"5.0" -> 5.0f
double/Double	"6.0" -> 6.0d
Enum subclass	"SECONDS" -> TimeUnit.SECONDS
java.time.Instant	"1970-01-01T00:00:00Z" -> Instant.ofEpochMilli(0)
java.time.LocalDate	"2017-10-24" -> LocalDate.of(2017, 10, 24)
java.time.LocalDateTime	"2017-03-14T12:34:56.789" -> LocalDateTime.of(2017, 3, 14, 12, 34, 56, 789_000_000)
java.time.LocalTime	"12:34:56.789" -> LocalTime.of(12, 34, 56, 789_000_000)
java.time.OffsetDateTime	"2017-03-14T12:34:56.789Z" -> OffsetDateTime.of(2017, 3, 14, 12, 34, 56, 789_000_000, ZoneOffset.UTC)
java.time.OffsetTime	"12:34:56.789Z" -> OffsetTime.of(12, 34, 56, 789_000_000, ZoneOffset.UTC)
java.time.Year	"2017" -> Year.of(2017)
java.time.YearMonth	"2017-10" -> YearMonth.of(2017, 10)
java.time.ZonedDateTime	"2017-10-24T12:34:56.789Z" -> ZonedDateTime.of(2017, 10, 24, 12, 34, 56, 789_000_000, ZoneOffset.UTC)

The following example shows several examples of implicit conversion. The first test
(testWithImplicitConversionToBoolean) declares a String source as "true", but
then, the expected argument type is Boolean. Similarly, the second test
("testWithImplicitConversionToInteger") makes an implicit conversion from
String to Integer. The third test (testWithImplicitConversionToEnum) converts the
input String to TimeUnit (enumeration), and finally the fourth test
(testWithImplicitConversionToLocalDate) produces a conversion to LocalDate:

```java
package io.github.bonigarcia;

import static org.junit.jupiter.api.Assertions.assertNotNull;
import static org.junit.jupiter.api.Assertions.assertTrue;

import java.time.LocalDate;
import java.util.concurrent.TimeUnit;
import org.junit.jupiter.params.ParameterizedTest;
import org.junit.jupiter.params.provider.ValueSource;

class ImplicitConversionParameterizedTest {

    @ParameterizedTest
    @ValueSource(strings = "true")
    void testWithImplicitConversionToBoolean(Boolean argument) {
        System.out.println("Argument " + argument + " is a type of "
            + argument.getClass());
        assertTrue(argument);
    }

    @ParameterizedTest
    @ValueSource(strings = "11")
    void testWithImplicitConversionToInteger(Integer argument) {
        System.out.println("Argument " + argument + " is a type of "
            + argument.getClass());
        assertTrue(argument > 10);
    }

    @ParameterizedTest
    @ValueSource(strings = "SECONDS")
    void testWithImplicitConversionToEnum(TimeUnit argument) {
        System.out.println("Argument " + argument + " is a type of "
            + argument.getDeclaringClass());
        assertNotNull(argument.name());
    }

    @ParameterizedTest
    @ValueSource(strings = "2017-07-25")
    void testWithImplicitConversionToLocalDate(LocalDate argument) {
```

```
        System.out.println("Argument " + argument + " is a type of "
            + argument.getClass());
        assertNotNull(argument);
    }

}
```

We can check the actual type of the argument in the console. Each test writes a line in the standard output with the value and the type of each argument:

```
--------------------------------------------------------
 T E S T S
--------------------------------------------------------
Running io.github.bonigarcia.ImplicitConversionParameterizedTest
Argument 11 is a type of class java.lang.Integer
Argument 2017-07-25 is a type of class java.time.LocalDate
Argument true is a type of class java.lang.Boolean
Argument SECONDS is a type of class java.util.concurrent.TimeUnit
Tests run: 4, Failures: 0, Errors: 0, Skipped: 0, Time elapsed: 0.353 sec - in
io.github.bonigarcia.ImplicitConversionParameterizedTest

Results :

Tests run: 4, Failures: 0, Errors: 0, Skipped: 0
```

Execution of parameterized tests using implicit argument conversion

Explicit conversion

If the implicit conversion provided by JUnit 5 is not enough to cover our needs, we can use the explicit conversion capability. Thanks to this feature, we can specify a class which is going to make the custom conversion of parameter types. This custom converter is identified with the annotation @ConvertWith, referring to the argument to be converted with. Consider the following example. This parameterized test declares a custom converter for its test method argument:

```
package io.github.bonigarcia;

import static org.junit.jupiter.api.Assertions.assertNotNull;

import java.util.concurrent.TimeUnit;
import org.junit.jupiter.params.ParameterizedTest;
import org.junit.jupiter.params.converter.ConvertWith;
import org.junit.jupiter.params.provider.EnumSource;

class ExplicitConversionParameterizedTest {
```

```
@ParameterizedTest
@EnumSource(TimeUnit.class)
void testWithExplicitArgumentConversion(
        @ConvertWith(CustomArgumentsConverter.class) String
        argument) {
    System.out.println("Argument " + argument + " is a type of "
        + argument.getClass());
    assertNotNull(argument);
}

}
```

Our custom converted is a class that extends the JUnit 5's `SimpleArgumentConverter`. This class overrides the method convert, in which the actual conversion takes place. In the example, we simply transform whatever argument source to `String`.

```
package io.github.bonigarcia;

import org.junit.jupiter.params.converter.SimpleArgumentConverter;

public class CustomArgumentsConverter extends SimpleArgumentConverter {

    @Override
    protected Object convert(Object source, Class<?> targetType) {
        return String.valueOf(source);
    }
}
```

All in all, when the test is executed, the seven enumeration constants defined in `TimeUnit` will be passed as arguments to the test, prior conversion to `String` in `CustomArgumentsConverter`:

```
-------------------------------------------------------
 T E S T S
-------------------------------------------------------
Running io.github.bonigarcia.ExplicitConversionParameterizedTest
Argument NANOSECONDS is a type of class java.lang.String
Argument MICROSECONDS is a type of class java.lang.String
Argument MILLISECONDS is a type of class java.lang.String
Argument SECONDS is a type of class java.lang.String
Argument MINUTES is a type of class java.lang.String
Argument HOURS is a type of class java.lang.String
Argument DAYS is a type of class java.lang.String
Tests run: 7, Failures: 0, Errors: 0, Skipped: 0, Time elapsed: 0.109 sec -
in io.github.bonigarcia.ExplicitConversionParameterizedTest

Results :

Tests run: 7, Failures: 0, Errors: 0, Skipped: 0
```

Execution of parameterized tests using explicit argument conversion

Custom names

The last feature related with parameterized tests in JUnit 5 has to do with the display name of each execution of tests. As we learned, a parameterized test is usually executed as several single tests. Therefore, for the shake of traceability, it is good practice to link each test execution with the argument source.

To that aim, the annotation `@ParameterizedTest` accepts an element called name in which we can specify a custom name (`String`) for the test execution. Moreover, in this String, we can use several built-in placeholders, as described in the following table:

Placeholder	Description
`{index}`	Current invocation index (first one is 1, second is 2, ...)
`{arguments}`	Comma-separated arguments complete list
`{0}`, `{1}`, ...	Value for an individual argument (first one is 0, second is 2, ...)

Let's see a simple example. The following class contains a parameterized test whose arguments are defined using a `@CsvSource` annotation. The test method accepts two arguments (`String` and `int`). In addition, we are specifying the element name of the annotation `@ParameterizedTest` with a custom message, using the placeholders for the current test invocation (`{index}`) and also for the values of each argument: the first one (`{0}`) and the second one (`{1}`):

```
package io.github.bonigarcia;

import org.junit.jupiter.api.DisplayName;
import org.junit.jupiter.params.ParameterizedTest;
import org.junit.jupiter.params.provider.CsvSource;

class CustomNamesParameterizedTest {

    @DisplayName("Display name of test container")
    @ParameterizedTest(name = "[{index}] first argument=\"{0}\", second
        argument={1}")
    @CsvSource({ "mastering, 1", "parameterized, 2", "tests, 3" })
    void testWithCustomDisplayNames(String first, int second) {
        System.out.println("Testing with parameters: " + first + " and " +
            second);
    }

}
```

When executing this test in an IDE (IntelliJ in the following screenshot), we can see how the display name is different for each test execution:

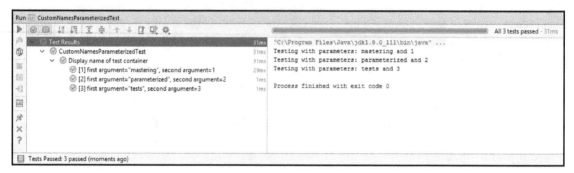

Execution of parameterized tests using custom names in IntelliJ IDE

Java 9

Java 9 was released for **General Availability (GA)** on September 21, 2017. There are many new features shipped with Java 9. Among them, modularity is the defining feature for Java 9.

So far, there has been a problem of modularity in Java, especially significant for large codebases. Every public class can be accessed by any other class in the classpath, leading to inadvertent usage of classes. In addition, the classpath presents potential problems, such as the inability to know whether or not there are duplicated JARs. To solve these problems, Java 9 provides the Java Platform Module System, which allows to create modular JAR files. This type of modules contains an additional module descriptor called `module-info.java`. The content of such files is quite simple: it declares dependencies to other modules using the keyword requires, and exports its own packages with the keyword `exports`. All non-exported packages are encapsulated in the module by default, for example:

```
module mymodule {
  exports io.github.bonigarcia;

  requires mydependency;
}
```

We can represent the relationship between these modules as follows:

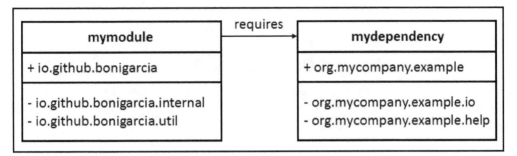

Example of relationship between modules in Java 9

Other new capabilities of Java 9 are summarized in the following list:

- The use modules allow to create a minimal runtime JDK optimized for the given application, instead of using a fully JDK installation. This can be achieve using the tool the *jlink* shipped with JDK 9.
- Java 9 provides an interactive environment to execute Java code, directly from the shell. This type of utility is commonly known as **Read-Eval-Print-Loop** (**REPL**), which is called **JShell** in JDK 9.
- Collection factory methods, Java 9 provides the capability of creating collections (for example, lists or sets) and populates them in a single line:

```
Set<Integer> ints = Set.of(1, 2, 3);
List<String> strings = List.of("first", "second");
```

- **Stream API improvements**: Streams was introduced in Java 8, and they allow to create declarative pipelines of transformations on collections. In Java 9, the methods `dropWhile`, `takeWhile`, and `ofNullable` are added to the Stream API.
- **Private interface methods**: Java 8 provides default methods on interfaces. The limitation so far is that default methods in Java 8 must be public. Now, in Java 9, these default methods can be also private, helping to structure better their implementation.
- **HTTP/2**: Java 9 supports out of the box, version 2 of HTTP and also WebSockets.
- **Multi release JARs**: This feature allows to create alternative versions of classes, depending on the version of the JRE executing the JAR. To that aim, under the folder `META-INF/versions/<java-version>`, we can specify different versions of compiled classes, which will used only when the JRE version matches the version.

- **Improved Javadoc**: Last but not least, Java 9 allows to create HTML5 compliant Javadoc with an integrated search capability.

JUnit 5 and Java 9 compatibility

Since M5, all JUnit 5 artifacts are shipped with compiled module descriptors for Java 9, declared in its JAR manifest (file MANIFEST.MF). For example, the content of the manifest for the artifact junit-jupiter-api M6 is the following:

```
Manifest-Version: 1.0
Implementation-Title: junit-jupiter-api
Automatic-Module-Name: org.junit.jupiter.api
Build-Date: 2017-07-18
Implementation-Version: 5.0.0-M6
Built-By: JUnit Team
Specification-Vendor: junit.org
Specification-Title: junit-jupiter-api
Implementation-Vendor: junit.org
Build-Revision: 3e6482ab8b0dc5376a4ca4bb42bef1eb454b6f1b
Build-Time: 21:26:15.224+0200
Created-By: 1.8.0_131 (Oracle Corporation 25.131-b11)
Specification-Version: 5.0.0
```

With regards to Java 9, the interesting thing is the declaration Automatic-Module-Name. This allows to test modules to require the JUnit 5 module simply by adding the following lines to its module descriptor file (module-info.java):

```
module foo.bar {
      requires org.junit.jupiter.api;
}
```

Beyond JUnit 5.0

JUnit 5.0 GA (General Availability) was released on September 10, 2017. Furthermore, JUnit is a living project, and new features are planned for the next release, that is, 5.1 (with no release agenda scheduled at the time of writing). The backlog for the next release of JUnit 5 can be seen on GitHub: https://github.com/junit-team/junit5/milestone/3. Among other, the following features are planned for JUnit 5.1:

- Scenario tests: This feature has to do with the capability of ordering different test methods within a class. To do that, the following annotations are planned:
  - `@ScenarioTest`: A class-level annotation used to denote that a test class contains steps that make up a single scenario test.
  - `@Step`: A method-level annotation used to denote that a test method is a single step within the scenario test.
  - Support for parallel tests execution: Concurrency is one of the main aspects to be improved in JUnit 5.1, and therefore the support of out of the box concurrent test execution is planned.
- Mechanism for terminating dynamic tests early: This is an enhancement of the JUnit 5.0 support for dynamic tests, introducing a timeout to stop the execution before it terminates itself (to avoid uncontrolled non-deterministic executions).
- Several improvements in test reporting, such as capturing `stdout/stderr` and include in test reports, provide reliable way to get the class (classname) of executed test methods, or specify the order of tests in test reports, among others.

Summary

This chapter contains a comprehensive summary of the advance capabilities to write rich Jupiter tests driven by examples. First, we have learned that parameters can be injected in constructor and methods in test classes. JUnit 5 provides three parameter resolvers out of the box, namely resolver for parameters of the type `TestInfo` (to retrieve information about the current test), resolver for parameters of the type `RepetitionInfo` (to retrieve information about the current repetition), and resolver for parameters of the type `TestReporter` (to publish additional data about the current test run).

Another new feature implemented in Jupiter is the concept of dynamic tests. So far in JUnit 3 and 4, tests are defined at compile time (that is static tests). Jupiter introduces the annotation `@TestFactory` that allows to generate test at runtime. Another new concept provided by the Jupiter programming model are the test templates. These templates re defined using the annotation `@TestTemplate` and are not regular test cases but rather a template for test cases.

JUnit 5 implements an enhancement support for parameterized tests. In order to implement this type of tests, the annotation @ParameterizedTest must be used. Together with this annotation, an argument provider should be also specified. To that aim, several annotations are provided in Jupiter: @ValueSource, @EnumSource, @MethodSource, @CsvSource, @CsvFileSource, and @ArgumentSource.

In the chapter 5, *Integration Of JUnit 5 With External Frameworks*, we are going to learn how JUnit 5 interacts with external frameworks. Concretely, we are going to review several JUnit 5 extension, which provides capabilities to use Mockito, Spring, Selenium, Cucumber, or Docker. Moreover, we present a Gradle plugin, which allows to execute tests within an Android project. Finally, we find out how to use several REST libraries (for example, REST Assured or WireMock) to test RESTful services.

5
Integration Of JUnit 5 With External Frameworks

If I have seen further than others, it is by standing upon the shoulders of giants.
- Isaac Newton

As described in `Chapter 2`, *What's New in JUnit*, the extension model of JUnit 5 allows us to extend the core functionality of JUnit 5 by a third party (tool vendor, developers, and so on). In the Jupiter extension model, an extension point is a callback interface that the extension implements and then registers (activates) in the JUnit 5 framework. As we will discover in this chapter, the JUnit 5 extension model can be used to provide seamless integration with existing third-party frameworks. Concretely, in this chapter, we review JUnit 5 extension for the following technologies:

- **Mockito**: Mock (test double) unit testing framework.
- **Spring**: A Java framework for building enterprise applications.
- **Selenium**: A testing framework to automate the navigation and assessment of web applications.
- **Cucumber**: Testing framework which allows us to create acceptance tests written following a **Behavior-Driven Development (BDD)** style.
- **Docker**: A software technology which allows us to pack and run any application as a lightweight and portable container.

Moreover, we discover that the JUnit 5 extension model is not the only way to integrate with the external world. Concretely, we study how JUnit 5 can be used together with the following:

- **Android** (mobile operating system based on Linux): We can run Jupiter tests in an Android project using a Gradle plugin for JUnit 5.
- **REST** (architectural style for designing distributed systems): We can interact and verify REST services simply using third-party libraries (such as REST Assured or WireMock), or using the fully integrated approach of Spring (tests together with the service implementation).

Mockito

Mockito (`http://site.mockito.org/`) is an open source mock unit testing framework for Java, first released in April 2008. Of course, Mockito is not the only mock framework for Java; there are others, such as the following:

- EasyMock (`http://easymock.org/`).
- JMock (`http://www.jmock.org/`).
- PowerMock (`http://powermock.github.io/`).
- JMockit (`http://jmockit.org/`).

We can say that, at the time of writing, Mockito is the preferred mock framework in Java tests for the most developers and testers. To justify that claim, we use the following screenshot, which shows the evolution of the terms Mockito, EasyMock, JMock, PowerMock, and JMockit in Google Trends (`https://trends.google.com/`) from 2004 to 2017. At the beginning of this period, we can see there was a significant interest on EasyMock and JMock; nevertheless, Mockito was more in demand compared with the rest of the frameworks:

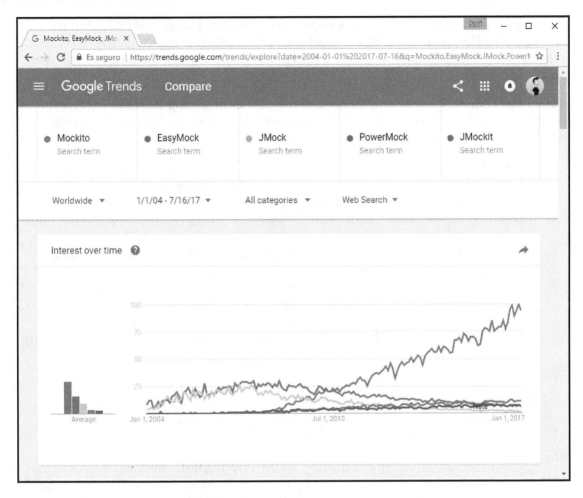

Google Trends evolution of Mockito, EasyMock, JMock, PowerMock, and JMockit

Mockito in a nutshell

As introduced in Chapter 1, *Retrospective on Software Quality and Java Testing*, there are different levels of software testing, such as unit, integration, system, or acceptance. Regarding unit tests, they should be executed in isolation for a single piece of software, for example, an individual class. The objective in this level of tests is to verify the functionality of the unit and not of its dependencies.

In other words, we want to test what is known as the **System Under Test (SUT)** but not its **Depended-On Components (DOCs)**. To achieve this isolation, we use typically *test doubles* to replace these DOCs. Mock objects are a kind of test double, which are programmed with expectations about the real DOC.

In few words, Mockito is a testing framework that allows mock object creation, stubbing, and verification. To that aim, Mockito provides an API to isolate the SUT and its DOCs. Generally speaking, using Mockito involves three different steps:

1. **Mocking objects**: In order to isolate our SUT, we use the Mockito API to create mocks of its associated DOC(s). This way, we guarantee that the SUT is not depending on its real DOC(s), and our unit test is actually focused on the SUT.

2. **Setting expectations**: The differential aspect of mocks object with respect to other test doubles (such as stub) is that mock objects can be programmed with custom expectations according to the needs of the unit test. This process in the Mockito jargon is known as stubbing methods, in which these methods belong to the mocks. By default, mock objects mimic the behavior of real objects. In practical terms, it means that mock objects return appropriate dummy values such as false for Boolean types, null for objects, 0 for integer or long return types, and so on. Mockito allows us to change this behavior with a rich API, which allows stubbing to return a specific value when a method is called.

 When a mock object is not programmed with any expectation (that is, it has no *stubbing method*), technically speaking, it is not a *mock* object but a *dummy* object (take a look at Chapter 1, *Retrospective on Software Quality and Java Testing* for the definition).

3. **Verification**: At the end of the day, we are creating tests, and thus, we need to implement some kind of verification for the SUT. Mockito provides a powerful API to carry out different types of verifications. With this API, we assess the interactions with the SUT and DOCs, verifying the invocation order with a mock, or capturing and verifying the argument passed to a stubbed method. Furthermore, the verification capabilities of Mockito can be complemented with the built-in assertion capabilities of JUnit or using a third-party assertion library (for example, Hamcrest, AssertJ, or Truth). See section *Assertions* within Chapter 3, *JUnit 5 Standard Tests*.

The following table summarizes the Mockito APIs grouped by the aforementioned phases:

Mockito API	Description	Phase
`@Mock`	This annotation identifies a mock object to be created by Mockito. This is used typically for DOC(s).	1.Mocking objects
`@InjectMocks`	This annotation identifies the object in which the mocks are going to be injected. This is used typically to the unit we want to test, that is, our SUT.	1.Mocking objects
`@Spy`	In addition to mocks, Mockito allows us to create spy objects (that is, a partial mock implementation, since they use the real implementation in non-stubbed methods).	1.Mocking objects
`Mockito.when(x).thenReturn(y)` `Mockito.doReturn(y).when(x)`	These methods allow us to specify the value (y) that should be returned by the stubbed method (x) of a given mock object.	2.Setting expectations (*stubbing methods*)

`Mockito.when(x).thenThrow(e)` `Mockito.doThrow(e).when(x)`	These methods allow us to specify the exception (e) that should be thrown when calling a stubbed method (x) of a given mock object.	2.Setting expectations (*stubbing methods*)
`Mockito.when(x).thenAnswer(a)` `Mockito.doAnswer(a).when(x)`	Unlike returning a hardcoded value, a dynamic user-defined logic (`Answer a`) is executed when a given method (x) of the mock is invoked.	2.Setting expectations (*stubbing methods*)
`Mockito.when(x).thenCallRealMethod()` `Mockito.doCallRealMethod().when(x)`	This method allows us the real implementation of a method instead the mocked one.	2.Setting expectations (*stubbing methods*)
`Mockito.doNothing().when(x)`	When using a spy, the default behavior is calling the real methods of the object. In order to avoid the execution of a `void` method x, this method is used.	2.Setting expectations (*stubbing methods*)

`BDDMockito.given(x).willReturn(y)`
`BDDMockito.given(x).willThrow(e)`
`BDDMockito.given(x).willAnswer(a)`
`BDDMockito.given(x).willCallRealMethod()`
	Behaviour-driven development is a test methodology in which tests are specified in terms of scenarios and implemented as *given* (initial context), *when* (event occurs), and *then* (ensure some outcomes). Mockito supports this type of tests through the class `BDDMockito`. The behavior of the stubbed methods (x) is equivalent to `Mockito.when(x)`.	2.Setting expectations (*stubbing methods*)

`Mockito.verify()`	This method verifies the invocation of mock objects. This verification can be optionally enhanced using the following methods: • `times(n)`: The stubbed method is invoked exactly `n` times. • `never()`: The stubbed method is never called. • `atLeastOnce()`: The stubbed method is invoked at least once. • `atLeast(n)`: The stubbed method is called at least n times. • `atMost(n)`: The stubbed method is called at the most n times. • `only()`: A mock fails if any other method is called on the mock object. • `timeout(m)`: This method is called in `m` milliseconds at the most.	3.Verification
`Mockito.verifyZeroInteractions()` `Mockito.verifyNoMoreInteractions()`	These two methods verify that a stubbed method has no interactions. Internally, they use the same implementation.	3.Verification

`@Captor`	This annotation allows us to define an `ArgumentChaptor` object, aimed to verify the arguments passed to a stubbed method.	3.Verification
`Mockito.inOrder`	It facilitates verifying whether interactions with a mock were performed in a given order.	3.Verification

The use of the different annotations depicted in preceding the table (`@Mock`, `@InjectMocks`, `@Spy`, and `@Captor`) is optional, although it is recommendable for the shake of test readability. In other words, there are alternatives to the use of annotation using different Mockito classes. For instance, in order to create a `Mock`, we can use the annotation `@Mock` as follows:

```
@Mock
MyDoc docMock;
```

The alternative to this would be using the method `Mockito.mock`, as follows:

```
MyDoc docMock = Mockito.mock(MyDoc.class)
```

The following sections contains comprehensive examples using the Mockito APIs described in preceding table within Jupiter tests.

JUnit 5 extension for Mockito

At the time of this writing, there is no official JUnit 5 extension to use Mockito in Jupiter tests. Nevertheless, the JUnit 5 team provides a simple ready to use Java class implementing a simple but effective extension for Mockito. This class can be found in the JUnit 5 user guide (`http://junit.org/junit5/docs/current/user-guide/`), and its code is the following:

```
import static org.mockito.Mockito.mock;

import java.lang.reflect.Parameter;
import org.junit.jupiter.api.extension.ExtensionContext;
import org.junit.jupiter.api.extension.ExtensionContext.Namespace;
```

```java
import org.junit.jupiter.api.extension.ExtensionContext.Store;
import org.junit.jupiter.api.extension.ParameterContext;
import org.junit.jupiter.api.extension.ParameterResolver;
import org.junit.jupiter.api.extension.TestInstancePostProcessor;
import org.mockito.Mock;
import org.mockito.MockitoAnnotations;
public class MockitoExtension
        implements TestInstancePostProcessor, ParameterResolver {

    @Override
    public void postProcessTestInstance(Object testInstance,
            ExtensionContext context) {
        MockitoAnnotations.initMocks(testInstance);
    }

    @Override
    public boolean supportsParameter(ParameterContext parameterContext,
      ExtensionContext extensionContext) {
      return
        parameterContext.getParameter().isAnnotationPresent(Mock.class);
    }

    @Override
    public Object resolveParameter(ParameterContext parameterContext,
            ExtensionContext extensionContext) {
        return getMock(parameterContext.getParameter(), extensionContext);
    }

    private Object getMock(Parameter parameter,
            ExtensionContext extensionContext) {
        Class<?> mockType = parameter.getType();
        Store mocks = extensionContext
                .getStore(Namespace.create(MockitoExtension.class,
                mockType));
        String mockName = getMockName(parameter);
        if (mockName != null) {
            return mocks.getOrComputeIfAbsent(mockName,
                    key -> mock(mockType, mockName));
        } else {
            return mocks.getOrComputeIfAbsent(mockType.getCanonicalName(),
                    key -> mock(mockType));
        }
    }

    private String getMockName(Parameter parameter) {
        String explicitMockName =
                parameter.getAnnotation(Mock.class).name()
                .trim();
```

```
        if (!explicitMockName.isEmpty()) {
            return explicitMockName;
        } else if (parameter.isNamePresent()) {
            return parameter.getName();
        }
        return null;
    }

}
```

This extension (among others) is planned to be released in the open source project JUnit Pioneer (http://junit-pioneer.org/). This project is maintained by Nicolai Parlog, Java developer and author of the blog CodeFX (https://blog.codefx.org/).

Inspecting the preceding class, we can check that it is simply a use case of the Jupiter extension model (described in chapter 2, *What's New In JUnit 5*, of this book), which implements the extensions callback `TestInstancePostProcessor` and `ParameterResolver`. Thanks to the first, after the test case is instantiated, the `postProcessTestInstance` method is invoked, and in the body of this method, the initialization of mocks is carried out:

```
MockitoAnnotations.initMocks(testInstance)
```

This has the same effect that using the JUnit 4 runner for Mockito: `@RunWith(MockitoJUnitRunner.class)`.

In addition, this extension also implements the interface `ParameterResolver`. That means that dependency injection at method level will be allowed in tests, which register the extension (`@ExtendWith(MockitoExtension.class)`). In particular, the annotation will inject mock objects for test parameters annotated with `@Mock` (located in package `org.mockito`).

Let's see some examples to clarify the use of this extension together with Mockito. As usual, we can find the source code of this examples on the GitHub repository https://github.com/bonigarcia/mastering-junit5. A copy of the preceding extension (`MockitoExtension`) is contained in the project `junit5-mockito`. To guide these examples, we implement a typical use case in software applications: the login of a user in a software system.

In this use case, we suppose that a user interacts with a system made up by three classes:

- `LoginController`: The class which receives the request from the user, returning a response as a result. This request is dispatched to the `LoginService` component.
- `LoginService`: This class implements the functionality of the use case. To that aim, it needs to confirm whether or not the user is authenticated in the system. To that, it needs to read the persistence layer, implemented in the `LoginRepository` class.
- `LoginRepository`: This class allows to access the persistence layer of the system, typically implemented by means of a database. This class can also be called **Data Access Object (DAO)**.

In terms of composition, the relationship of these three classes are is following:

Login use case class diagram (composition relationship among the classes)

The sequence diagram of the two basic operations involved in the use case (login and logout) is depicted in the following chart:

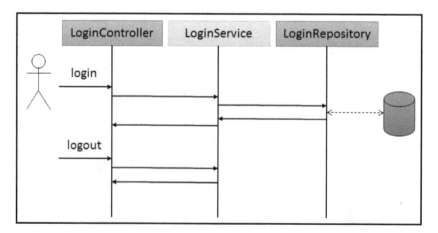

Login use case sequence diagram

We implement this example with several simple Java classes. First, the LoginController uses the LoginService by composition:

```java
package io.github.bonigarcia;

public class LoginController {
    public LoginService loginService = new LoginService();

    public String login(UserForm userForm) {
        System.out.println("LoginController.login " + userForm);
        try {
            if (userForm == null) {
                return "ERROR";
            } else if (loginService.login(userForm)) {
                return "OK";
            } else {
                return "KO";
            }
        } catch (Exception e) {
            return "ERROR";
        }
    }

    public void logout(UserForm userForm) {
        System.out.println("LoginController.logout " + userForm);
        loginService.logout(userForm);
    }
}
```

The UserForm object is a simple Java class, sometimes called **Plain-Old Java Object** (**POJO**), with two properties username and password:

```java
package io.github.bonigarcia;

public class UserForm {

    public String username;
    public String password;

    public UserForm(String username, String password) {
        this.username = username;
        this.password = password;
    }

    // Getters and setters

    @Override
    public String toString() {
```

```
        return "UserForm [username=" + username + ", password=" + password
                + "]";
    }
}
```

Then, the service depends on the repository (LoginRepository) for data access. In this example, the service also implements a user registry using a Java list in which the authenticated users are stored:

```
package io.github.bonigarcia;

import java.util.ArrayList;
import java.util.List;

public class LoginService {

    private LoginRepository loginRepository = new LoginRepository();
    private List<String> usersLogged = new ArrayList<>();

    public boolean login(UserForm userForm) {
        System.out.println("LoginService.login " + userForm);

        // Preconditions
        checkForm(userForm);

        // Same user cannot be logged twice
        String username = userForm.getUsername();
        if (usersLogged.contains(username)) {
            throw new LoginException(username + " already logged");
        }

        // Call to repository to make logic
        boolean login = loginRepository.login(userForm);

        if (login) {
            usersLogged.add(username);
        }

        return login;
    }

    public void logout(UserForm userForm) {
        System.out.println("LoginService.logout " + userForm);

        // Preconditions
        checkForm(userForm);

        // User should be logged beforehand
```

```
        String username = userForm.getUsername();
        if (!usersLogged.contains(username)) {
            throw new LoginException(username + " not logged");
        }

        usersLogged.remove(username);
    }

    public int getUserLoggedCount() {
        return usersLogged.size();
    }

    private void checkForm(UserForm userForm) {
        assert userForm != null;
        assert userForm.getUsername() != null;
        assert userForm.getPassword() != null;
    }

}
```

Finally, the `LoginRepository` is as follows. For the sake of simplicity, instead of accessing a real database, this component implements a map in which the credentials of the hypothetical user of the system are stored (where `key`= username, and `value`=password):

```
package io.github.bonigarcia;

import java.util.HashMap;
import java.util.Map;

public class LoginRepository {

    Map<String, String> users;

    public LoginRepository() {
        users = new HashMap<>();
        users.put("user1", "p1");
        users.put("user2", "p3");
        users.put("user3", "p4");
    }

    public boolean login(UserForm userForm) {
        System.out.println("LoginRepository.login " + userForm);
        String username = userForm.getUsername();
        String password = userForm.getPassword();
        return users.keySet().contains(username)
                && users.get(username).equals(password);
    }
```

```
    }
```

Now, we are going to test our system using JUnit 5 and Mockito. First of all, we test the controller component. Since we are doing unit tests, we need to isolate the `LoginController` login from the rest of the system. To do that, we need to mock its dependencies, in this example, the `LoginService` component. Using the SUT/DOC terminology explained at the beginning, in this test, our SUT is the class `LoginController` and its DOC is the class `LoginService`.

To implement our test with JUnit 5, first we need to register the `MockitoExtension` with `@ExtendWith`. Then, we declare the SUT with `@InjectMocks` (class `LoginController`) and its DOC with `@Mock` (class `LoginService`). We implement two tests (`@Test`). First one (`testLoginOk`) specifies when the method login of mock `loginService` is called, this method should return true. After that, the SUT is actually exercised, and its response is verified (in this case, the returned String must be `OK`). Moreover, the Mockito API is used again to assess that no more interactions with the mock `LoginService` is done. The second test (`testLoginKo`) is equivalent, but stubbing the method login to return false and therefore the response of the SUT (`LoginController`) must be `KO` in this case:

```java
package io.github.bonigarcia;

import static org.junit.jupiter.api.Assertions.assertEquals;
import static org.mockito.Mockito.verify;
import static org.mockito.Mockito.verifyNoMoreInteractions;
import static org.mockito.Mockito.verifyZeroInteractions;
import static org.mockito.Mockito.when;

import org.junit.jupiter.api.Test;
import org.junit.jupiter.api.extension.ExtendWith;
import org.mockito.InjectMocks;
import org.mockito.Mock;
import io.github.bonigarcia.mockito.MockitoExtension;

@ExtendWith(MockitoExtension.class)
class LoginControllerLoginTest {

    // Mocking objects
    @InjectMocks
    LoginController loginController;

    @Mock
    LoginService loginService;

    // Test data
    UserForm userForm = new UserForm("foo", "bar");
```

```
@Test
void testLoginOk() {
    // Setting expectations (stubbing methods)
    when(loginService.login(userForm)).thenReturn(true);

    // Exercise SUT
    String reseponseLogin = loginController.login(userForm);

    // Verification
    assertEquals("OK", reseponseLogin);
    verify(loginService).login(userForm);
    verifyNoMoreInteractions(loginService);
}

@Test
void testLoginKo() {
    // Setting expectations (stubbing methods)
    when(loginService.login(userForm)).thenReturn(false);

    // Exercise SUT
    String reseponseLogin = loginController.login(userForm);

    // Verification
    assertEquals("KO", reseponseLogin);
    verify(loginService).login(userForm);
    verifyZeroInteractions(loginService);
}

}
```

If we execute this test, simply inspecting the traces on the standard output we can check that the SUT have been actually executed. In addition, we assure that the verification stage has been succeeded in both tests since both of them have passed:

```
-------------------------------------------------------------
 T E S T S
-------------------------------------------------------------
Running io.github.bonigarcia.LoginControllerLoginTest
LoginController.login UserForm [username=foo, password=bar]
LoginController.login UserForm [username=foo, password=bar]
Tests run: 2, Failures: 0, Errors: 0, Skipped: 0, Time elapsed: 0.739 sec -
in io.github.bonigarcia.LoginControllerLoginTest

Results :

Tests run: 2, Failures: 0, Errors: 0, Skipped: 0
```

Execution of unit test of *LoginControllerLoginTest* with JUnit 5 and Mockito

Let's move now to other example in which the negative scenarios (that is, error situations) are tested for the component `LoginController`. The following class contains two tests, first one (`testLoginError`) is devoted to assess the response of the system (it should be ERROR) when a null form is used. In the second test (`testLoginException`), we program the method login of the mock `loginService` to raise an exception when any form is used first. Then, we exercise the SUT (`LoginController`) and assess that the response is actually an ERROR:

 Note that we are using the argument matcher any (provided out of the box by Mockito) when setting the expectations for the mock method.

```java
package io.github.bonigarcia;

import static org.junit.jupiter.api.Assertions.assertEquals;
import static org.mockito.ArgumentMatchers.any;
import static org.mockito.Mockito.when;

import org.junit.jupiter.api.Test;
import org.junit.jupiter.api.extension.ExtendWith;
import org.mockito.InjectMocks;
import org.mockito.Mock;
import io.github.bonigarcia.mockito.MockitoExtension;

@ExtendWith(MockitoExtension.class)
class LoginControllerErrorTest {

    @InjectMocks
    LoginController loginController;

    @Mock
    LoginService loginService;

    UserForm userForm = new UserForm("foo", "bar");

    @Test
    void testLoginError() {
        // Exercise
        String response = loginController.login(null);

        // Verify
        assertEquals("ERROR", response);
    }

    @Test
```

```
    void testLoginException() {
        // Expectation
        when(loginService.login(any(UserForm.class)))
                .thenThrow(IllegalArgumentException.class);

        // Exercise
        String response = loginController.login(userForm);

        // Verify
        assertEquals("ERROR", response);
    }

}
```

Again, when running the tests in the shell, we can confirm that both of tests are correctly executed and the SUT is exercised:

```
-------------------------------------------------------
 T E S T S
-------------------------------------------------------
Running io.github.bonigarcia.LoginControllerErrorTest
LoginController.login UserForm [username=foo, password=bar]
LoginController.login null
Tests run: 2, Failures: 0, Errors: 0, Skipped: 0, Time elapsed: 1.088 sec -
in io.github.bonigarcia.LoginControllerErrorTest

Results :

Tests run: 2, Failures: 0, Errors: 0, Skipped: 0
```

Execution of unit test of *LoginControllerErrorTest* with JUnit 5 and Mockito

Let's see an example using the BDD style. To that aim, the class BDDMockito is used. Notice that the static method given of this class is imported in the example. Then, four tests are implemented. In fact, these four tests are exactly the same implemented in the previous examples (LoginControllerLoginTest and LoginControllerErrorTest), but this time using the BDD style and a more compact style (one-liner commands).

```
package io.github.bonigarcia;

import static org.junit.jupiter.api.Assertions.assertEquals;
import static org.mockito.ArgumentMatchers.any;
import static org.mockito.BDDMockito.given;

import org.junit.jupiter.api.Test;
import org.junit.jupiter.api.extension.ExtendWith;
import org.mockito.InjectMocks;
import org.mockito.Mock;
```

```java
import io.github.bonigarcia.mockito.MockitoExtension;

@ExtendWith(MockitoExtension.class)
class LoginControllerBDDTest {

    @InjectMocks
    LoginController loginController;

    @Mock
    LoginService loginService;

    UserForm userForm = new UserForm("foo", "bar");

    @Test
    void testLoginOk() {
        given(loginService.login(userForm)).willReturn(true);
        assertEquals("OK", loginController.login(userForm));
    }

    @Test
    void testLoginKo() {
        given(loginService.login(userForm)).willReturn(false);
        assertEquals("KO", loginController.login(userForm));
    }

    @Test
    void testLoginError() {
        assertEquals("ERROR", loginController.login(null));
    }

    @Test
    void testLoginException() {
        given(loginService.login(any(UserForm.class)))
                .willThrow(IllegalArgumentException.class);
        assertEquals("ERROR", loginController.login(userForm));
    }

}
```

The execution of this test class supposes that four tests are executed. As shown in the following screenshot, all of them pass:

```
-----------------------------------------------------
 T E S T S
-----------------------------------------------------
Running io.github.bonigarcia.LoginControllerBDDTest
LoginController.login UserForm [username=foo, password=bar]
LoginController.login UserForm [username=foo, password=bar]
LoginController.login UserForm [username=foo, password=bar]
LoginController.login null
Tests run: 4, Failures: 0, Errors: 0, Skipped: 0, Time elapsed: 0.565 sec -
in io.github.bonigarcia.LoginControllerBDDTest

Results :

Tests run: 4, Failures: 0, Errors: 0, Skipped: 0
```

Execution of unit test of *LoginControllerBDDTest* with JUnit 5 and Mockito

Let's move now to the next component of our system: `LoginService`. In the following example, we aim to unit test that component, and thus first we use the annotation `@InjectMocks` to inject the SUT in our test. Then, the DOC (`LoginRepository`) is mocked using the annotation `@Mock`. The class contains three tests. The first (`testLoginOk`) is devoted to verify the answer of the SUT when a correct form is received. The second test (`testLoginKo`) verifies the opposite scenario. Finally, the third test also verifies an error situation of the system. The implementation of this service keeps a registry of the users logged, and will not allowed to login the same user twice. For this reason, we implemented a test (`testLoginTwice`), which verifies that the exception `LoginException` is raised when the same user tries to login twice:

```
package io.github.bonigarcia;

import static org.junit.jupiter.api.Assertions.assertFalse;
import static org.junit.jupiter.api.Assertions.assertThrows;
import static org.junit.jupiter.api.Assertions.assertTrue;
import static org.mockito.ArgumentMatchers.any;
import static org.mockito.Mockito.atLeast;
import static org.mockito.Mockito.times;
import static org.mockito.Mockito.verify;
import static org.mockito.Mockito.when;

import org.junit.jupiter.api.Test;
import org.junit.jupiter.api.extension.ExtendWith;
import org.mockito.InjectMocks;
```

```java
import org.mockito.Mock;
import io.github.bonigarcia.mockito.MockitoExtension;

@ExtendWith(MockitoExtension.class)
class LoginServiceTest {

    @InjectMocks
    LoginService loginService;

    @Mock
    LoginRepository loginRepository;

    UserForm userForm = new UserForm("foo", "bar");

    @Test
    void testLoginOk() {
        when(loginRepository.login(any(UserForm.class))).thenReturn(true);
        assertTrue(loginService.login(userForm));
        verify(loginRepository, atLeast(1)).login(userForm);
    }

    @Test
    void testLoginKo() {
        when(loginRepository.login(any(UserForm.class))).thenReturn(false);
        assertFalse(loginService.login(userForm));
        verify(loginRepository, times(1)).login(userForm);
    }

    @Test
    void testLoginTwice() {
        when(loginRepository.login(userForm)).thenReturn(true);
        assertThrows(LoginException.class, () -> {
            loginService.login(userForm);
            loginService.login(userForm);
        });
    }

}
```

As usual, the execution of the test in shell gives us an idea of how things have gone. We can check that the login service has been exercised four times (since in the third test, we did twice). But due to the fact that the LoginException was expected, that test is succeeded (as well the other two):

```
------------------------------------------------------------
 T E S T S
------------------------------------------------------------
Running io.github.bonigarcia.LoginServiceTest
LoginService.login UserForm [username=foo, password=bar]
LoginService.login UserForm [username=foo, password=bar]
LoginService.login UserForm [username=foo, password=bar]
LoginService.login UserForm [username=foo, password=bar]
Tests run: 3, Failures: 0, Errors: 0, Skipped: 0, Time elapsed: 0.757 sec -
in io.github.bonigarcia.LoginServiceTest

Results :

Tests run: 3, Failures: 0, Errors: 0, Skipped: 0
```

Execution of unit test of *LoginServiceTest* with JUnit 5 and Mockito

The following class provides a simple example for capturing the argument of a mock object. We define a class property of type ArgumentCaptor<UserForm>, which is annotated with @Captor. Then, in the body of the test, the SUT (LoginService in this case) is exercised and the argument of the method login are captured. Finally, the value of this argument is assessed:

```
package io.github.bonigarcia;

import static org.junit.jupiter.api.Assertions.assertEquals;
import static org.mockito.Mockito.verify;

import org.junit.jupiter.api.Test;
import org.junit.jupiter.api.extension.ExtendWith;
import org.mockito.ArgumentCaptor;
import org.mockito.Captor;
import org.mockito.InjectMocks;
import org.mockito.Mock;
import io.github.bonigarcia.mockito.MockitoExtension;

@ExtendWith(MockitoExtension.class)
class LoginServiceChaptorTest {

    @InjectMocks
    LoginService loginService;
```

```
@Mock
LoginRepository loginRepository;

@Captor
ArgumentCaptor<UserForm> argCaptor;

UserForm userForm = new UserForm("foo", "bar");

@Test
void testArgumentCaptor() {
    loginService.login(userForm);
    verify(loginRepository).login(argCaptor.capture());
    assertEquals(userForm, argCaptor.getValue());
}

}
```

Once again, in the console, we check that the SUT was exercised and the test is declared as successful:

```
-------------------------------------------------------------
 T E S T S
-------------------------------------------------------------
Running io.github.bonigarcia.LoginServiceChaptorTest
LoginService.login UserForm [username=foo, password=bar]
Tests run: 1, Failures: 0, Errors: 0, Skipped: 0, Time elapsed: 0.674 sec -
in io.github.bonigarcia.LoginServiceChaptorTest

Results :

Tests run: 1, Failures: 0, Errors: 0, Skipped: 0
```

Execution of unit test of *LoginServiceChaptorTest* with JUnit 5 and Mockito

The last example we see in this chapter related to Mockito has to do with the use of an spy. As introduced before, by default, an spy uses the real implementation in non-stubbed methods. Therefore, if we do not stub methods in an spy object, what we get is the real object in our test. This is what happens in the next example. As we can see, we are using the LoginService as our SUT, and then we spy the object LoginRepository. Due to the fact that in the body of the tests we are not programming expectations in the spy object, we are assessing the real system in the test.

All in all, the test data is prepared to get a login correct (using username as `user` and password as `p1`, which is present in the hardcoded values in the real implementation of `LoginRepository`), and then some dummy values for an unsuccessful login:

```
package io.github.bonigarcia;

import static org.junit.jupiter.api.Assertions.assertFalse;
import static org.junit.jupiter.api.Assertions.assertTrue;

import org.junit.jupiter.api.Test;
import org.junit.jupiter.api.extension.ExtendWith;
import org.mockito.InjectMocks;
import org.mockito.Spy;
import io.github.bonigarcia.mockito.MockitoExtension;

@ExtendWith(MockitoExtension.class)
class LoginServiceSpyTest {

    @InjectMocks
    LoginService loginService;

    @Spy
    LoginRepository loginRepository;

    UserForm userOk = new UserForm("user1", "p1");
    UserForm userKo = new UserForm("foo", "bar");

    @Test
    void testLoginOk() {
        assertTrue(loginService.login(userOk));
    }

    @Test
    void testLoginKo() {
        assertFalse(loginService.login(userKo));
    }
}
```

In the shell, we can check that both tests were correctly executed, and in this case, the real components (both `LoginService` and `LoginRepository`) were actually exercised:

```
- - - - - - - - - - - - - - - - - - - - - - - - - - - - - - - - - - - - - - - - - -
 T E S T S
- - - - - - - - - - - - - - - - - - - - - - - - - - - - - - - - - - - - - -
Running io.github.bonigarcia.LoginServiceSpyTest
LoginService.login UserForm [username=foo, password=bar]
LoginRepository.login UserForm [username=foo, password=bar]
LoginService.login UserForm [username=user1, password=p1]
LoginRepository.login UserForm [username=user1, password=p1]
Tests run: 2, Failures: 0, Errors: 0, Skipped: 0, Time elapsed: 0.709 sec -
in io.github.bonigarcia.LoginServiceSpyTest

Results :

Tests run: 2, Failures: 0, Errors: 0, Skipped: 0
```

Execution of unit test of *LoginServiceSpyTest* with JUnit 5 and Mockito

 These examples demonstrate several of the capabilities of Mockito, but of course not all. For further information, visit the official Mockito reference at `http://site.mockito.org/`.

Spring

Spring (`https://spring.io/`) is an open source Java framework for building enterprise applications. It was first written by Rod Johnson together with his book *Expert One-on-One J2EE Design and Development* in October 2002. The original motivation of Spring was getting rid of the complexity of J2EE, providing a light-weight infrastructure aimed to ease the development of enterprise application using simple POJOs as building blocks.

Spring in a nutshell

The core technology of the Spring Framework is known as **Inversion of Control (IoC)**, which is the process of instantiating objects outside the class in which these objects are actually used. These objects are known as beans or components in the Spring jargon and are created as *singleton* objects by default. The entity in charge of the creation of beans is known as the Spring IoC container. This is achieved by **Dependency Injection (DI)**, which is the process of providing dependencies of one object instead of constructing them itself.

IoC and DI are often used interchangeably. Nevertheless, as depicted in the paragraph earlier, these concepts are not exactly the same (IoC is achieved through DI).

As depicted in the next part of this section, Spring is a modular framework. The core functionally of Spring (that is, IoC) is provided in the `spring-context` module. This module provides the ability of creating **application context**, that is, the Spring's DI container. There are many different ways to define application contexts in Spring. Two of the most significant types are the following:

- `AnnotationConfigApplicationContext`: Application context, which accepts annotated classes to identify the Spring beans to be executed in the container. In this type of context, beans are identified by annotating plain classes with the annotation `@Component`. It is not the only one to declare a class as a Spring bean. There are further stereotypes annotations: `@Controller` (stereotype for presentation layer, used in the web module, MVC), `@Repository` (stereotype for the persistence layer, used in the data access module, called Spring Data), and `@Service` (used in the service layer). These three annotations are used to separate the layers of an application. Finally, classes annotated with `@Configuration` allows to define Spring beans by annotating methods with `@Bean` (the object returned by these methods will be Spring beans living in the container):

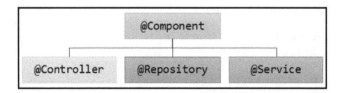

Spring stereotypes used to define beans

- `ClassPathXmlApplicationContext`: Application context, which accepts bean definitions declared in an XML file located in the project classpath.

The annotation-based context configuration was introduced in Spring 2.5. The Spring IoC container is totally decoupled from the format in which configuration metadata (that is, bean definition) is actually written. Nowadays many developers chose annotation-based configuration rather than XML based. For this reason, in this book, we are going to use only annotation-based context configuration in the examples.

Let's see a simple example. First of all, we need to include the `spring-context` dependency in our project. For example, as a Maven dependency:

```
<dependency>
    <groupId>org.springframework</groupId>
    <artifactId>spring-context</artifactId>
    <version>${spring-context.version}</version>
</dependency>
```

Then, we create an executable Java class (that is, with a main method). Notice that in this class there is one annotation at class level: `@ComponentScan`. This is a very important annotation in Spring, since it allows to declare the package in which Spring will look for beans definition in the form of annotations. If specific packages are not defined (just like in the example), scanning will occur from the package of the class that declares this annotation (in the example the package `io.github.bonigarcia`). In the body of the main method, we create the Spring application context with `AnnotationConfigApplicationContext`. From that context, we get the Spring component whose class is `MessageComponent`, and we write the result of its `getMessage()` method on the standard output:

```java
package io.github.bonigarcia;

import org.springframework.context.annotation.AnnotationConfigApplicationContext;
import org.springframework.context.annotation.ComponentScan;

@ComponentScan
public class MySpringApplication {

    public static void main(String[] args) {
        try (AnnotationConfigApplicationContext context = new
                AnnotationConfigApplicationContext(
                MySpringApplication.class)) {
            MessageComponent messageComponent = context
                    .getBean(MessageComponent.class);
            System.out.println(messageComponent.getMessage());
        }
    }

}
```

The bean `MessageComponent` is defined in the following class. Notice that it is declared as the Spring component simply using the annotation `@Component` at class level. Then, in this example, we are injecting another Spring component called `MessageService` using the class constructor:

```
package io.github.bonigarcia;

import org.springframework.beans.factory.annotation.Autowired;
import org.springframework.stereotype.Component;

@Component
public class MessageComponent {

    private MessageService messageService;

    public MessageComponent(MessageService messageService) {
        this.messageService = messageService;
    }

    public String getMessage() {
        return messageService.getMessage();
    }

}
```

At this point, it is worth reviewing the different manners to carry out dependency injection of Spring components:

1. Field injection: The injected component is a class field annotated with `@Autowired`, just like the example before. As a benefit, this kind of injection removes clutter code such as setter methods or constructor parameters.
2. Setter injection: The injected component is declared as a field in the class, and then a setter for this field is created and annotated with `@Autowired`.

3. Constructor injection: The dependency is injected in the class constructor, which is annotated with `@Autowired` (**3-a** in the diagram here). This is the way shown in the example earlier. As of Spring 4.3, it is not required anymore to annotate the constructor with `@Autowired` to carry out the injection (**3-b**).

The latest way of injection (**3-b**) was several benefits, such as the promotion of testability without the need of reflection mechanism (implemented, for example, by mocking library). In addition, it can make developers to think over the design of the class, since many injected dependencies suppose many constructor parameters, and this should be avoided (*God object* anti-pattern).

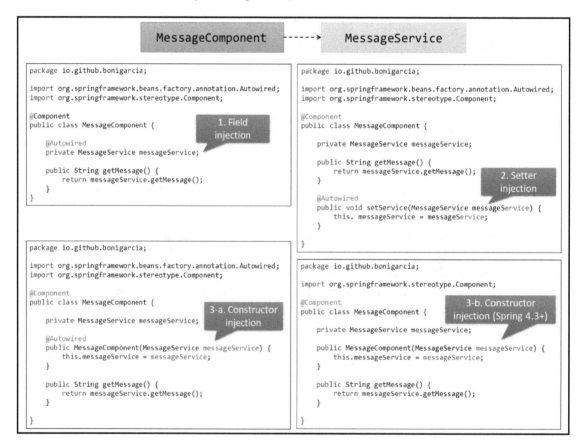

Different ways of dependency injection (Autowired) in Spring

The last component in our example is named `MessageService`. Note that is also a Spring component, this time annotated with `@Service` to remark its service nature (from a functional perspective, it would be same than annotating the class with `@Component`):

```
package io.github.bonigarcia;

import org.springframework.stereotype.Service;

@Service
public class MessageService {

    public String getMessage() {
        return "Hello world!";
    }

}
```

Now, if we execute the main class of this example (called `MySpringApplication`, see the source code here), we create an annotation-based application context with a try with resources (this way the application context will be closed at the end). The Spring IoC container will create two beans: `MessageService` and `MessageComponet`. Using the application context, we seek the bean `MessageComponet` and invoke its method `getMessage`, which is finally written in the standard output:

```
package io.github.bonigarcia;

import
org.springframework.context.annotation.AnnotationConfigApplicationContext;
import org.springframework.context.annotation.ComponentScan;

@ComponentScan
public class MySpringApplication {

    public static void main(String[] args) {
        try (AnnotationConfigApplicationContext context = new
                AnnotationConfigApplicationContext(
                MySpringApplication.class)) {
            MessageComponent messageComponent = context
                    .getBean(MessageComponent.class);
            System.out.println(messageComponent.getMessage());
        }
    }

}
```

Spring modules

The Spring framework is modular, allowing developers to use only the needed modules provided by the framework. The complete list of this modules can be found on `https://spring.io/projects`. The following table summarizes some of the most important ones:

Spring project	Logo	Description
Spring Framework		Provides core support for DI, transaction management, web applications (Spring MCV), data access, messaging, and so on.
Spring IO Platform		Brings together the core Spring APIs into a cohesive and versioned foundational platform for modern applications.
Spring Boot		Simplifies the creation of standalone, production-grade Spring-based applications with the minimal configuration. It follows the convention-over-configuration approach.
Spring Data		Simplifies data access by means of comprehensive APIs to work with the relational databases, NoSQL, map-reduce algorithms, and so on.

Spring Cloud		Provides a set of libraries and common patterns for building and deploying distributed systems and microservices.
Spring Security		Provides customizable authentication and authorization capabilities for Spring-based applications.
Spring Integration		Provides a lightweight, POJO-based messaging for Spring-based applications to integrate with external systems.
Spring Batch		Provides a lightweight framework designed to enable the development of robust batch applications for operations of enterprise systems.

Introduction to Spring Test

Spring a module called `spring-test`, which supports unit and integration testing of Spring components. Among other features, this module provides the ability to create Spring application context for testing purposes or create mock objects that to test our code in isolation. There are different annotations supporting this testing capabilities. A list of the most significant one is the following:

- `@ContextConfiguration`: This annotation is used to determine how to load and configure an `ApplicationContext` for integration tests. For example, it allows to load the application context from annotated classes (using the element classes) or bean definitions declared in XML files (using the element locations).
- `@ActiveProfiles`: This annotation is used to instruct the container about which definition profiles should be active during the application context loading (for example, development and test profiles).
- `@TestPropertySource`: This annotation is used to configure the locations of the properties files and the inline properties to be added.
- `@WebAppConfiguration`: This annotation is used to instruct the Spring context that `ApplicationContext` loaded is `WebApplicationContext`.

In addition, the `spring-test` module offers several capabilities to carry out different actions typically required in tests, namely:

- The `org.springframework.mock.web` package contains a set of Servlet API mock objects, useful for testing web contexts. For instance, the object `MockMvc` allows to perform HTTP requests (`POST`, `GET`, `PUT`, `DELETE`, and so on) and verify the response (status code, content type, or response body).
- The `org.springframework.mock.jndi` package contains an implementation of the **Java Naming and Directory Interface (JNDI)** SPI, which can be used to set up a simple JNDI environment for tests. For instance, using the class `SimpleNamingContextBuilder` we can make a JNDI data source available in our tests.
- The `org.springframework.test.jdbc` package contains the class `JdbcTestUtils`, which is a collection of JDBC utility functions aimed to simplify standard database access.
- The `org.springframework.test.util` package contains the class `ReflectionTestUtils`, which is a collection of utility methods to set a non-public field or invoke a private/protected setter method when testing the application code.

Testing Spring Boot applications

As introduced before, Spring Boot is a project of the Spring portfolio aimed to simplify the development of Spring applications. The main benefits of using Spring Boot are summarized as follows:

- A Spring Boot application is just a Spring `ApplicationContext` in which the principal convention over configuration is used. Thank to this, it is faster to get started with the Spring development.
- The annotation `@SpringBootApplication` is used to identify the main class in a Spring Boot project.
- A range of non-functional features are provided out of the box: embedded servlet containers (Tomcat, Jetty, and Undertow), security, metrics, health checks, or externalized configuration.
- A creation of standalone running applications that just run using the command `java -jar` (even for web applications).
- Spring Boot **command line interface** (**CLI**) allows to run Groovy scripts for quickly prototyping with Spring.
- Spring Boot works in the same way as any standard Java library, that is, to use it, we simply need to add the appropriate `spring-boot-*.jar` in our project classpath (typically using build tools such as Maven or Gradle). Spring Boot provides a number of *starters* aimed to ease the process of adding the different libraries to the classpath. The following table contains several of those starters:

Name	Description
`spring-boot-starter`	Core starter, including auto-configuration support and logging
`spring-boot-starter-batch`	Starter for using Spring Batch
`spring-boot-starter-cloud-connectors`	Starter for using Spring Cloud Connectors, which simplifies connecting to services in Cloud platforms like Cloud Foundry and Heroku
`spring-boot-starter-data-jpa`	Starter for using Spring Data JPA with Hibernate
`spring-boot-starter-integration`	Starter for using Spring Integration
`spring-boot-starter-jdbc`	Starter for using JDBC with the Tomcat JDBC connection pool

spring-boot-starter-test	Starter for testing Spring Boot applications with libraries, including JUnit, Hamcrest, and Mockito
spring-boot-starter-thymeleaf	Starter for building MVC web applications using Thymeleaf views
spring-boot-starter-web	Starter for building web, including REST, applications using Spring MVC. Uses Tomcat as the default embedded container
spring-boot-starter-websocket	Starter for building WebSocket applications using Spring Framework's WebSocket support

 For complete information about Spring Boot visit the official reference: https://projects.spring.io/spring-boot/.

Spring Boot provides different capabilities to simplify the tests. For instance, it provides the @SpringBootTest annotation, which is used at classlevel in test classes. This annotation will create ApplicationContext for these tests (similarly to @ContextConfiguration but for Spring Boot based applications). As we have seen in the section before, in the spring-test module, we use the annotation @ContextConfiguration(classes=...) to specify, which bean definition (Spring @Configuration) to be loaded. When testing Spring Boot applications this is often not required. Spring Boot's tests annotations will search the primary configuration automatically if not explicitly define one. The search algorithm works up from the package that contains the test until it finds a @SpringBootApplication annotated class.

Spring Boot also facilitates the use of mocks for Spring components. To that, the annotation @MockBean is provided. This annotation allows defining a Mockito mock for a bean inside our ApplicationContext. It can be new beans, but also to it can replace a single existing bean definition. Mock beans are automatically reset after each test method. This method is usually known as in-container testing, in counterpart to out-of-container, in which a mock library (example, Mockito) is used to unit test the Spring components in isolation and without the need of a Spring ApplicationContext. For example of both types of unit tests for Spring applications is shown in the next section.

JUnit 5 extension for Spring

In order to integrate the `spring-test` capabilities into JUnit 5's Jupiter programming model, `SpringExtension` has been developed. This extension is part of the `spring-test` module, as of Spring 5. Let's see several examples of JUnit 5 and Spring 5 together.

Let's suppose we want to make an integration in-container test of the Spring application described in the former section, made up of three classes: `MySpringApplication`, `MessageComponent`, and `MessageService`. As we have learned, in order to implement a Jupiter test against this application, we need to make the following steps:

1. Annotate our test class with `@ContextConfiguration` to specify which `ApplicationContext` needs to be loaded.
2. Annotate our test class with `@ExtendWith(SpringExtension.class)` to enable `spring-test` into Jupiter.
3. Inject the Spring component we want to assess in our test class.
4. Implement our test (`@Test`).

For example:

```java
package io.github.bonigarcia;

import static org.junit.jupiter.api.Assertions.assertEquals;

import org.junit.jupiter.api.Test;
import org.junit.jupiter.api.extension.ExtendWith;
import org.springframework.beans.factory.annotation.Autowired;
import org.springframework.test.context.ContextConfiguration;
import org.springframework.test.context.junit.jupiter.SpringExtension;

@ExtendWith(SpringExtension.class)
@ContextConfiguration(classes = { MySpringApplication.class })
class SimpleSpringTest {

    @Autowired
    public MessageComponent messageComponent;

    @Test
    public void test() {
        assertEquals("Hello world!", messageComponent.getMessage());
    }

}
```

This is a very simple example in which the Spring component called `MessageComponent` is assessed. When this test is started, our `ApplicationContext` is initiated with and all our Spring components inside. After that, in this example, the bean `MessageComponent` is injected in the test, which is assessed simply calling the method `getMessage()` and verifying its response.

It is worth to review which dependencies are needed for this test. When using Maven, these dependencies are the following:

```
<dependencies>
    <dependency>
        <groupId>org.springframework</groupId>
        <artifactId>spring-context</artifactId>
        <version>${spring.version}</version>
    </dependency>
    <dependency>
        <groupId>org.springframework</groupId>
        <artifactId>spring-test</artifactId>
        <version>${spring.version}</version>
        <scope>test</scope>
    </dependency>
    <dependency>
        <groupId>org.junit.jupiter</groupId>
        <artifactId>junit-jupiter-api</artifactId>
        <version>${junit.jupiter.version}</version>
        <scope>test</scope>
    </dependency>
</dependencies>
```

On the other side, if we use Gradle, the dependencies clause would be as follows:

```
dependencies {
    compile("org.springframework:spring-context:${springVersion}")
    testCompile("org.springframework:spring-test:${springVersion}")
    testCompile("org.junit.jupiter:junit-jupiter-
api:${junitJupiterVersion}")
    testRuntime("org.junit.jupiter:junit-jupiter-
engine:${junitJupiterVersion}")
}
```

Note that in both cases the `spring-context` dependency is needed to implement the application, and then we need `spring-test` and `junit-jupiter` to test it. In order to implement the equivalent application and test, but this time using Spring Boot, first we would need to change our `pom.xml` (when using Maven):

```xml
<project xmlns="http://maven.apache.org/POM/4.0.0"
xmlns:xsi="http://www.w3.org/2001/XMLSchema-instance"
    xsi:schemaLocation="http://maven.apache.org/POM/4.0.0
http://maven.apache.org/xsd/maven-4.0.0.xsd">
    <modelVersion>4.0.0</modelVersion>
    <groupId>io.github.bonigarcia</groupId>
    <artifactId>junit5-spring-boot</artifactId>
    <version>1.0.0</version>

    <parent>
        <groupId>org.springframework.boot</groupId>
        <artifactId>spring-boot-starter-parent</artifactId>
        <version>2.0.0.M3</version>
    </parent>

    <properties>
        <junit.jupiter.version>5.0.0</junit.jupiter.version>
        <junit.platform.version>1.0.0</junit.platform.version>
        <java.version>1.8</java.version>
        <maven.compiler.target>${java.version}</maven.compiler.target>
        <maven.compiler.source>${java.version}</maven.compiler.source>
        <project.build.sourceEncoding>UTF-8</project.build.sourceEncoding>
<project.reporting.outputEncoding>UTF-8</project.reporting.outputEncoding>
    </properties>

    <dependencies>
        <dependency>
            <groupId>org.springframework.boot</groupId>
            <artifactId>spring-boot-starter</artifactId>
        </dependency>
        <dependency>
            <groupId>org.springframework.boot</groupId>
            <artifactId>spring-boot-starter-test</artifactId>
            <scope>test</scope>
        </dependency>
        <dependency>
            <groupId>org.junit.jupiter</groupId>
            <artifactId>junit-jupiter-api</artifactId>
            <version>${junit.jupiter.version}</version>
            <scope>test</scope>
        </dependency>
    </dependencies>
```

```
        <build>
            <plugins>
                <plugin>
                    <artifactId>maven-surefire-plugin</artifactId>
                    <dependencies>
                        <dependency>
                            <groupId>org.junit.platform</groupId>
                            <artifactId>junit-platform-surefire-
provider</artifactId>
                            <version>${junit.platform.version}</version>
                        </dependency>
                        <dependency>
                            <groupId>org.junit.jupiter</groupId>
                            <artifactId>junit-jupiter-engine</artifactId>
                            <version>${junit.jupiter.version}</version>
                        </dependency>
                    </dependencies>
                </plugin>
                <plugin>
                    <groupId>org.springframework.boot</groupId>
                    <artifactId>spring-boot-maven-plugin</artifactId>
                    <executions>
                        <execution>
                            <goals>
                                <goal>repackage</goal>
                            </goals>
                        </execution>
                    </executions>
                </plugin>
            </plugins>
        </build>

        <repositories>
            <repository>
                <id>spring-milestones</id>
                <url>https://repo.spring.io/libs-milestone</url>
            </repository>
        </repositories>

        <pluginRepositories>
            <pluginRepository>
                <id>spring-milestones</id>
                <url>https://repo.spring.io/milestone</url>
            </pluginRepository>
        </pluginRepositories>

</project>
```

Or our `build.gradle` (when using Gradle):

```
buildscript {
    ext {
        springBootVersion = '2.0.0.M3'
        junitPlatformVersion = '1.0.0'
    }

    repositories {
        mavenCentral()
        maven {
            url 'https://repo.spring.io/milestone'
        }
    }

    dependencies {
        classpath("org.springframework.boot:spring-boot-gradle-
plugin:${springBootVersion}")
        classpath("org.junit.platform:junit-platform-gradle-
plugin:${junitPlatformVersion}")
    }
}

repositories {
    mavenCentral()
    maven {
        url 'https://repo.spring.io/libs-milestone'
    }
}

apply plugin: 'java'
apply plugin: 'eclipse'
apply plugin: 'idea'
apply plugin: 'org.springframework.boot'
apply plugin: 'io.spring.dependency-management'
apply plugin: 'org.junit.platform.gradle.plugin'

jar {
    baseName = 'junit5-spring-boot'
    version = '1.0.0'
}

compileTestJava {
    sourceCompatibility = 1.8
    targetCompatibility = 1.8
    options.compilerArgs += '-parameters'
}
```

```
dependencies {
    compile('org.springframework.boot:spring-boot-starter')
    testCompile("org.springframework.boot:spring-boot-starter-test")
    testCompile("org.junit.jupiter:junit-jupiter-
api:${junitJupiterVersion}")
    testRuntime("org.junit.jupiter:junit-jupiter-
engine:${junitJupiterVersion}")
}
```

In order to transform our raw Spring application into Spring Boot, our components (in the example called MessageComponent and MessageService) would be exactly the same, but our main class would change a bit (see here). Notice that we use the annotation @SpringBootApplication at class level, implementing the main method with the typically bootstrapping mechanism of Spring Boot. Just for logging purposes, we are implementing a method annotated with @PostConstruct. This method will be triggered just before the application context is started:

```
package io.github.bonigarcia;

import javax.annotation.PostConstruct;
import org.slf4j.Logger;
import org.slf4j.LoggerFactory;
import org.springframework.beans.factory.annotation.Autowired;
import org.springframework.boot.SpringApplication;
import org.springframework.boot.autoconfigure.SpringBootApplication;

@SpringBootApplication
public class MySpringBootApplication {
    final Logger log =
LoggerFactory.getLogger(MySpringBootApplication.class);

    @Autowired
    public MessageComponent messageComponent;

    @PostConstruct
    private void setup() {
        log.info("*** {} ***", messageComponent.getMessage());
    }

    public static void main(String[] args) throws Exception {
        new SpringApplication(MySpringBootApplication.class).run(args);
    }

}
```

The implementation of the test would be straightforward. The only change we need to do is to annotate the test with `@SpringBootTest` instead of `@ContextConfiguration` (Spring Boot automatically looks for and starts our `ApplicationContext`):

```
package io.github.bonigarcia;

import static org.junit.jupiter.api.Assertions.assertEquals;

import org.junit.jupiter.api.Test;
import org.junit.jupiter.api.extension.ExtendWith;
import org.springframework.beans.factory.annotation.Autowired;
import org.springframework.boot.test.context.SpringBootTest;
import org.springframework.test.context.junit.jupiter.SpringExtension;

@ExtendWith(SpringExtension.class)
@SpringBootTest
class SimpleSpringBootTest {

    @Autowired
    public MessageComponent messagePrinter;

    @Test
    public void test() {
        assertEquals("Hello world!", messagePrinter.getMessage());
    }

}
```

Executing the test in the console, we can see that actually the application is started before the test (notice the unmistakable spring ASCII banner at the beginning).

After that, our test uses the `ApplicationContext` to verify one Spring component, and as a result the test is succeeded:

Execution of test using Spring Boot

To finish with this part, we see a simple web application implemented with Spring Boot. With respect to the dependencies, the only change we need to do is to include the started `spring-boot-starter-web` (instead of the generic `spring-boot-starter`). That's it, we can start implementing our Spring-based web application.

We are going to implement a very simple `@Controller`, that is, the Spring bean, which handles the request from the browsers. In our example, the only URL mapped by the controller is the default resource `/`:

```
package io.github.bonigarcia;

import static org.springframework.web.bind.annotation.RequestMethod.GET;

import org.springframework.beans.factory.annotation.Autowired;
import org.springframework.stereotype.Controller;
import org.springframework.web.bind.annotation.RequestMapping;

@Controller
public class WebController {

    @Autowired
    private PageService pageService;

    @RequestMapping(value = "/", method = GET)
    public String greeting() {
        return pageService.getPage();
    }

}
```

This component injects a service called `PageService`, responsible of returning the actual page to be loaded in response to the request to `/`. The content of this service is also very simple:

```
package io.github.bonigarcia;

import org.springframework.stereotype.Service;

@Service
public class PageService {

    public String getPage() {
        return "/index.html";
    }

}
```

By convention (we are using Spring Boot here), the static resource for Spring-based web applications are located in a folder called `static` within the project classpath. Following the structure of Maven/Gradle project, this folder is located in the `src/main/resources` path (see screenshot below). Note that there are two pages there (we switch from one to the other in the tests, stay tuned):

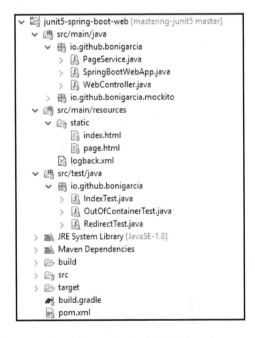

Content of the example project *junit5-spring-boot-web*

Let's move on not the interesting part: the tests. We are implementing three Jupiter tests in this project. The first one is devoted to verify a direct call to the page `/index.html`. As depicted before, this test needs to use the Spring extension (`@ExtendWith(SpringExtension.class)`) and be declared as Spring Boot test (`@SpringBootTest`). To carry out the request to web application, we use an instance of the `MockMvc`, verifying the response in several ways (HTTP response code, content-type, and response content body). This instance is automatically configured using the Spring Boot annotation `@AutoConfigureMockMvc`.

> Out of Spring Boot, instead of using `@AutoConfigureMockMvc`, the object `MockMvc` can be created using a builder class called `MockMvcBuilders`. In this case, the application context is used as parameter for that builder.

```java
package io.github.bonigarcia;

import static org.hamcrest.core.StringContains.containsString;
import static
org.springframework.test.web.servlet.request.MockMvcRequestBuilders.get;
import static
org.springframework.test.web.servlet.result.MockMvcResultMatchers.content;
import static
org.springframework.test.web.servlet.result.MockMvcResultMatchers.status;

import org.junit.jupiter.api.Test;
import org.junit.jupiter.api.extension.ExtendWith;
import org.springframework.beans.factory.annotation.Autowired;
import
org.springframework.boot.test.autoconfigure.web.servlet.AutoConfigureMockMvc;
import org.springframework.boot.test.context.SpringBootTest;
import org.springframework.test.context.junit.jupiter.SpringExtension;
import org.springframework.test.web.servlet.MockMvc;

@ExtendWith(SpringExtension.class)
@SpringBootTest
@AutoConfigureMockMvc
class IndexTest {

    @Autowired
    MockMvc mockMvc;

    @Test
    void testIndex() throws Exception {
        mockMvc.perform(get("/index.html")).andExpect(status().isOk())
                .andExpect(content().contentType("text/html")).andExpect(
```

```
        content().string(containsString("This is index
        page")));
    }

}
```

Again, running this test in the shell, we check that the application is actually executed. By default, the embedded Tomcat listens the port `8080`. After that, test is executed successfully:

Console output of in-container first test

Second test is similar, but as a differential factor it uses the test capability `@MockBean` to override a spring component (in this example, `PageService`) by a mock. In the body of the test, first we stub the method `getPage` of the mock to change the default response of the component to `redirect:/page.html`. As a result, when requesting the resource `/` in the test with the object `MockMvc`, we will obtain an HTTP 302 response (redirect) to the resource `/page.html` (which is actually an existing page, as shown in the project screenshot):

```java
package io.github.bonigarcia;

import static org.mockito.Mockito.doReturn;
import static
org.springframework.test.web.servlet.request.MockMvcRequestBuilders.get;
import static
org.springframework.test.web.servlet.result.MockMvcResultMatchers.redirecte
dUrl;
import static
org.springframework.test.web.servlet.result.MockMvcResultMatchers.status;

import org.junit.jupiter.api.Test;
import org.junit.jupiter.api.extension.ExtendWith;
import org.springframework.beans.factory.annotation.Autowired;
```

```
import
org.springframework.boot.test.autoconfigure.web.servlet.AutoConfigureMockMv
c;
import org.springframework.boot.test.context.SpringBootTest;
import org.springframework.boot.test.mock.mockito.MockBean;
import org.springframework.test.context.junit.jupiter.SpringExtension;
import org.springframework.test.web.servlet.MockMvc;

@ExtendWith(SpringExtension.class)
@SpringBootTest
@AutoConfigureMockMvc
class RedirectTest {

    @MockBean
    PageService pageService;

    @Autowired
    MockMvc mockMvc;

    @Test
    void test() throws Exception {
        doReturn("redirect:/page.html").when(pageService).getPage();
        mockMvc.perform(get("/")).andExpect(status().isFound())
                .andExpect(redirectedUrl("/page.html"));
    }

}
```

Similarly, in the shell we can confirm that the test starts the Spring application and then it is executed correctly:

Console output of in-container second test

The last test in this project is an example of an *out-of-container* test. In the previous test examples, the Spring context was used within the test. On the other side, the following relies completely in Mockito to exercise the components of the system, this time without starting the Spring application context. Note that we are using the `MockitoExtension` extension here, using the component `WebController` as our SUT (`@InjectMocks`) and the component `PageService` as DOC (`@Mock`):

```java
package io.github.bonigarcia;

import static org.junit.jupiter.api.Assertions.assertEquals;
import static org.mockito.Mockito.times;
import static org.mockito.Mockito.verify;
import static org.mockito.Mockito.when;

import org.junit.jupiter.api.Test;
import org.junit.jupiter.api.extension.ExtendWith;
import org.mockito.InjectMocks;
import org.mockito.Mock;
import io.github.bonigarcia.mockito.MockitoExtension;

@ExtendWith(MockitoExtension.class)
class OutOfContainerTest {

    @InjectMocks
    private WebController webController;

    @Mock
    private PageService pageService;

    @Test
    void test() {
        when(pageService.getPage()).thenReturn("/my-page.html");
        assertEquals("/my-page.html", webController.greeting());
        verify(pageService, times(1)).getPage();
    }

}
```

This time, in the execution of the test, we do not see spring traces since the application container was not started before executing the test:

```
-------------------------------------------------------------
 T E S T S
-------------------------------------------------------------
Running io.github.bonigarcia.OutOfContainerTest
Tests run: 1, Failures: 0, Errors: 0, Skipped: 0, Time elapsed: 0.645 sec -
in io.github.bonigarcia.OutOfContainerTest

Results :

Tests run: 1, Failures: 0, Errors: 0, Skipped: 0
```

Console output of out-of-container test

Selenium

Selenium (http://www.seleniumhq.org/) is an open source web testing framework, since its inception in 2008 has established itself as the *de facto* web automation library. In the next section, we are going to review the main features of Selenium and how to use it from JUnit 5 tests.

Selenium in a nutshell

Selenium is composed by different projects. First, we found the Selenium IDE. It is a Firefox plugin implementing the **Record and Playback (R&P)** pattern for web applications. Thus, it allows to record manual interactions with Firefox and the playback that recording in an automated fashion.

The second project was named **Selenium Remote Control (RC)**. This component was capable of driving different types of browser automatically using different programming languages, such as Java, C#, Python, Ruby, PHP, Perl, or JavaScript. This component injected a JavaScript library (called Selenium Core) in the SUT. This library was controlled with an intermediate component called **Selenium RC Server** which receives requests from the test code (see the following figure). Selenium RC had important security problems due to same-origin policy.

For that reason, it was deprecated on 2016 in favor of Selenium WebDriver:

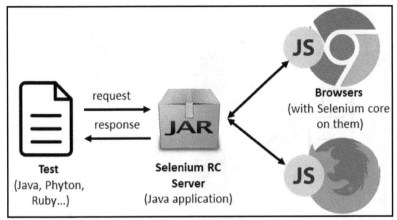

Selenium RC schema

 We review Selenium RC just to introduce Selenium WebDriver. Nowadays, Selenium RC is deprecated and its use is highly discouraged.

From a functional point of view, Selenium WebDriver is equivalent to RC (that is, allows to control browsers using code). As a differential aspect, Selenium WebDriver makes calls to the browser using each browser's native support for automation. The language bindings provided by Selenium WebDriver (labeled as Test in next figure) communicates with and a browser-specific binary, which acts as a bridge between real browser. For instance, this binary is called *chromedriver* (`https://sites.google.com/a/chromium.org/chromedriver/`) for Chrome and *geckodriver* (`https://github.com/mozilla/geckodriver`) for Firefox. The communication between the Test and the driver is done with JSON messages over HTTP using the so-called JSON Wire Protocol.

This mechanism, originally proposed by the WebDriver team is standardized in the W3C WebDriver API (`https://www.w3.org/TR/webdriver/`):

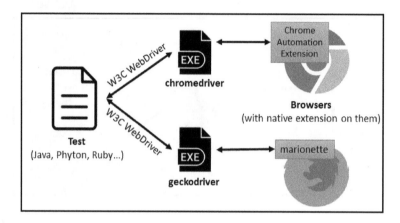

Selenium WebDriver schema

The last project of the Selenium portfolio is called Selenium Grid. It can be seen as extension of Selenium WebDriver, since it allows distributing browser execution on remote machines. There are a number of Nodes, each running on different operating systems and with different browsers. The Hub server keeps a track of the nodes and proxies requests to them (see figure below):

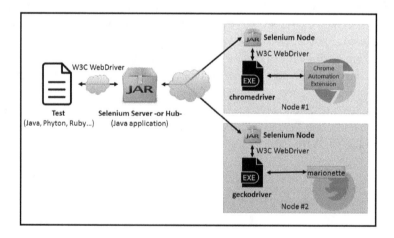

Selenium Grid schema

The following table summarizes the main features of the WebDriver API:

WebDriver feature and description	Example
WebDriver object creation: It allows to create WebDriver instances, which are used from the test code to control a browser remotely.	```WebDriver driver = new FirefoxDriver();

WebDriver driver = new ChromeDriver();

WebDriver driver = new OperaDriver();``` |
| Navigation:
It allows to navigate to a given URL. | ```driver.get("http://junit.org/junit5/");``` |
| Locate elements:
It allows to identify elements with a web page (WebElement) using different strategies: by id, name, class name, CSS selector, link text, tag name, or XPath | ```WebElement webElement =
driver.findElement(By.id("id"));

driver.findElement(By.name("name"));
driver.findElement(By.className("class"));
driver.findElement(By.cssSelector("cssInput"));
driver.findElement(By.linkText("text"));
driver.findElement(By.tagName("tag name"));
driver.findElement(By.xpath("/html/body/div[4]"));``` |
| Interact with elements:
From a given WebElement, we can carry out different types of automated interaction, such as click elements, type text or clear input fields, read attributes, and so on. | ```webElement.click();
webElement.sendKeys("text");
webElement.clear();
String text = webElement.getText();
String href = webElement.getAttribute("href");
String css = webElement.getCssValue("css");
Dimension dim = webElement.getSize();
boolean enabled = webElement.isEnabled();
boolean selected = webElement.isSelected();
boolean displayed = webElement.isDisplayed();``` |
| Handle waits:
WebDriver can handle wait both explicit and implicitly. | ```// Explicit
WebDriverWait wait = new WebDriverWait(driver, 30);
wait.until(ExpectedConditions);

// Implicit wait
driver.manage().timeouts().implicitlyWait(30,
SECONDS);``` |

XPath (XML Path Language) is a language to build expressions to parse and process XML-like documents (for example, HTML)

JUnit 5 extension for Selenium

In order to simplify the use of Selenium WebDriver in JUnit 5, the open source JUnit 5 extension called `selenium-jupiter` can be used. This extension has been built using the dependency injection capability provided by the extension model of JUnit 5. Thanks to this feature, different types objects can be injected in JUnit 5 in `@Test` methods as parameters. Concretely, `selenium-jupiter` allows to inject subtypes of the `WebDriver` interface (for example, `ChromeDriver`, `FirefoxDriver`, and so on).

Using `selenium-jupiter` is very easy. First, we need to import the dependency in our project (typically as test dependency). In Maven, it is done as follows:

```
<dependency>
        <groupId>io.github.bonigarcia</groupId>
        <artifactId>selenium-jupiter</artifactId>
        <version>${selenium-jupiter.version}</version>
        <scope>test</scope>
</dependency>
```

`selenium-jupiter` depends on several libraries, which are added in our project as transitive dependencies, namely:

- `Selenium-java` (`org.seleniumhq.selenium:selenium-java`): Java library for Selenium WebDriver.
- `WebDriverManager` (`io.github.bonigarcia:webdrivermanager`): Java library for automatic Selenium WebDriver binaries management in runtime for Java (https://github.com/bonigarcia/webdrivermanager).
- Appium (`io.appium:java-client`): Java client for Appium, testing framework that extends Selenium to automate testing of native, hybrid, and mobile web apps (http://appium.io/).

Once `selenium-jupiter` is included in our project, we need to declare `selenium-jupiter` extension in our JUnit 5 test, simply annotating it with `@ExtendWith(SeleniumExtension.class)`. Then, we need to include one or more parameters in our `@Test` methods whose types implement the WebDriver interface, and `selenium-jupiter` control the lifecycle of the WebDriver object internally. He WebDriver subtypes supported by `selenium-jupiter` are the following:

- `ChromeDriver`: This is used to control Google Chrome browser.
- `FirefoxDriver`: This is used to control Firefox browser.
- `EdgeDriver`: This is used to control Microsoft Edge browser.
- `OperaDriver`: This is used to control Opera browser.
- `SafariDriver`: This is used to control Apple Safari browser (only possible in OSX El Capitan or greater).
- `HtmlUnitDriver`: This is used to control HtmlUnit (headless browser, that is, a browser without GUI).
- `PhantomJSDriver`: This is used to control PhantomJS (another headless browser).
- `InternetExplorerDriver`: This is used to control Microsoft Internet Explorer. Although this browser is supported, Internet Explorer is deprecated (in favor of Edge) and its use is highly discouraged.
- `RemoteWebDriver`: This is used to control remote browsers (Selenium Grid).
- `AppiumDriver`: This is used to control mobile devices (Android and iOS).

Consider the following class, which uses `selenium-jupiter`, that is, declaring the Selenium extension using `@ExtendWith(SeleniumExtension.**class**)`. This example defines three tests, which are going be executed using local browsers. First one (named `testWithChrome`) uses Chrome as browsers. To that aim, and thanks to the dependency injection feature of `selenium-jupiter`, the method simply needs to declare a method argument using the type `ChromeDriver`. Then, in the body of the test, the `WebDriver` API is invoked in that object. Note that this test simple opens a web page and asserts that the title is as expected. Next, test (`testWithFirefoxAndOpera`) is similar, but this time using two different browsers at the same time: Firefox (using an instance of `FirefoxDriver`) and Opera (using an instance of `OperaDriver`). The third and last test (`testWithHeadlessBrowsers`) declares and uses two headless browsers (`HtmlUnit` and `PhantomJS`):

```
package io.github.bonigarcia;

import static org.junit.jupiter.api.Assertions.assertNotNull;
```

```java
import static org.junit.jupiter.api.Assertions.assertTrue;

import org.junit.jupiter.api.Test;
import org.junit.jupiter.api.extension.ExtendWith;
import org.openqa.selenium.chrome.ChromeDriver;
import org.openqa.selenium.firefox.FirefoxDriver;
import org.openqa.selenium.htmlunit.HtmlUnitDriver;
import org.openqa.selenium.opera.OperaDriver;
import org.openqa.selenium.phantomjs.PhantomJSDriver;

@ExtendWith(SeleniumExtension.class)
public class LocalWebDriverTest {

    @Test
    public void testWithChrome(ChromeDriver chrome) {
        chrome.get("https://bonigarcia.github.io/selenium-jupiter/");
        assertTrue(chrome.getTitle().startsWith("selenium-jupiter"));
    }

    @Test
    public void testWithFirefoxAndOpera(FirefoxDriver firefox,
            OperaDriver opera) {
        firefox.get("http://www.seleniumhq.org/");
        opera.get("http://junit.org/junit5/");
        assertTrue(firefox.getTitle().startsWith("Selenium"));
        assertTrue(opera.getTitle().equals("JUnit 5"));
    }

    @Test
    public void testWithHeadlessBrowsers(HtmlUnitDriver htmlUnit,
            PhantomJSDriver phantomjs) {
        htmlUnit.get("https://bonigarcia.github.io/selenium-jupiter/");
        phantomjs.get("https://bonigarcia.github.io/selenium-jupiter/");
        assertTrue(htmlUnit.getTitle().contains("JUnit 5 extension"));
        assertNotNull(phantomjs.getPageSource());
    }

}
```

 In order to execute properly this test class, the required browsers (Chrome, Firefox, and Opera) should be installed beforehand running it. On the other hand, the headless browsers (HtmlUnit and PhantomJS) are consumed as Java dependencies, and so there is no need to install them manually.

Let's see another example, this time using remote browsers (that is, Selenium Grid). Again, this class uses the `selenium-jupiter` extension. The test (`testWithRemoteChrome`) declares a single parameter called `remoteChrome`, of type `RemoteWedbrider`. This argument is annotated with `@DriverUrl` and `@DriverCapabilities`, specifying the Selenium Server (or Hub) URL and the required capabilities respectively. Regarding the capabilities, we are configuring to use a Chrome browser version 59:

 To run this test properly, a Selenium Server should up and running in the localhost, and a node (Chrome 59) needs to be registered in the Hub.

```java
package io.github.bonigarcia;

import static org.junit.jupiter.api.Assertions.assertTrue;

import org.junit.jupiter.api.Test;
import org.junit.jupiter.api.extension.ExtendWith;
import org.openqa.selenium.remote.RemoteWebDriver;

@ExtendWith(SeleniumExtension.class)
public class RemoteWebDriverTest {

    @Test
    void testWithRemoteChrome(
            @DriverUrl("http://localhost:4444/wd/hub")
            @DriverCapabilities(capability = {
                @Capability(name = "browserName", value ="chrome"),
                @Capability(name = "version", value = "59") })
                RemoteWebDriver remoteChrome)
            throws InterruptedException {
        remoteChrome.get("https://bonigarcia.github.io/selenium-
            jupiter/");
        assertTrue(remoteChrome.getTitle().contains("JUnit 5
            extension"));
    }

}
```

In the last example of this section, we use `AppiumDriver`. Concretely, we set up as capabilities the use of a Chrome browser in an Android emulated device (`@DriverCapabilities`). Again, this emulator needs to be up and running in the machine running the test beforehand:

```java
package io.github.bonigarcia;

import static org.junit.jupiter.api.Assertions.assertTrue;

import org.junit.jupiter.api.Test;
import org.junit.jupiter.api.extension.ExtendWith;
import org.openqa.selenium.By;
import org.openqa.selenium.WebElement;
import org.openqa.selenium.remote.DesiredCapabilities;
import io.appium.java_client.AppiumDriver;

@ExtendWith(SeleniumExtension.class)
public class AppiumTest {

    @DriverCapabilities
    DesiredCapabilities capabilities = new DesiredCapabilities();
    {
        capabilities.setCapability("browserName", "chrome");
        capabilities.setCapability("deviceName", "Android");
    }

    @Test
    void testWithAndroid(AppiumDriver<WebElement> android) {
        String context = android.getContext();
        android.context("NATIVE_APP");
        android.findElement(By.id("com.android.chrome:id/terms_accept"))
                .click();
        android.findElement(By.id("com.android.chrome:id/negative_button"))
                .click();
        android.context(context);
        android.get("https://bonigarcia.github.io/selenium-jupiter/");
        assertTrue(android.getTitle().contains("JUnit 5 extension"));
    }

}
```

For further examples of `selenium-jupiter`, visit `https://bonigarcia.github.io/selenium-jupiter/`.

Cucumber

Cucumber (`https://cucumber.io/`) is testing framework aimed to automate acceptance tests written following a **Behavior-Driven Development** (**BDD**) style. Cucumber has been written in Ruby, although implementations for other languages (including Java, JavaScript, and Python) are available.

Cucumber in a nutshell

Cucumber executes tests specified written in language called Gherkin. It is a plaint-text natural language (for example, English or one of other 60+ languages supported by Cucumber) with a given structure. Gherkin has been designed to be used by non-programmers, typically customers, business analysis, managers, and so on.

 The extension for Gherkin files is `.feature`.

In a Gherkin file, non-blank lines can start with a keyword, followed by text in natural language. The main keywords are the following:

- **Feature**: High-level description of the software feature to be tested. It can be seen as a use case description.
- **Scenario**: Concrete example that illustrates a business rule. Scenarios follow the same pattern:
    - Describe initial context.
    - Describe an event.
    - Describe the expected outcome.

These actions are known in the Gherkin jargon as steps, which are mainly **Given**, **When**, or **Then**:

There are two additional steps: **And** (used for logical and for different steps) and **But** (used in for negative form of **And**).

- **Given**: Preconditions and initial state before the start of a test.
- **When**: Actions taken by a user during a test.
- **Then**: Outcome from actions taken in the **When** clause.
- **Background**: To avoid repeat steps in different scenarios, the keyword background allows to declared these steps, which are reused in subsequent scenarios.
- **Scenario Outline**: Scenarios in which steps are marked with variables (using the symbols < and >).
- **Examples**: A scenario outline declaration is always followed by one or more examples sections, which is a container table with values for the declared variables in the **Scenario Outline**.

When one line does not start with a keyword, that line is not interpreted by Cucumber. It is used to custom description.

Once we defined our features to be tested we need what it is called *steps definition*, which allows to translate plain text Gherkin into actions that actually exercise our SUT. In Java, it can be easily done by annotations to annotate methods for the step implementation: `@Given`, `@Then`, `@When`, `@And`, and `@But`. The string value of each step can contain regular expression which are mapped as fields in the method. See an example in the next section.

JUnit 5 extension for Cucumber

The latest versions of the Cucumber artifacts for Java incorporates a JUnit 5 extension for Cucumber. This section contains a complete example of a feature defined in Gherkin and the JUnit 5 to execute it with Cucumber. As usual, the source code of this example is hosted on GitHub (`https://github.com/bonigarcia/mastering-junit5`).

The structure of the project containing this example is as follows:

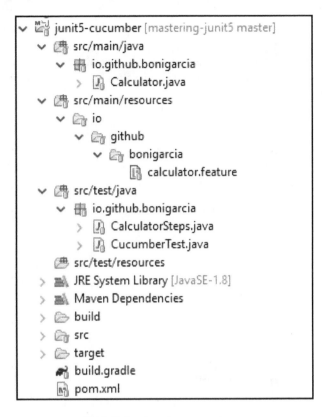

JUnit 5 with Cucumber project structure and content

First of all, we need to create our Gherkin file, which is aimed to test a simple calculator system. This calculator will be the SUT or our test. The content of our feature file is as follows:

```
Feature: Basic Arithmetic
  Background: A Calculator
    Given a calculator I just turned on
  Scenario: Addition
    When I add 4 and 5
    Then the result is 9
  Scenario: Substraction
    When I substract 7 to 2
    Then the result is 5
  Scenario Outline: Several additions
    When I add <a> and <b>
    Then the result is <c>
```

```
Examples: Single digits
  | a | b | c  |
  | 1 | 2 | 3  |
  | 3 | 7 | 10 |
```

Then, we need to implement our steps definition. As described earlier, we use annotations and regular expression to map the text contained in the Gherkin file to the actual exercise of SUT depending on the step:

```java
package io.github.bonigarcia;

import static org.junit.jupiter.api.Assertions.assertEquals;

import cucumber.api.java.en.Given;
import cucumber.api.java.en.Then;
import cucumber.api.java.en.When;

public class CalculatorSteps {

    private Calculator calc;

    @Given("^a calculator I just turned on$")
    public void setup() {
        calc = new Calculator();
    }

    @When("^I add (\\d+) and (\\d+)$")
    public void add(int arg1, int arg2) {
        calc.push(arg1);
        calc.push(arg2);
        calc.push("+");
    }

    @When("^I substract (\\d+) to (\\d+)$")
    public void substract(int arg1, int arg2) {
        calc.push(arg1);
        calc.push(arg2);
        calc.push("-");
    }

    @Then("^the result is (\\d+)$")
    public void the_result_is(double expected) {
        assertEquals(expected, calc.value());
    }

}
```

Of course, we still need to implement our JUnit 5 test. To achieve the integration of Cucumber and JUnit 5, the Cucumber extension needs to be registered in our class by means of `@ExtendWith(CucumberExtension.`**`class`**`)`. Internally, `CucumberExtension` implements the `ParameterResolver` callback of the Jupiter extension model. The objective is to inject the corresponding tests of the Cucumber feature as Jupiter `DynamicTest` objects in the tests. Notice in the example how a `@TestFactory` is used.

Optionally, we can annotate our test class with `@CucumberOptions`. This annotation allows to configure the Cucumber settings for our test. The allowed elements for this annotation are:

- `plugin`: Built-in formatter: pretty, progress, JSON, usage, among others. Default: `{}`.
- `dryRun`: Checks if all steps have definitions. Default: `false`.
- `features`: Paths of the features files. Default: `{}`.
- `glue`: Paths for step definitions. Default: `{}`.
- `tags`: Tags in the features to be executed. Default `{}`.
- `monochrome`: Displays console output in a readable way. Default: `false`.
- `format`: Reports formatter to be used. Default: `{}`.
- `strict`: Fails if there are undefined or pending steps. Default: `false`.

```
package io.github.bonigarcia;

import java.util.List;
import java.util.stream.Collectors;
import java.util.stream.Stream;
import org.junit.jupiter.api.DynamicTest;
import org.junit.jupiter.api.TestFactory;
import org.junit.jupiter.api.extension.ExtendWith;
import cucumber.api.CucumberOptions;
import cucumber.api.junit.jupiter.CucumberExtension;

@CucumberOptions(plugin = { "pretty" })
@ExtendWith(CucumberExtension.class)
public class CucumberTest {

    @TestFactory
    public Stream<DynamicTest> runCukes(Stream<DynamicTest> scenarios) {
        List<DynamicTest> tests = scenarios.collect(Collectors.toList());
        return tests.stream();
    }

}
```

At this point, we are able to execute our Cucumber suite with JUnit 5. In the following example we see the output when running the test with Gradle:

```
Command Prompt                                                    —   □   ×

D:\dev\mastering-junit5\junit5-cucumber>gradle test
Starting a Gradle Daemon, 3 incompatible and 1 stopped Daemons could not be reused, use --status for details
:compileJava
:processResources
:classes
:compileTestJava
:processTestResources NO-SOURCE
:testClasses
:junitPlatformTest
Feature: Basic Arithmetic

  Background: A Calculator
    Given a calculator I just turned on

  Scenario: Addition
    When I add 4 and 5
    Then the result is 9

  Background: A Calculator
    Given a calculator I just turned on

  Scenario: Substraction
    When I substract 7 to 2
    Then the result is 5

  Background: A Calculator
    Given a calculator I just turned on

  Scenario Outline: Several additions
    When I add 1 and 2
    Then the result is 3

  Background: A Calculator
    Given a calculator I just turned on

  Scenario Outline: Several additions
    When I add 3 and 7
    Then the result is 10

Test run finished after 500 ms
[         3 containers found      ]
[         0 containers skipped    ]
[         3 containers started    ]
[         0 containers aborted    ]
[         3 containers successful ]
[         0 containers failed     ]
[         4 tests found           ]
[         0 tests skipped         ]
[         4 tests started         ]
[         0 tests aborted         ]
[         4 tests successful      ]
[         0 tests failed          ]

:test SKIPPED

BUILD SUCCESSFUL

Total time: 16.328 secs
D:\dev\mastering-junit5\junit5-cucumber>
```

Execution of JUnit 5 using Cucumber with Gradle

Docker

Docker (`https://www.docker.com/`) is an open source software technology, which allows to pack and run any application as a lightweight and portable container. It provides a command-line program, a background daemon, and a set of remote services that simplifies the life cycle of containers.

Docker in a nutshell

Historically, UNIX-style operating systems used the term jail to describe modified isolated runtime environments. The **Linux Containers** (**LXC**) project started in 2008 and brought together cgroups, kernel namespaces, or chroot (among others) to provide complete isolation execution. The problem with LXC is the difficulty, and for that reason, the Docker technology emerged.

Docker hides in underlying complexity of the aforementioned resource isolation features of the Linux kernel (cgroups, kernel namespaces, and so on) to allow independent containers to run within a single Linux instance. Docker provides a high-level API, which allows to pack, ship and run any application as a container.

In Docker, a container contains an application and its dependencies together. Multiple containers can run on the same machine and share the same OS kernel with other containers. Each container is running as isolated process in user space.

Unlike **virtual machines** (**VMs**), in Docker containers there is no need of using a hypervisor, which is the software that allows to create and runs VM (example; VirtualBox, VMware, QEMU or Virtual PC).

The architecture of VM and container are depicted in the following diagram:

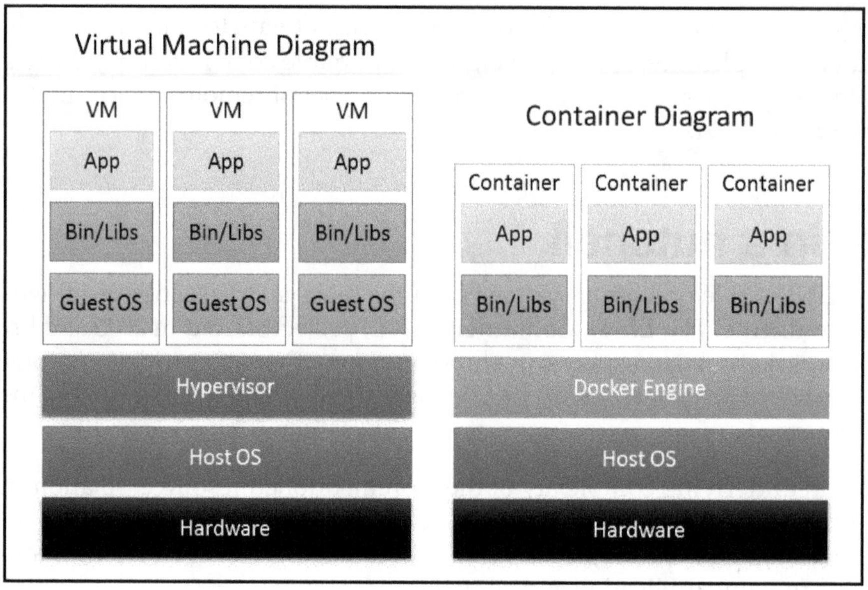

Virtual machine versus container

The Docker platform has two components: the Docker Engine, which is responsible for creating and running containers; and the Docker Hub (`https://hub.docker.com/`), a cloud service for distributing containers. The Docker Hub provides an enormous number of public container images for download. The Docker Engine is a client-server application composed by three major components:

- A server implemented as a daemon process (the `dockerd` command).
- A REST API, which specifies interfaces that programs can use to talk to the daemon and instruct it what to do.
- A **command line interface** (**CLI**) client (the `docker` command).

JUnit 5 extension for Docker

Nowadays, containers are changing the way we develop, distribute, and run software. This is especially interesting for **Continuous Integration** (**CI**) testing environment, in which the convergence with Docker has a direct impact on the improvement of efficiency.

Regarding JUnit 5, at the moment of this writing there is an open source JUnit 5 extension for Docker, named JUnit5-Docker (`https://faustxvi.github.io/junit5-docker/`). This extension acts as client of the Docker engine and allows to start a Docker container (downloaded from the Docker Hub), before running the tests of a class. That container is stopped at the end of the tests. In order to use JUnit5-Docker, first we need to add the dependency in our project. In Maven:

```
<dependency>
    <groupId>com.github.faustxvi</groupId>
    <artifactId>junit5-docker</artifactId>
    <version>${junit5-docker.version}</version>
    <scope>test</scope>
</dependency>
```

In Gradle:

```
dependencies {
    testCompile("com.github.faustxvi:junit5-docker:${junitDockerVersion}")
}
```

The use of JUnit5-Docker is quite straightforward. We simply need to annotate our test class with `@Docker`. The elements available in this annotation are the following:

- `image`: Docker image to be started.
- `ports`: Port mapping for the Docker container. This is required since at least one port must be visible for the container to be useful.
- `environments`: Optional environment variables to pass to the docker container. Default: `{}`.
- `waitFor`: Optional log to wait for before running the tests. Default: `@WaitFor(NOTHING)`.
- `newForEachCase`: Boolean flag, which determines if the container should be recreated for each test case. This value will be false if it should be created only once for the test class. Default: `true`.

Consider the following example. This test class uses the `@Docker` annotation to start a MySql container (container image MySQL) and the beginning of each test. The internal container port is `3306`, which will be mapped to the host port `8801`. Then, several environment attributes are defined (MySql root password, default database, and user name and password). The execution of the test will not start until the trace *mysqld: ready for connections* appears in the container log (which indicates that the MySql instance is up and running). In the body of the test, we start a JDBC connection against the MySQL instance running in the container.

This test has been executed in a Windows machine. For that reason, the host of the JDBC URL is 192.168.99.100, which is the IP for the Docker Machine. It is a tool which allows to install Docker Engine on virtual hosts, such as Windows or Mac (`https://docs.docker.com/machine/`). In a Linux machine, this IP could be 127.0.0.1 (localhost).

```java
package io.github.bonigarcia;

import static org.junit.jupiter.api.Assertions.assertFalse;

import java.sql.Connection;
import java.sql.DriverManager;
import org.junit.jupiter.api.Test;
import com.github.junit5docker.Docker;
import com.github.junit5docker.Environment;
import com.github.junit5docker.Port;
import com.github.junit5docker.WaitFor;

@Docker(image = "mysql", ports = @Port(exposed = 8801, inner = 3306),
environments = {
        @Environment(key = "MYSQL_ROOT_PASSWORD", value = "root"),
        @Environment(key = "MYSQL_DATABASE", value = "testdb"),
        @Environment(key = "MYSQL_USER", value = "testuser"),
        @Environment(key = "MYSQL_PASSWORD", value = "secret"), },
            waitFor = @WaitFor("mysqld: ready for connections"))

public class DockerTest {

    @Test
    void test() throws Exception {
        Class.forName("com.mysql.jdbc.Driver");
        Connection connection = DriverManager.getConnection(
                "jdbc:mysql://192.168.99.100:8801/testdb", "testuser",
                "secret");
        assertFalse(connection.isClosed());
        connection.close();
    }

}
```

The execution of this test in the Docker Windows terminal is as follows:

Execution of test using JUnit5-Docker extension

Android

Android (https://www.android.com/) is an open source mobile operating system based on a modified version of Linux. It was originally developed by a startup named Android, acquired and championed by Google in 2005.

According to the report by Gartner Inc. (American IT research and advisory company), in 2017 Android and iOS account more than 99% of global smartphone sales, as shown in the following chart:

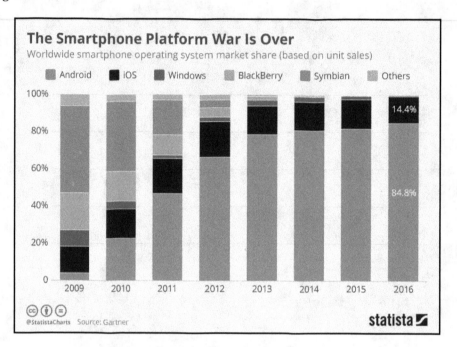

Smartphone operative system market. Picture created by www.statista.com.

Android in a nutshell

Android is a Linux-based software stack divided into several layers. Those layers, from down to top are the following:

- **Linux kernel**: This is the foundation of the Android platform. This layer contains all the low-level device drivers for the various hardware components of an Android device.
- **Hardware Abstraction Layer (HAL)**: This layer provides standard interfaces that expose hardware capabilities to the higher-level Java API framework.
- **Android Runtime (ART)**: It provides a runtime environment for .dex files, a bytecode format designed for minimal memory footprint. ART was the first release on Android 5.0 (see table below). Prior to that version, Dalvik was the Android runtime.

- **Native C/C++ libraries**: This layer contains native libraries written in C and C++, such as OpenGL ES for high-performance 2D and 3D graphics processing.
- **Java API framework**: The entire feature-set of Android is available for developers through APIs written in Java. These APIs are the building block for creating Android apps, for instance: the View System (for apps UIs), the Resource Manager (for I18N, graphics, layouts), the Notification Manager (for custom alerts in the status bar), the Activity Manager (to manage the apps lifecycle), or the Content Provider (to enable apps access data from other apps, such as the Contacts, and so on).
- **Apps**: Android comes with a set of core apps, such as Phone, Contacts, Browser, and so on. In addition, many others apps can be downloaded and installed from Google Play (formerly Android Market):

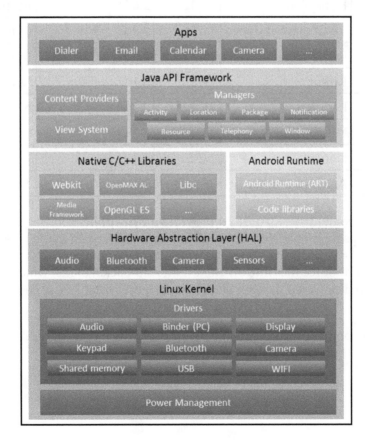

Android layered architecture

Android has gone through quite a number of updates since its first release, as described in the following table:

Android version	Codename	API level	Linux kernel version	Release date
1.5	Cupcake	3	2.6.27	April 30, 2009
1.6	Donut	4	2.6.29	September 15, 2009
2.0, 2.1	Eclair	5, 6, 7	2.6.29	October 26, 2009
2.2	Froyo	8	2.6.32	May 20, 2010
2.3	Gingerbread	9, 10	2.6.35	December 6, 2010
3.0, 3.1, 3.2	Honeycomb	11, 12, 13	2.6.36	February 22, 2011
4.0	Ice Cream Sandwich	14, 15	3.0.1	October 18, 2011
4.1, 4.2, 4.3	Jelly Bean	16, 17, 18	3.0.31, 3.0.21, 3.4.0	July 9, 2012
4.4	KitKat	19, 20	3.10	October 31, 2013
5.0, 5.1	Lollipop	21, 22	3.16.1	November 12, 2014
6.0	Marshmallow	23	3.18.10	October 5, 2015
7.0, 7.1	Nougat	24, 25	4.4.1	August 22, 2016
8.0	Android O	26	TBA	TBA

From a developer point of view, Android provides a rich application framework, which allows to build apps for mobile devices. Android apps are written in the Java programming language. The Android **Software Development Kit** (**SDK**) compile out Java code along with any data and resource files into an `.apk` (Android package) file, which contains can be installed in Android-powered devices, such as smartphones, tablets, smart TVs, or smartwatches.

For complete information about Android development, visit `https:// developer.android.com/`.

Android Studio is the official IDE for Android development. It is built based on IntelliJ IDEA. In Android Studio, the build process of Android projects is managed by the Gradle build system. During the Android Studio installation, two additional tools can be also installed:

- **Android SDK**: This contains all of the packages and tools required to develop Android apps. The SDK Manager allows to download and install SDK for different versions (see the preceding table).
- **Android Virtual Device** (**AVD**): This is an emulator that allows us to model an actual device. The AVD Manager allows to download and install different emulated Android virtual devices grouped into four categories: phones, tables, TV, and wears.

Gradle plugin for JUnit 5 in Android projects

At the time of this writing, there is no official support for JUnit 5 in Android projects. To solve this problem, an open source Gradle plugin named `android-junit5` has been created (`https://github.com/aurae/android-junit5`). To use this plugin, first we need to specify the proper dependency in our `build.gradle` file:

```
buildscript {
    dependencies {
        classpath "de.mannodermaus.gradle.plugins:android-junit5:1.0.0"
    }
}
```

In order to use this plugin in our project, we need to extend our project capabilities using the clause `apply plugin` in our `build.gradle` file:

```
apply plugin: "com.android.application"
apply plugin: "de.mannodermaus.android-junit5"

dependencies {
    testCompile junitJupiter()
}
```

The `android-junit5` plugin configures the `junitPlatform` task, attaching automatically attaches both the Jupiter and Vintage engines during the test execution phase. As an example, consider the following project example, as usual hosted on GitHub (https://github.com/bonigarcia/mastering-junit5/tree/master/junit5-android). The following is a screenshot of this project imported in Android Studio:

Android project compatible with JUnit 5 on IntelliJ

Now, we are going to create an Android JUnit run configuration of Android Studio. As can be seen in the screenshot, we use the option `All in package` referred to the package containing the tests (`io.github.bonigarcia.myapplication` in this example):

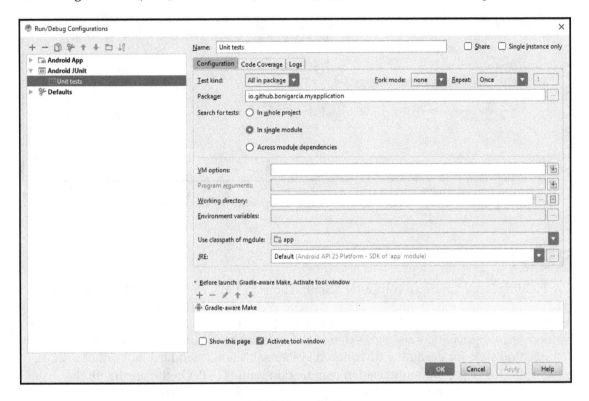

Android JUnit run configuration

If we launch the aforementioned run configuration, all the tests of the project will be executed. These tests can use the JUnit 4 programming model (Vintage) and even the JUnit 5 (Jupiter) in a seamless way:

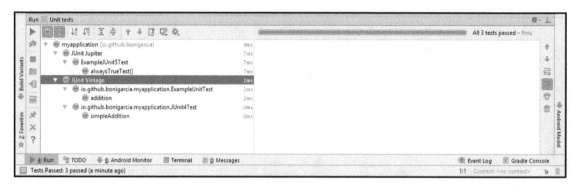

Execution on Jupiter and Vintage tests within an Android project in IntelliJ

REST

Roy Fielding is an American computer scientist born in 1965. He is one of the authors of the HTTP protocol and the co-authors of the Apache Web server. In the year 2000, Fielding coined the term REST (short for REpresentational State Transfer) in his doctoral dissertation entitled *Architectural Styles and the Design of Network-based Software Architecture*. REST is an architectural style for designing distributed systems. It's not a standard, but rather a set of constraints. REST is commonly used in conjunction with HTTP. On the one hand, the implementations which follows the strict principles of REST are often referred as RESTful. On the other hand, those which follow a loose adherence of such principles are called RESTlike.

REST in a nutshell

REST follows a client-server architecture. The server is in charge of handling a set of services, listening for requests made by clients. The communication between client and server must be stateless, meaning that server do not store any record from the clients and therefore each request done from the client must contain all the information required for the server to process it separately.

The building blocks of REST architectures are named resources. Resources define the type of information that is going to be transferred. Resources should be identified in a unique way. In HTTP, the way to access the resource it to provide its full URL, also known as API endpoint. Each resource has a representation, which is a machine-readable explanation of the current state of a resource. Nowadays, representations are usually with JSON, but it can be done in other formats such as XML or YAML.

Once we identified the resources and the representation format, we need to specify what can be done with them, that is, the actions. Actions could potentially be anything, although there is a set of common actions that any resource-oriented system should provide: CRUD (create, retrieve, update, and delete) actions. REST actions can be mapped to the HTTP methods (so-called verbs), as follows:

- GET: Reads a resource.
- POST: Sends a new resource to the server.
- PUT: Updates a given resource.
- DELETE: Deletes a resource.
- PATCH: update partially a resource.
- HEAD: Asks if a given resource exists without returning any of its representations.
- OPTIONS: Retrieves a list of available verbs on a given resource.

In REST, it is important the notion of *idempotency*. For example, GET, DELETE, or PUT are said to be idempotent, since the effect of these requests should be the same whether the command is sent one or several times. On the other hand, POST is not idempotent, since it creates a different resource each time it is requested.

REST, when based on HTTP can benefit on standard HTTP status codes. A status code is a number that summarizes the response associated to it. The typical HTTP status code reused in REST are:

- 200 OK: The request went fine and the content requested was returned. Normally used on GET requests.
- 201 Created: The resource was created. Useful on responses to POST or PUT requests.
- 204 No content: The action was successful, but there is no content returned. Useful for actions that do not require a response body, such as a DELETE.
- 301 Moved permanently: This resource was moved to another location and the location is returned.
- 400 Bad request: The request issued has problems (for example, lacking some required parameters).

- `401 Unauthorized`: Useful for authentication when the requested resource is not accessible to the user owning the request.
- `403 Forbidden`: The resource is not accessible, but unlike 401, authentication will not affect the response.
- `404 Not found`: The URL provided does not identify any resource.
- 405 Method not allowed. The HTTP verb used on a resource is not allowed. (for example, a PUT on a read-only resource).
- `500 Internal server error`: A generic error code when an unexpected condition in the server side.

The following picture shows an example of client-server interaction with REST. The body of the HTTP messages uses JSON both for requests and responses:

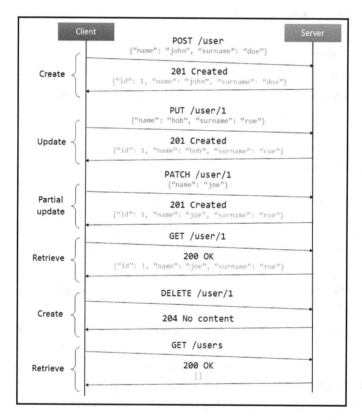

REST sequence diagram example

Using REST test libraries with Jupiter

REST APIs are becoming more and more pervasive nowadays. For that reason, a proper strategy for assessing REST services is desirable. In this section, we are going to learn how to use several test libraries in our JUnit 5 tests.

First of all, we can use the open source library REST Assured (`http://rest-assured.io/`). REST Assured allows the validation of REST services by means of a fluent API inspired in dynamic languages such as Ruby or Groovy. To use REST Assured in our test project, we simply need to add the proper dependency in Maven:

```
<dependency>
    <groupId>io.rest-assured</groupId>
    <artifactId>rest-assured</artifactId>
    <version>${rest-assured.version}</version>
    <scope>test</scope>
</dependency>
```

or in Gradle:

```
dependencies {
    testCompile("io.rest-assured:rest-assured:${restAssuredVersion}")
}
```

After that, we can use the REST Assured API. The following class contains two test examples. First sends a request to the free online REST service `http://echo.jsontest.com/`. Then verifies if the response code and the body content are as expected. The second test consumes another free online REST service (`http://services.groupkt.com/`) and also verifies the response:

```java
package io.github.bonigarcia;

import static io.restassured.RestAssured.given;
import static org.hamcrest.Matchers.equalTo;

import org.junit.jupiter.api.Test;

public class PublicRestServicesTest {

    @Test
    void testEchoService() {
        String key = "foo";
        String value = "bar";
        given().when().get("http://echo.jsontest.com/" + key + "/" + value)
                .then().assertThat().statusCode(200).body(key,
                equalTo(value));
    }
```

```
@Test
void testCountryService() {
    given().when()
            .get("http://services.groupkt.com/country/get/iso2code/ES")
            .then().assertThat().statusCode(200)
            .body("RestResponse.result.name", equalTo("Spain"));
}

}
```

Running this test in console with Maven, we can check that both tests succeed:

```
-------------------------------------------------------------
 T E S T S
-------------------------------------------------------------
Running io.github.bonigarcia.PublicRestServicesTest
Tests run: 2, Failures: 0, Errors: 0, Skipped: 0, Time elapsed: 2.943 sec -
in io.github.bonigarcia.PublicRestServicesTest

Results :

Tests run: 2, Failures: 0, Errors: 0, Skipped: 0
```

Execution of test using REST Assured

In the second example, we are going to study, in addition to the test, we are also going to implement the server side, that is, the REST service implementation. To that aim, we are going to use Spring MVC and Spring Boot, previously introduced on this chapter (see section *Spring*).

The implementation of REST services in Spring is quite straightforward. First, we simply need to annotate a Java class with @RestController. In the body of this class, we need to add methods annotated with @RequestMapping. These methods will listen to the different URLs (endpoints) implemented in our REST API. The accepted elements for the @RequestMapping are:

- value: This is the path mapping URL.
- method: This finds the HTTP request methods to map to.
- params: This finds parameters of the mapped request, narrowing the primary mapping.
- headers: his finds the headers of the mapped request.

- `consumes`: This finds consumable media types of the mapped request.
- `produces`: This finds producible media types of the mapped request.

As can be seen inspecting the code of the following class, our service example implements three different operations: `GET /books` (to read all book in the system), `GET /book/{index}` (to read a book given its identifier), and `POST /book` (to create a book).

```java
package io.github.bonigarcia;

import java.util.List;
import org.springframework.beans.factory.annotation.Autowired;
import org.springframework.http.HttpStatus;
import org.springframework.http.ResponseEntity;
import org.springframework.web.bind.annotation.PathVariable;
import org.springframework.web.bind.annotation.RequestBody;
import org.springframework.web.bind.annotation.RequestMapping;
import org.springframework.web.bind.annotation.RequestMethod;
import org.springframework.web.bind.annotation.RestController;

@RestController
public class MyRestController {

    @Autowired
    private LibraryService libraryService;

    @RequestMapping(value = "/books", method = RequestMethod.GET)
    public List<Book> getBooks() {
        return libraryService.getBooks();
    }

    @RequestMapping(value = "/book/{index}", method = RequestMethod.GET)
    public Book getTeam(@PathVariable("index") int index) {
        return libraryService.getBook(index);
    }

    @RequestMapping(value = "/book", method = RequestMethod.POST)
    public ResponseEntity<Boolean> addBook(@RequestBody Book book) {
        libraryService.addBook(book);
        return new ResponseEntity<Boolean>(true, HttpStatus.CREATED);
    }

}
```

Since we are implementing a Jupiter test for Spring, we need to use the `SpringExtension` and also the `SpringBootTest` annotation. As a novelty, we are going to inject a test component provided by `spring-test`, named `TestRestTemplate`.

This component is a wrapper of the standard Spring's `RestTemplate` object, which allows to implement REST clients in a seamless way. In our test, it requests to our service (which is started before executing the tests), and responses are used to verify the outcome.

Notice that the object `MockMvc` (explained in the section *Spring*) could be also used to test REST services. The difference with respect to `TestRestTemplate` is that the former is used to test from the client-side (that is, response code, body, content type, and so on), while the the latter is used to test the service from the server side. For instance, in the example here, the responses to the service calls (`getForEntity` and `postForEntity`) are Java objects, whose scope is only the server side (in the client side, this information is serialized as JSON).

```java
package io.github.bonigarcia;

import static org.junit.Assert.assertEquals;
import static
org.springframework.boot.test.context.SpringBootTest.WebEnvironment.RANDOM_
PORT;
import static org.springframework.http.HttpStatus.CREATED;
import static org.springframework.http.HttpStatus.OK;

import java.time.LocalDate;
import org.junit.jupiter.api.Test;
import org.junit.jupiter.api.extension.ExtendWith;
import org.springframework.beans.factory.annotation.Autowired;
import org.springframework.boot.test.context.SpringBootTest;
import org.springframework.boot.test.web.client.TestRestTemplate;
import org.springframework.http.ResponseEntity;
import org.springframework.test.context.junit.jupiter.SpringExtension;

@ExtendWith(SpringExtension.class)
@SpringBootTest(webEnvironment = RANDOM_PORT)
class SpringBootRestTest {

    @Autowired
    TestRestTemplate restTemplate;

    @Test
    void testGetAllBooks() {
        ResponseEntity<Book[]> responseEntity = restTemplate
                .getForEntity("/books", Book[].class);
        assertEquals(OK, responseEntity.getStatusCode());
        assertEquals(3, responseEntity.getBody().length);
    }
```

```
@Test
void testGetBook() {
    ResponseEntity<Book> responseEntity = restTemplate
            .getForEntity("/book/0", Book.class);
    assertEquals(OK, responseEntity.getStatusCode());
    assertEquals("The Hobbit", responseEntity.getBody().getName());
}

@Test
void testPostBook() {
    Book book = new Book("I, Robot", "Isaac Asimov",
            LocalDate.of(1950, 12, 2));
    ResponseEntity<Boolean> responseEntity = restTemplate
            .postForEntity("/book", book, Boolean.class);
    assertEquals(CREATED, responseEntity.getStatusCode());
    assertEquals(true, responseEntity.getBody());
    ResponseEntity<Book[]> responseEntity2 = restTemplate
            .getForEntity("/books", Book[].class);
    assertEquals(responseEntity2.getBody().length, 4);
}

}
```

As shown in the screenshot below, our Spring application is started before running our tests, which are executed successfully:

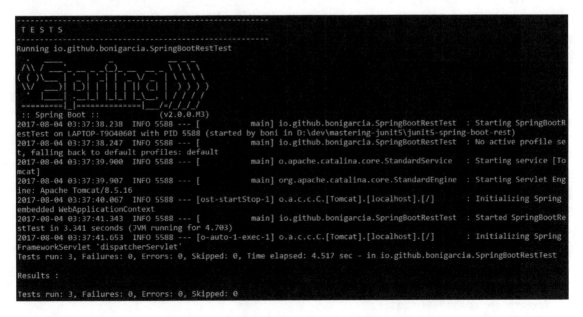

Output of Jupiter test using TestRestTemplate to verify a REST service.

To conclude this section, we see an example in which the library WireMock (`http://wiremock.org/`) is used. This library allows to mock REST services, that is, a so-called HTTP *mock server*. This mock server captures incoming requests to the service, providing stubbed responses. This capability is very useful to test a system which consumes a REST service, but the service is not available during the tests (or we can test the component that calls the service in isolation).

As usual, we see an example to demonstrate its usage. Let's suppose we have a system which consumes a remote REST service. To implement a client for that service we use Retrofit 2 (`http://square.github.io/retrofit/`), which is a highly configurable HTTP client for Java. We define the interface to consume this service as illustrated in the class below. Notice that the service exposes three endpoints aimed to read a remote file (open file, read stream, and close stream):

```
package io.github.bonigarcia;

import okhttp3.ResponseBody;
import retrofit2.Call;
import retrofit2.http.POST;
import retrofit2.http.Path;

public interface RemoteFileApi {

    @POST("/api/v1/paths/{file}/open-file")
    Call<ResponseBody> openFile(@Path("file") String file);

    @POST("/api/v1/streams/{streamId}/read")
    Call<ResponseBody> readStream(@Path("streamId") String streamId);

    @POST("/api/v1/streams/{streamId}/close")
    Call<ResponseBody> closeStream(@Path("streamId") String streamId);

}
```

Then we implement the class which consumes the REST service. In this example, it is a simple Java class which connects to the remote service given its URL passed as constructor parameter:

```
package io.github.bonigarcia;

import java.io.IOException;
import okhttp3.ResponseBody;
import retrofit2.Call;
import retrofit2.Response;
import retrofit2.Retrofit;
import retrofit2.adapter.rxjava.RxJavaCallAdapterFactory;
```

```
import retrofit2.converter.gson.GsonConverterFactory;

public class RemoteFileService {

    private RemoteFileApi remoteFileApi;

    public RemoteFileService(String baseUrl) {
        Retrofit retrofit = new Retrofit.Builder()
                .addCallAdapterFactory(RxJavaCallAdapterFactory.create())
                .addConverterFactory(GsonConverterFactory.create())
                .baseUrl(baseUrl).build();
        remoteFileApi = retrofit.create(RemoteFileApi.class);
    }

    public byte[] getFile(String file) throws IOException {
        Call<ResponseBody> openFile = remoteFileApi.openFile(file);
        Response<ResponseBody> execute = openFile.execute();
        String streamId = execute.body().string();
        System.out.println("Stream " + streamId + " open");

        Call<ResponseBody> readStream = remoteFileApi.readStream(streamId);
        byte[] content = readStream.execute().body().bytes();
        System.out.println("Received " + content.length + " bytes");

        remoteFileApi.closeStream(streamId).execute();
        System.out.println("Stream " + streamId + " closed");

        return content;
    }

}
```

Finally, we implement a JUnit 5 test to verify our service. Notce that we are creating the mock server (**new** `WireMockServer`) and stubbing the REST service calls using the static methods `stubFor(...)` provided by WireMock in the setup of the test (`@BeforeEach`). Since in this case, the SUT is very simple and it has no DOCs, we directly instantiate the class `RemoteFileService` also in the setup of each test, using the mock server URL as constructor argument. Finally, we test our service (which uses the mock server) simply exercising the object called `wireMockServer`, in this example, by calling to the method `getFile` and assessing its output.

```
package io.github.bonigarcia;

import static com.github.tomakehurst.wiremock.client.WireMock.aResponse;
import static com.github.tomakehurst.wiremock.client.WireMock.configureFor;
import static com.github.tomakehurst.wiremock.client.WireMock.post;
import static com.github.tomakehurst.wiremock.client.WireMock.stubFor;
```

```
import static com.github.tomakehurst.wiremock.client.WireMock.urlEqualTo;
import static
com.github.tomakehurst.wiremock.core.WireMockConfiguration.options;
import static org.junit.jupiter.api.Assertions.assertEquals;

import java.io.IOException;
import java.net.ServerSocket;
import org.junit.jupiter.api.AfterEach;
import org.junit.jupiter.api.BeforeEach;
import org.junit.jupiter.api.Test;
import com.github.tomakehurst.wiremock.WireMockServer;

public class RemoteFileTest {

    RemoteFileService remoteFileService;
    WireMockServer wireMockServer;

    // Test data
    String filename = "foo";
    String streamId = "1";
    String contentFile = "dummy";

    @BeforeEach
    void setup() throws Exception {
        // Look for free port for SUT instantiation
        int port;
        try (ServerSocket socket = new ServerSocket(0)) {
            port = socket.getLocalPort();
        }
        remoteFileService = new RemoteFileService("http://localhost:" +
            port);

        // Mock server
        wireMockServer = new WireMockServer(options().port(port));
        wireMockServer.start();
        configureFor("localhost", wireMockServer.port());

        // Stubbing service
        stubFor(post(urlEqualTo("/api/v1/paths/" + filename + "/open-
            file"))
            .willReturn(aResponse().withStatus(200).withBody(streamId)));
        stubFor(post(urlEqualTo("/api/v1/streams/" + streamId +
            "/read"))
            .willReturn(aResponse().withStatus(200).withBody(contentFile)));
        stubFor(post(urlEqualTo("/api/v1/streams/" + streamId + /close"))
            .willReturn(aResponse().withStatus(200)));
    }
```

```
@Test
void testGetFile() throws IOException {
    byte[] fileContent = remoteFileService.getFile(filename);
    assertEquals(contentFile.length(), fileContent.length);
}

@AfterEach
void teardown() {
    wireMockServer.stop();
}

}
```

Executing the test in the console, in the traces we can see how the internal HTTP server controlled by WireMock is started before the test execution. Then, the three REST operations (open stream, read bytes, close stream) are executed by the test, and finally the mock server is disposed:

```
----------------------------------------------------
 T E S T S
----------------------------------------------------
Running io.github.bonigarcia.RemoteFileTest
[main] INFO org.eclipse.jetty.util.log - Logging initialized @1456ms
[main] INFO org.eclipse.jetty.server.Server - jetty-9.2.22.v20170606
[main] INFO org.eclipse.jetty.server.handler.ContextHandler - Started o.e.j.s.ServletContextHandler@4b79ac84{/__admi
n,null,AVAILABLE}
[main] INFO org.eclipse.jetty.server.handler.ContextHandler - Started o.e.j.s.ServletContextHandler@740d2e78{/,null,
AVAILABLE}
[main] INFO org.eclipse.jetty.server.NetworkTrafficServerConnector - Started NetworkTrafficServerConnector@4f9a2c08{
HTTP/1.1}{0.0.0.0:57253}
[main] INFO org.eclipse.jetty.server.Server - Started @1583ms
[qtp1812823171-18] INFO /__admin - RequestHandlerClass from context returned com.github.tomakehurst.wiremock.http.Ad
minRequestHandler. Normalized mapped under returned 'null'
[qtp1812823171-21] INFO / - RequestHandlerClass from context returned com.github.tomakehurst.wiremock.http.StubReque
stHandler. Normalized mapped under returned 'null'
Stream 1 open
Received 5 bytes
Stream 1 closed
[main] INFO org.eclipse.jetty.server.NetworkTrafficServerConnector - Stopped NetworkTrafficServerConnector@4f9a2c08{
HTTP/1.1}{0.0.0.0:57253}
[main] INFO org.eclipse.jetty.server.handler.ContextHandler - Stopped o.e.j.s.ServletContextHandler@740d2e78{/,null,
UNAVAILABLE}
[main] INFO org.eclipse.jetty.server.handler.ContextHandler - Stopped o.e.j.s.ServletContextHandler@4b79ac84{/__admi
n,null,UNAVAILABLE}
Tests run: 1, Failures: 0, Errors: 0, Skipped: 0, Time elapsed: 1.976 sec - in io.github.bonigarcia.RemoteFileTest

Results :

Tests run: 1, Failures: 0, Errors: 0, Skipped: 0
```

Execution of test using a mock REST server using WireMock

Summary

This section provides a detailed insight of how JUnit 5 can be used in conjunction with third-party frameworks, libraries, and platforms. Thanks to the Jupiter extension model, developers can create extensions which allows seamless integration with external frameworks to JUnit 5. First, we have seen the *MockitoExtension*, an extension provided by the JUnit 5 team to use Mockito (a notorious mock framework for Java) in Jupiter tests. Then, we have used the *SpringExtension*, which is the official extension provided in the version 5 of the Spring Framework. This extension integrates Spring into the JUnit 5 programming model. This way, we are able to use Spring's application contexts (that is, the Spring's DI container) in our tests.

We have also reviewed the *SeleniumExtension* implemented by *selenium-jupiter*, an open source project providing a JUnit 5 extension for Selenium WebDriver (testing framework for web applications). Thank to thins extension, we can use different browsers to interact automatically with web applications and emulated mobile devices (using Appium). Then, we have seen the *CucumberExtension*, allows to specify JUnit 5 acceptance tests following a BDD style using the Gherkin language. Finally, we have seen how the open source JUnit5-Docker extension can be used to start Docker containers (downloading the image from Docker Hub) before the execution of our JUnit 5 tests.

Moreover, we discovered that the extension model is not the only way of interacting with external technologies by JUnit tests. For example, in order to run Jupiter tests in an Android project, we can use the `android-junit5` plugin. On the other hand, even though there is no custom extension for assessing REST services using JUnit 5, the integration with such libraries is strait forward: we simply need to include the proper dependency in our project and use it in our tests (for example, REST Assured, Spring, or WireMock).

6

From Requirements To Test Cases

Program testing can be used to show the presence of bugs, but never to show their absence!
- Edsger Dijkstra

This chapter provides a base of knowledge aimed to help software engineers to write meaningful test cases. The starting point for this process is the understanding of the requirements of the system being tested. Without that information, it is not feasible to design nor implement valuable tests. After that, several actions might be executed before the actual coding of the tests, namely, test planning and test design. Once we start the test coding process, we need to have in mind a set of principles to write code right, and also a set of anti-patterns and bad smells to be avoided. All this information is provided in this chapter in form of the following sections:

- **The importance of requirements**: This section provides a general overview of the software development process, started by the statement of some needs to be covered by a software system, and followed by several stages, typically including analysis, design, implementation, and tests.

- **Test planning**: A document called *test plan* can be generated at the beginning of a software project. This section reviews the structure of a test plan according to the IEEE 829 Standard for Test Documentation. As we will discover, the complete statement of a test plan is a very fine-grained process, especially recommended for large projects in which the communication among the team is a key aspect for the success of the project.

- **Test design:** Before starting the coding of the tests, it is always a good practice to think about the blueprint of these tests. In this section, we review the major aspects to be taken into consideration to design properly our tests. We put the accent on the test data (expected outcome), which feed the test assertions. In this regard, we review some black-box data generation techniques (equivalence partitioning and boundary analysis) and white-box (test coverage).
- **Software testing principles**: This section provides a set of best-practices which can help us write our tests.
- **Test anti-patterns**: Finally, the opposite side is also reviewed: what are the patterns and code smells to be avoided when writing our test cases.

The importance of requirements

Software systems are built to satisfy some kind of need to a group of consumers (final users or customer). Understanding those needs is one of most challenging problems in software engineering due to the fact that it is quite common that consumer needs are nebulous (especially in the early stages of the project). Moreover, it is also common that these needs can be deeply changed throughout the project lifetime. Fred Brooks, a well-known software engineer, and computer scientist, defines this problem in his seminal book *The Mythical Man-Month (1975):*

> *The hardest single part of building a software system is deciding precisely what to build. No other part of the conceptual work is as difficult as establishing the detailed technical requirements ... No other part of the work so cripples the resulting system if done wrong. No other part is as difficult to rectify later.*

In any case, consumer's needs are the touchstone for any software project. From these needs, a list of features can emerge. We define a feature as a high-level description of a software system functionality. From each feature, one or more requirements (functional and non-functional) should be derived. A requirement is everything that be true about the software, in order to meet the consumer's expectations. Scenarios (real-life examples rather than abstract descriptions) can be useful for adding details to the requirements description. The group of requirements and/or list of features of the software system are often known as specification.

In software engineering, the stage of defining the requirements is called **requirements elicitation**. In this stage, software engineers need to clarify *what* problem they are trying to solve. At the end of this phase, it is a common practice to start the modeling of the system. To that aim, a modeling language (typically UML) is employed to create a group of diagrams. The UML diagrams, which typically fits in the elicitation stage is the use case diagram (model of the functionality of the system and its relationship with the involved actors).

 Modeling is not always carried out in all software projects. For example, agile methodologies are more based on the principle of sketching rather than in a formal modeling strategy.

After elicitation, requirements should be refined in the **analysis** stage. In this phase, the stated requirements are analysed in order to resolve incomplete, ambiguous of contradictory issues. As a result, in this stage it is likely to continue modeling, using for example high-level class diagrams not linked to any specific technology yet. Once the analysis is clear (that is, the *what* of the system), we need to find out *how* to implement it. This stage is known as **design**. In the design phase, the guidelines of the project should be established. To that aim, an architecture of the software system is typically derived from the requirements. Again, the modeling techniques are broadly employed to carry out different aspects of the design. There is a bunch of UML diagrams that can be used at this point, including structural diagrams (component, deployment, object, package, and profile diagram) and behavioral diagrams (activity, communication, sequence, or state diagram). From the design, the actual **implementation** (that is, coding) can start.

The amount of modeling carried out in the design stage varies significantly depending on different factors, including the type and size of the company producing the software (multinationals, SMEs, governmental, and so on), the development process (waterfall, spiral, prototyping, agile, and so on), the type of project (enterprise, open source, and so on), the type of software (custom made software, commercial off-the-shelf, and so on), and even the background of the people involved (experience, career, and so on). All in all, the designs need to be understood as a way of communication between the different roles of software engineers participating in the project. Typically, the bigger the project, the more necessary a fine-grained design based on different modeling diagrams is.

Concerning **tests**, in order to make a proper test plan (see next section for further details), again we need to use the requirements elicitation data, that is, the list of requirements and/or features. In other words, in order to verify our system, we need to to know beforehand what we expect from it. Using the classic definition proposed by Barry Boehm (see `chapter 1`, *Retrospective On Software Quality And Java Testing*), verification is used to answer the question *Are we building the product right?* To that, we need to know the requirements, or at least, the desired features. In addition to verification, it would be desirable to carry out some validation (according to Boehm: *Are we building the right product?*). This is necessary since sometimes there is a gap between what has been specified (the features and requirements) and the real needs of the consumer. Therefore, validation is a high-level assessment method, and to carry out it, the final consumer can be involved (validating the software system once it is deployed). All these ideas are depicted in the following picture:

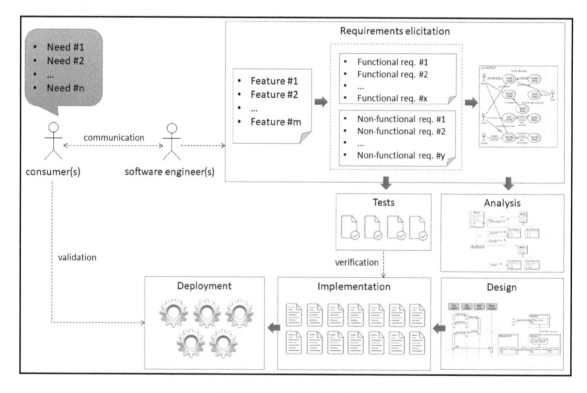

Software engineering generic development process

There is no universal workflow for the terms presented so far (communication, requirement elicitation, analysis, design, implementation/test, and deployment). In the preceding diagram, it follows a linear process flows, nevertheless, in practice, it can follow an iterative, evolutionary, or parallel workflow.

To illustrate the potential problems involved in the different phases in software engineer (analysis, design, implementation, and so on), it is worth to review the classical cartoon *How project really works?* The original source of this picture is unknown (there are versions dating back to the 1960s). In 2007, a site called *Project Cartoon* emerged (`http://www.projectcartoon.com/`), allowing to customize the original cartoon with new scenes. The following chart is the version 1.5 of the cartoon provided on that site:

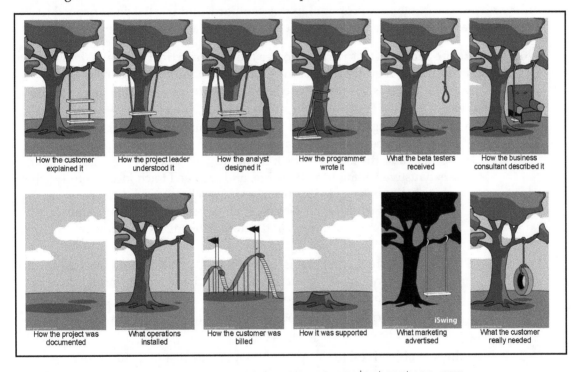

How projects really work, version 1.5 (illustrated created by `www.projectcartoon.com`)

If we think about this picture, we discover that the root of the problems comes from the requirements, badly explained by the customer at the beginning, and worst understood by the project leader. From that point, the whole software engineering process turns into the *Chinese whispers* children game. To solve all these problems is out of the scope of this book, but as a good start, we need to take special care in the requirements, which guide the whole process, including, of course, the tests.

Test planning

A first step in the testing path can be the generation of a document called *test plan*, which is the blueprint to conduct software testing. This document describes the objective, scope, approach, focus, and distribution of the testing efforts. The process of preparing such document is a useful way to think about the needs to verify of a software system. Again, this document is especially useful when the size of the SUT and the involved team is large, due to the fact that the separation of work in different roles makes the communication a potential deterrent for the success of the project.

A way to create a test plan is to follow the IEEE 829 Standard for Test Documentation. Although this standard might be too much formal for the most of software projects, it might be worth to review the guidelines proposed in this standard, and use the parts needed (if any) in our software projects. The steps proposed in IEEE 829 are the following:

1. **Analyze the product**: This part reinforces the idea of extracting the understanding the requirements of the system from the consumer needs. As already explained, it is not possible to test a software if no information about it is available.

2. **Design the test strategy**: This part of the plan contains several parts, including:
   - Define scope of testing, that is, the system components to be tested (in scope) and those parts which do not (out of scope). As explained later, exhaustive testing is not feasible, and we need to choose carefully what is going to be tested. This is not a simple choice, and it can be determined by different factors, such as precise customer requests, project budget and timing, and skills of the involved software engineers.
   - Identify testing type, that is, which levels of tests should be conducted (unit, integration, system, acceptance) and which test strategy (black box, white box, non-functional).
   - Document risks, that is, potential problems which might cause different issues in the project.

3. **Define the test objectives**: In this part of the plan, the list of features to be tested are listed together with the target of testing each one.

4. **Define the test criteria**: These criteria are typically made up by two parts, namely:
    - Suspension criteria, for instance the percentage of failed tests in which the development of new features is suspended until the team solves all the failures.
    - Exit criteria, for example, the percentage of critical tests that should be passed to proceed to next phase of development.

5. **Resource planning**: This part of the plan is devoted to summarize the resources required to carry out the testing activities. It could be personnel, equipment, or infrastructure.

6. **Plan test environment**: It consists of the software and hardware setup on which test are going to be executed.

7. **Schedule and estimation**: In this phase, managers are supposed to break out the whole project into small tasks estimating the efforts (person-month).

8. **Determine test deliverables**: Determine all the documents that has to be maintained to support the testing activities.

As can be seen, test planning is a complex task, typically carried out in large projects by managers. In the rest of this chapter we continue discovering how to write test cases, but hereinafter from a point of view closest to the actual test coding.

Test design

In order to design properly a test, we need to define specifically what needs to be implemented. To that aim, it is important to remember what is the generic structure of a test, already explained in `chapter 1`, *Retrospective On Software Quality And Java Testing*. Therefore, for each test we need to define:

- What is test fixture, that is, the required state in the SUT to carry out the test? This is done at the beginning of the test in the stage called setup. At the end of the test, the test fixture might be released in the stage called teardown.
- What is the SUT, and if we are doing unit tests, which are its DOC(s)? Unit test should be in isolation and therefore we need to define test doubles (typically mocks or spies) for the DOC(s).

- What are the assertions? This a key part of tests. Without assertions, we cannot claim that a test is actually made. In order to design assertion, it is worth to recall which is its generic structure. In short, an assertion consists in the comparison of some expected value (test data) and the actual outcome obtained from the SUT. If any of the assertions is negative, the test will be declared as failed (test verdict):

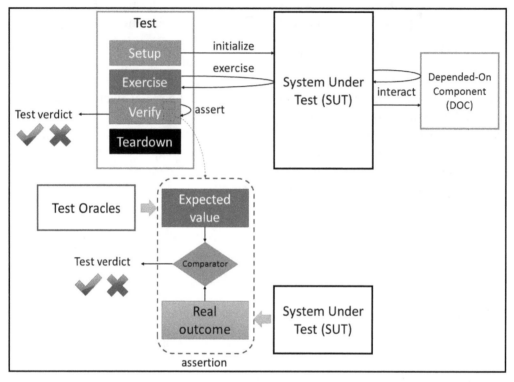

Test cases and assertions general schema

Test data plays a crucial role in the testing process. The source of test data is often called test oracles, and typically can be extracted from the requirements. Nevertheless, there are some others commonly used sources for tests oracles, for example:

- A different program, which produces the expected output (inverse relationship).
- A heuristic or statistical oracle that provides approximate results.
- Values based on the experience of human experts.

Moreover, test data can be derived, depending on the underlying testing technique. When using black-box testing, that is, exercise some specific requirement based using some input and expecting some output, different techniques can be employed, such as equivalence partitioning or boundary analysis. On the other side, if we are using white-box testing, the structure is the basis for our test and therefore the test coverage will be key to select the test input which maximizes these coverage rates. In the following sections, these techniques are reviewed.

Equivalence partitioning

Equivalence partitioning (also known as equivalence class partitioning) is a black-box technique (that is, it relies in the requirements of the system) aimed to reduce the number of tests that should be executed against a SUT. This technique was first defined by Glenford Myers in 1978 as:

> "A technique that partitions the input domain of a program into a finite number of classes [sets], it then identifies a minimal set of well-selected test cases to represent these classes."

In other words, equivalence partitioning provides a criteria to answer the question *How many tests do we need?* The idea is to divide all possible input test data (which often is a enormous number of combinations) in a set of values for which we assume to be processed in the same way by the SUT. We call equivalence classes to these sets of values. The idea is that testing one representative value within the equivalence class is consider sufficient because it is assumed that all the values are processed in the same way by the SUT.

Typically, the equivalence classes for a given SUT can be grouped in two types: valid and invalid inputs. The equivalence partitioning testing theory ensures that only one test case of each partition is needed to evaluate the behavior of the program for the related partition (both the valid and the invalid classes). The following process describes how to systematically carry out the equivalence partitioning for a given SUT:

1. First, we determine the domain of all possible valid inputs for a SUT. To find out these values, we rely on the specification (features or functional requirements). Our SUT is supposed to process these values (valid equivalence class) correctly.
2. If our specification establishes that some elements of the equivalence class are processed differently, they should assigne to another equivalence class.
3. The values outside this domain can be seen as another equivalence class, this time for invalid inputs.

4. For every single equivalence class, a representative value is chosen. This decision is an heuristic process typically based on the tester experience.

5. For every test input, the proper test output is also selected, and with these values we will be able to complete our test case (test exercise and assertions).

Boundary analysis

As any programmer knows, faults often appear at the boundary of a equivalence class (for example, the initial value of an array, the maximum value for a given range, and so on). Boundary value analysis is a method, which complements equivalence partitioning by looking at the boundaries of the test input. It was defined by the National Institute of Standards and Technology (NIST) in 1981 as:

> *"A selection technique in which test data are chosen to lie along 'boundaries' of the input domain [or output range] classes, data structures, and procedure parameters."*

All in all, to apply boundary value analysis in our tests, we need to evaluate our SUT exactly in the borders of our equivalence class. Therefore, typically two tests cases are derived using this approach: the upper and the lower boundary of the equivalence class.

Test coverage

Test coverage is the rate of code in SUT that is exercised for any of their tests. Test coverage is very useful to finding untested parts of our SUT. Therefore, it can be the perfect white box technique (structural) to complement the black box (functional). As a general rule, a test coverage rate of 80% or above is considered reasonable.

There are different Java libraries, which allows to make test coverage in a simple manner, for instance:

- Cobertura (`http://cobertura.github.io/cobertura/`): It is an open source reporting tool, which can be executed using Ant, Maven, or directly using the command line.

- EclEmma (`http://www.eclemma.org/`): It is an open source code coverage tool for Eclipse. As of Eclipse 4.7 (Oxygen), EclEmma is integrated out of the box in the IDE. The following screenshot shows an example on how EclEmma highlights the code coverage on a Java class in Eclipse:

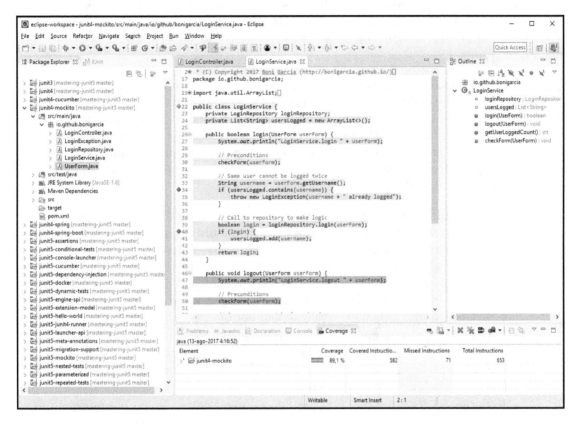

Test coverage with EclEmma in Eclipse 4.7 (Oxygen)

- JaCoCo (`http://www.jacoco.org/jacoco/`): It is an open source code coverage library created by the EclEmma team based on other old coverage library called EMMA (`http://emma.sourceforge.net/`). JaCoCo is available as a Maven dependency.
- Codecov (`https://codecov.io/`): It is a cloud solution offering a friendly code coverage web dashboard. It is free for open source projects.

Software testing principles

Exhaustive testing is the name given to a test approach, which uses all possible combinations of test inputs to verify a software system. This approach is only applicable to tiny software systems or components with a close finite number of possible of operations and allowed data. In the majority of software systems, it is not feasible to verify every possible permutation and input combination, and therefore exhaustive testing is just a theoretical approach.

For that reason, it is said that the absence of defects in a software system cannot be proved. This was stated by the computer science pioneer Edsger W. Dijkstra (see quote at beginning of this chapter). Thus, testing is, at best, sampling, and it must be carried out in any software project to reduce the risk of system failures (see chapter 1, *Retrospective On Software Quality And Java Testing*, to recall the software defect taxonomy). Since we cannot test everything, we need to test properly. In this section, we review a set of best practices to write effective and efficient test cases, namely:

- **Tests should be simple**: The software engineer writing the test (call him or her tester, programmer, developer, or whatever) should avoid attempting to test his or her program. In regards to testing, the right answer to the question *Who watches the watchmen?* Should be nobody. Our test logic should be simple enough to avoid any kind of meta-testing, since this would lead to a recursive problem out of any logic. Indirectly, if we keep tests simple, we also obtain another desirable feature: tests will be easy to maintain.
- **Do not implement simple tests**: One thing is make simple tests, and another very different stuff is to implement dummy code, such as getter or setters. As introduced before, test is at best sampling, and we cannot waste precious time in assessing such kind of part of our codebase.
- **Easy to read**: The first step is to provide a meaningful name for our test method. In addition, thanks to the JUnit 5 @DisplayName annotation, we can provide a rich textual description, which defines without Java naming constraints the goal of the test.
- **Single responsibility principle**: This is a general principle of computer programming that states that every class should have responsibility of a single functionality. It is closely related to the metric of cohesion. This principle is very important to be accomplished when coding tests: a single test should be only referred to a given system requirement.

- **Test data is key**: As described in the section before, the expected outcome from the SUT is a central part of the tests. The correct management of these data is critical to create effective tests. Fortunately, JUnit 5 provides a rich toolbox to handle test data (see section *Parameterized tests* in `chapter 4`, *Simplifying Testing With Advanced JUnit Features*).

- **Unit test should be executed very fast**: A commonly accepted rule of thumb for the duration of unit test is that a unit test should last a second at the most. To accomplish that goal, it is also required that unit test isolates properly the SUT, doubling properly its DOCs.

- **Test must be repeatable**: Defects should be reproduced as many times as required for developers to find the cause of the bug. This is the theory, but unfortunately this is not always applicable. For example, in multi-threaded SUT (a real-time or server-side software systems), race conditions are likely to occur. In those situations, non-deterministic defects (often called *heisenbugs*) might be experienced.

- **We should test positive and the negative scenarios**: This mean that we need to write tests with for input condition that assess the expected outcome, but we also need to verify what the program is not supposed to do. In addition to meet its requirements, programs must be tested to avoid unwanted side effects.

- **Testing cannot be done only for the sake of coverage**: Just because all parts of the code have been touched by some tests, we cannot assure that those parts have been thoroughly tested. For that to be true, tests have to analyzed in terms of reduction of risks.

The psychology of testing

From a psychological point of view, the objective of testing should be executing a software system with the intent of finding defects. Understanding the motivation of that claim can make the difference in the success of our tests.

Human beings tend to be goal oriented. If we carry out tests to demonstrate that a program has no errors, we will tend to implement tests selecting test data with a low probability of causing program failures. On the other hand, if the objective is to demonstrate that a program has errors, we will increase the probability of finding them, adding more value to the program than the former approach. For that reason, testing is often considered as a destructive process, since testers are supposed to prove that the SUT has errors.

Moreover, trying to demonstrate that errors are present in the software is a goal feasible, while trying to demonstrate their absence, as explained before, it is impossible. Again, psychology studies tell us that people perform poorly when they know that a task is infeasible.

Test anti-patterns

In software design, a pattern is a reusable solution to solve recurring problems. There are a bunch of them, including for example singleton, factory, builder, facade, proxy, decorator, or adapter, to name a few. Anti-patterns are also patterns, but undesirable ones. Concerning to testing, it is worth to know some of these anti-patterns to avoid them in our tests:

- **Second class citizens**: Test code containing a lot of duplicated code, making it hard to maintain.
- **The free ride** (also known as *Piggyback*): Instead of writing a new method to verify another feature/requirement, a new assertion is added to an existing test.
- **Happy path**: It only verifies expected results without testing for boundaries and exceptions.
- **The local hero**: A test dependent to some specific local environment. This anti-pattern can be summarized in the phrase *It works in my machine.*
- **The hidden dependency**: A test that requires some existing data populated somewhere before the test runs.
- **Chain gang**: Tests that must be run in a certain order, for example, changing the SUT to a state expected by the next one.
- **The mockery**: A unit test that contains too much test doubles that the SUT is not even tested at all, instead of returning data from test doubles.
- **The silent catcher**: A test that passes even if an unintended exception actually occurs.
- **The inspector**: A test that violates encapsulation that any refactor in the SUT requires reflecting those changes in the test.
- **Excessive setup**: A test that requires a huge setup in order to start the exercise stage.
- **Anal probe**: A test which has to use unhealthy ways to perform its task, such as reading private fields using reflection.
- **The test with no name**: Test methods name with no clear indicator about what it is being tested (for example, identifier in a bug tracking tool).
- **The slowpoke**: A unit test which lasts over few seconds.

- **The flickering test**: A test which contains race conditions within the proper test, making it to fail from time to time.
- **Wait and see**: A test that needs to wait a specific amount of time (for example, `Thread.sleep()`) before it can verify some expected behavior.
- **Inappropriately shared fixture**: Tests that use a test fixture without even need the setup/teardown.
- **The giant**: A test class that contains a huge number of tests methods (God Object).
- **Wet floor**: A test that creates persisted data but it is not clean up at when finished.
- **The cuckoo**: A unit test which establishes some kind of fixture before the actual test, but then the test discards somehow the fixture.
- **The secret catcher**: A test that is not making any assertion, relying on an exception to be thrown and reporting by the testing framework as a failure.
- **The environmental vandal**: A test which requires the use of given environment variables (for instance, a free port number to allows simultaneous executions).
- **Doppelganger**: Copying parts of the code under test into a new class to make visible for the test.
- **The mother hen**: A fixture which does more than the test needs.
- **The test it all**: Tests that should not break the Single Responsibility Principle.
- **Line hitter**: A test without any kind of real verification of the SUT.
- **The conjoined twins**: Tests that are called *unit tests* but are really integration tests since there is no isolation between the SUT and the DOC(s).
- **The liar**: A test that does not test what was supposed to test.

Code smells

Code smells (also known as *bad smell* when referred to software) are undesirable symptoms within the source code. Code smells are not problematic per se, but they can evidence some kind of issue nearby.

As described in previous sections, tests should be simple and easy to read. With that promises, code smells should be present in our tests under no circumstances. All in all, generic code smells might be avoided in our tests. Some of the most common code smells are the following:

- **Duplicated code**: Cloned code is always a bad idea in software, since it breaks the principle **Don't Repeat Yourself** (**DRY**). This problem is even worst in tests, since test logic must be crystal clear.
- **High complexity**: Too many branches or loops may be potentially simplified into smaller pieces.
- **Long method**: A method that has grown too large is always problematic, and it is a very bad symptom when this method is a test.
- **Unappropriated naming convention**: Variables, class, and method names should be concise. It is considered a bad smell to use very long identifiers, but also use excessive short (or meaningless) ones.

Summary

The starting point for the test design should be the list of requirements. If these requirements have not been formally elicited, at least we need to know the SUT features, which reflects the software needs. From this point, several strategies can be carried out. As usual, there is no unique path to reach our goal, which in the end should be reducing the risks of the project.

This chapter reviewed a process aimed to create effective and efficient tests cases. This process involves the analysis of requirements, definition of a test plan, design of test cases, and finally writing the test cases. We should be aware that, even though software testing is technical task, it involves some important considerations of human psychology. These factors should be known by software engineers and testers in order to follow know best practices and also avoiding common mistakes.

In chapter 7, *Testing management*, we are going to understand how software testing activities are managed in a living software project. To that, first we review when and how to carry out testing in the common software development processes, such as waterfall, spiral, iterative, spiral, agile, or test-driven development. Then, the server-side infrastructure (such as Jenkins or Travis) aimed to automate the software development process in the context of JUnit 5 is reviewed. Finally, we learn how to keep track of the defects found with the Jupiter tests using the so-called issue tracking systems and test reporting libraries.

7

Testing Management

The important thing is not to stop questioning.
- Albert Einstein

This is the final chapter of the book, and its objective is to guide how to understand when and how software testing activities are managed in a living software project. To that aim, this chapter is structured into the following sections:

- **Software development processes**: In this section we study when tests are executed in different methodologies: **Behavior-Driven Development** (**BDD**), **Test-Driven Development** (**TDD**), **Test-First Development** (**TFD**) and **Test-Last Development** (**TLD**).

- **Continuous Integration** (**CI**): In this section, we will discover CI, the software development practice, in which the process of build, test, and integration is carried out continuously. The common trigger of this process is usually the commit of new changes (patches) to a source code repository (for example, GitHub). In addition, in this section, we will learn how to extend CI, reviewing the concept of Continuous Delivery and Continuous Deployment. Finally, we present two of the most important build server nowadays: Jenkins and Travis CI.

- **Test reporting**: In this section, we will first discover the XML format in which the xUnit framework usually reports the execution of tests. The problem with this format is that it is not human readable. For this reason, there are tools which covert this XML into a friendlier format, typically HTML. We review two alternatives: Maven Surefire Report and Allure.

- **Defect tracking systems**: In this section, we review several issue trackes: JIRA, Bugzilla, Redmine, MantisBT, and GitHub issues.

- **Static analysis**: In this section, on the one hand we review several automated analysis tools (*linters*) such as Checkstyle, FindBugs, PMD, and SonarQube. On the other side, we describe several peer review tools, such as Collaborator, Crucible, Gerrit, and GitHub pull requests reviews.
- **Putting all, pieces together**: To conclude the book, in the final section we present a complete example application in which different types of tests (unit, integration, and end-to-end) are performed using some of the main concepts presented along this book.

Software development processes

In software engineering, the software development process (also known as the software development life cycle) is the name given to the workflow for the activities, actions, and tasks required to create software systems. As introduced in `Chapter 6`, *From Requirements to Test Cases*, the usual phases in any software development process are:

- Definition of *what*: Requirements elicitation, analysis and use case modeling.
- Definition of *how*: The system architecture and modeling of structural and behavioral diagrams.
- The actual software development (coding).
- The set of activities that makes the software available for use (release, installation, activation, and so on).

The timing in which tests are designed and implemented in the overall software development process results in different test methodologies, namely (see diagram after the list):

- **Behavior-Driven Development (BDD)**: At the beginning of the analysis phase, conversations between the software consumer (final user or costumer) and some of the development team (typically, project leader, manager, or analysts) took place. These conversations are used to concretize scenarios (that is, concrete examples to build up a common understanding of the system features). These examples form the basis to develop acceptance tests using tools such as Cucumber (for more details about it, take a look to `Chapter 5`, *Integration of JUnit 5 with external frameworks*.) The description of acceptance tests in BDD (for example, using Gherkin in Cucumber) produces both automated tests and documentation that accurately describe the application features. The BDD approach is naturally aligned with iterative or Agile methodologies, since it is very difficult to define requirements upfront, and these evolve as the team learns more about the project.

The term *agile* was popularized with the inception of the Agile manifesto in 2001 (http://agilemanifesto.org/). It was written by 17 software practitioners (Kent Beck, James Grenning, Robert C. Martin, Mike Beedle, Jim Highsmith, Steve Mellor, Arie van Bennekum, Andrew Hunt, Ken Schwaber, Alistair Cockburn, Ron Jeffries, Jeff Sutherland, Ward Cunningham, Jon Kern, Dave Thomas, Martin Fowler, and Brian Marick), and includes a list of 12 principles to guide an iterative and people-centric software development process. Based on these principles, several software development frameworks emerged, such as SCRUM, Kanban, or extreme programming (XP).

- **Test-Driven Development (TDD)**: TDD is a methodology in which tests are designed and implemented before the actual software design. The idea is to convert the requirements obtained in the analysis stage to specific test cases. Then, the software is designed and implemented to pass these tests. TDD is part of the XP methodology.

- **Test-First Development (TFD)**: In this methodology, tests are implemented after the design stage, but before the actual implementation of the SUT. This allows to assure that the software units have been understood correctly before its actual implementation. This methodology is followed in the Unified Process, which is a popular iterative and incremental software development process. The **Rational Unified Process** (**RUP**) is a well-known framework implementation of the Unified Process. In addition to TFD, RUP also supports other methodologies such as TDD and TLD.

- **Test-Last Development (TLD)**: In this methodology, the implementation of the test is carried out after the implementation of the actual software (SUT). This test methodology is followed by classic software development processes, such as waterfall (sequential), incremental (multi-waterfall) or spiral (risk-oriented multi-waterfall).

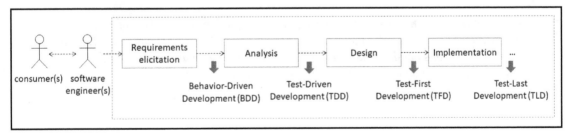

Test methodologies during the software development processes

There is no universal accepted definitions of the terms presented so far. These concepts are subject to continuous evolution and debate, just like the software engineering itself. Consider this to be a proposal, which fits into a large number of software projects.

Regarding who is responsible for coding the tests, there is a universally accepted consensus. It is broadly recommended that unit tests should be written by SUT developers. In some cases, especially in small teams, these developers are also responsible for other kinds of tests.

In addition, the role of an independent test group (often called testers or a QA team) is also a common practice, especially in large teams. One of the objective of this role separation is to remove the conflict of interests that may be present otherwise. We cannot forget that testing is understood as a destructive activity from a physiological point of view (the objective is finding defects). This independent test group is usually in charge on the integration, system, and non-functional tests. In this case, both groups of engineers should work closely; while tests are conducted, developers should be available to correct faults and minimize future errors.

Finally, high-level acceptance tests are usually conducted in heterogeneous groups involving non-programmers (customers, business analysis, managers, and so on) together with software engineers or testers (for example, for implement the step definition in Cucumber).

Continuous Integration

The concept of CI was first coined on 1991 by Grady Booch (American software engineer, best known for the development of UML together with Ivar Jacobson and James Rumbaugh). The **Extreme Programming** (**XP**) methodology adopted this term, making it very popular. According to Martin Fowler, CI is defined as follows:

> *Continuous Integration is a software development practice where members of a team integrate their work frequently, usually each person integrates at least daily - leading to multiple integrations per day. Each integration is verified by an automated build (including test) to detect integration errors as quickly as possible.*

In CI systems, we can identify different parts. First, we need a source code repository, which is a file archive to host the source code of our software project, typically using a version control system. Nowadays, the preferred version control system is Git (originally developed by Linus Torvalds) over older solutions, such as CVS or SVN. At the moment of this writing, the leading version control repository is GitHub (`https://github.com/`), which as its name indicates it is based on Git. Besides, there are other alternatives, such as GitLab (`https://gitlab.com`), BitBucket (`https://bitbucket.org/`), or SourceForge (`https://sourceforge.net/`). The latter was the leading forge in the past, but is nowadays less used.

A copy of the source code repository is synchronized in the local environment of developers. The coding work is done against this local copy. Developers are supposed to commit new changes (known as *patches*) to the remote repository in a daily basis. Frequent commits allow to avoid conflict errors due to the mutual modification of the same parts of a given file.

The basic idea of CI is that every commit should execute the build and test the software with the new changes. For that reason, we need a server-side infrastructure which automates this process. This infrastructure is known as build server (or directly CI server). Two of the most important build servers nowadays are Jenkins and Travis CI. Details of both of them are provided in next subsections. As a result of the build process, the build server should notify the result of the process to the origin developer. If tests were successful, the patch is merged in the codebase:

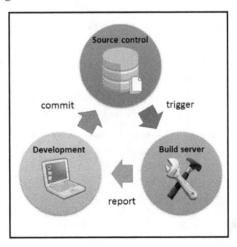

Continuous Integration process

Close to CI, the term DevOps has gained momentum. DevOps comes from *development* and *operations*, and it is the name given to a software development process that emphasizes the communication and collaboration different teams in a project software: development (software engineering), QA (**quality assurance**), and operations (infrastructure). The term DevOps is also referred to a job position, typically in charge of the setup, monitoring an operation of the build servers:

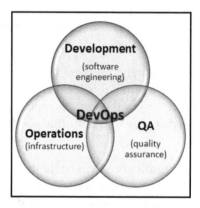

DevOps are in between development, operations and QA

As shown in the next figure, the concept of CI can be extended to:

- **Continuous Delivery**: When the CI pipeline finish correctly, at least a release of software will be deployed to a test environment (for instance, deploying an SNAPSHOT artifact to a Maven archiver). In this phase, acceptance tests can also be executed.
- **Continuous Deployment**: As the final step in the automation toolchain, the release of the software can be released to a production environment (for example, deploying a web application to the production server for each commit, which achieves to pass the complete pipeline).

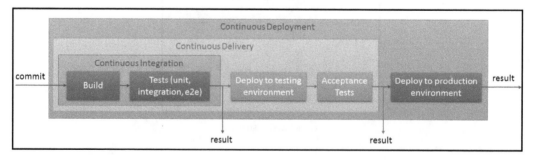

Continuous Integration, Continuous Delivery, and Continuous Deployment chain

Jenkins

Jenkins (`https://jenkins.io/`) is an open source build server which supports building, deploying, and automating any project. Jenkins has been developed in Java, and it can be managed easily using its web interface. The global configuration of a Jenkins instance includes information about JDK, Git, Maven, Gradle, Ant, and Docker.

 Jenkins was originally developed as the Hudson project by Sun Microsystems in 2004. After the acquisition of Sun by Oracle, the Hudson project was forked to an open source project, renamed to Jenkins. Both names (Hudson and Jenkins) were meant to sound like stereotypical English butler names. The idea is they help developers carry out tedious tasks, just like a helpful butler.

In Jenkins, builds are typically triggered by new commits in version control systems. In addition, builds can be started by other mechanisms, such as scheduled cron task or even manually using the Jenkins interface.

Jenkins is highly extensible thanks to its plugin architecture. Thanks to those, Jenkins has been extended to a rich plugin ecosystem made by vast number of third-party frameworks, libraries, systems, and so on. This is maintained by the open source community. The Jenkins plugin portfolio is available on `https://plugins.jenkins.io/`.

At the heart of Jenkins, we find the concept of job. A job is a runnable entity monitored by Jenkins. As shown in the screenshot here, a Jenkins job is composed of four groups:

- **Source code management**: This is the URL of the source code repository (Git, SVN, and so on)
- **Build trigger**: This is the mechanism starting the build process, such as new changes in the source code repository, external scripts, periodically, and so on.
- **Build environment**: Optional setup, for example, delete workspace before build start, abort the build when stuck, and so on.

- **Collection of steps of the jobs**: These steps can be done with Maven, Gradle, Ant, or shell commands. After those, post-build actions can be configured, for example, to archive an artifact, to publish JUnit test report (we will describe this feature later in this chapter), email notifications, and so on.

Jenkins job configuration

Another interesting way of configuring a job is using a Jenkins *pipeline*, which is the description of the build workflow using the Pipeline DSL (a domain-specific language based on Groovy). A Jenkins pipeline description is typically stored in a file called Jenkinsfile, which can be under the control of the source code repository. In short, a Jenkins pipeline is declarative chain of stages composed of steps. For example:

```
pipeline {
    agent any
```

```
stages {
    stage('Build') {
        steps {
            sh 'make'
        }
    }
    stage('Test') {
        steps {
            sh 'make check'
            junit 'reports/**/*.xml'
        }
    }
    stage('Deploy') {
        steps {
            sh 'make publish'
        }
    }
}
}
```

Travis CI

Travis CI (`https://travis-ci.org/`) is a distributed build server used to build and test software projects hosted on GitHub. Travis supports open source projects with no charge.

The configuration of Travis CI is done using a file named *.travis.yaml*. The content of this file is structured using different keywords, including:

- `language`: Project language, that is, java, node_js, ruby, python, or php among others (the complete list is available on `https://docs.travis-ci.com/user/languages/`).
- `sudo`: Flag value to set if superuser privileges are needed (for example to install Ubuntu packages).
- `dist`: Builds can be executed on Linux environments (Ubuntu Precise 12.04 or Ubuntu Trusty 14.04).
- `addons`: Declarative shortcuts to basic operations of the apt-get commands.
- `install`: First part of the Travis build life cycle, in which the installation of the required dependencies is done. This part can be optionally initiated using `before_install`.
- `script`: Actual execution of the build. This phase can be optionally surrounded by `before_script` and `after_script`.

- `deploy`: Finally, the deployment of the build can be optionally made in this phase. This stage has its own life cycle controlled with `before_deploy` and `after_deploy`.

> YAML is lightweight markup language used broadly for configuration files due to its minimalist syntax. It was originally defined as Yet Another Markup Language, but then it was repurposed to YAML Ain't Markup Language to distinguish its purpose as data oriented.

The following snippet shows an example of `.travis.yaml`:

```
language: java
sudo: false
dist: trusty

addons:
    firefox: latest
    apt:
        packages:
            - google-chrome-stable
    sonarcloud:
        organization: "bonigarcia-github"
        token:
            secure: "encripted-token"

before_script:
    - export DISPLAY=:99.0
    - sh -e /etc/init.d/xvfb start &
    - sleep 3

script:
    - mvn test sonar:sonar
    - bash <(curl -s https://codecov.io/bash)
```

Travis CI provides a web dashboard in which we can check the status of the current and past build generated in the projects using Travis CI of our GitHub account:

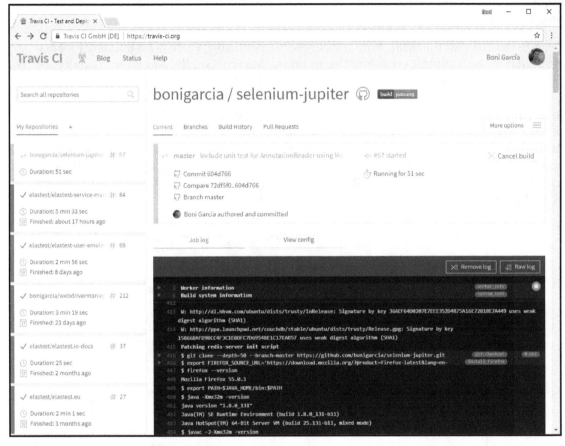

Travis CI dashboard

Test reporting

From its initial versions, the JUnit testing framework introduced an XML file format to report the execution of test suites. Over the years, this XML format has become a *de facto* standard for reporting test results, broadly adopted in the xUnit family.

These XML can be processed by different programs to display the results in a human-friendly format. This is for example what build servers do. For example, Jenkins implements a tool called `JUnitResultArchiver`, which parses to HTML the XML files resulting from the test execution of a job.

Despite the fact that this XML format has become pervasive, there is no universal formal definition for it. JUnit test executors (for example, Maven, Gradle, and so on) usually use its own XSD (XML Schema Definition). For instance, the structure of this XML report in Maven (`http://maven.apache.org/surefire/maven-surefire-plugin/`) is as depicted in the following diagram. Note that a test suite is composed by a set of properties and a set of test cases. Each test case can be declared as a failure (test with some assertion failed), skipped (test ignored), and an error (test with an unexpected exception). If none of these states appear in the body of the test suite, then the test is interpreted as successful. Finally, for each test case the XML also stores the standard output (*system-out*) and the standard error output (*system-err*):

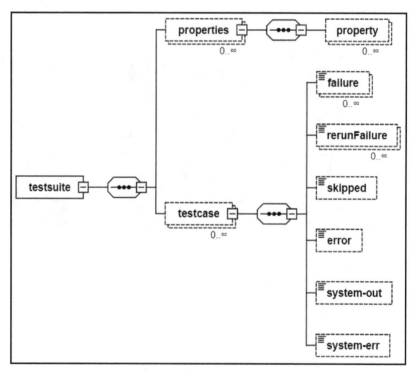

Schema representation for Maven Surefire XML reports

The *rerunFailure* is a custom state implemented by Maven Surefire for retrying flaky (intermittent) tests (`http://maven.apache.org/surefire/ maven-surefire-plugin/examples/rerun-failing-tests.html`).

With regards to JUnit 5, the Maven and Gradle plugins used to run Jupiter tests (`maven- surefire-plugin` and `junit-platform-gradle-plugin` respectively) write the results of the test execution following this XML format. In the following sections, we are going to see how to transform this XML output to a human readable HTML report.

Maven Surefire Report

By default, `maven-surefire-plugin` generates the XML resulting from a test suite execution as `${basedir}/target/surefire-reports/TEST-*.xml`. This XML output can be easily parsed to HTML using the plugin `maven-surefire-report-plugin`. To that, we simply need to declare this plugin in the reporting clause of our `pom.xml`, as follows:

```
<reporting>
    <plugins>
        <plugin>
            <groupId>org.apache.maven.plugins</groupId>
            <artifactId>maven-surefire-report-plugin</artifactId>
            <version>${maven-surefire-report-plugin.version}</version>
        </plugin>
    </plugins>
</reporting>
```

This way, when we invoque the Maven lifecycle for documentation (`mvn site`), an HTML page with the test result will be included in the general report.

See an example of the report, made using the project `junit5-reporting` within the GitHub repository examples (`https://github.com/bonigarcia/mastering-junit5`):

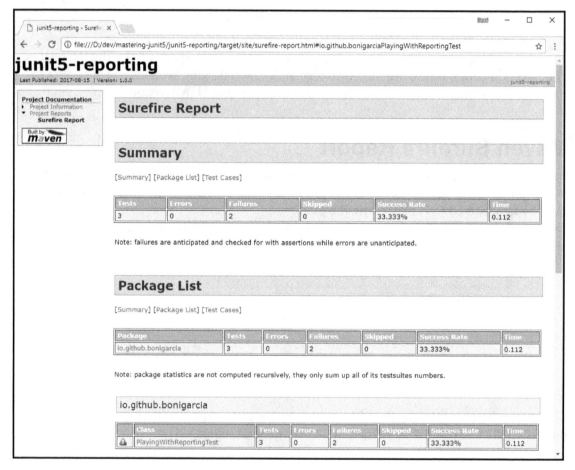

HTML report generated by maven-surefire-report-plugin

Allure

Allure (`http://allure.qatools.ru/`) is a light-weight open source framework for generating test reports for different programming languages, including Java, Python, JavaScript, Ruby, Groovy, PHP, .NET, and Scala. Generaliy speaking, Allure uses the XML test output and transforms it in an HTML5-rich report.

Allure provides support for JUnit 5 projects. This can be done using both Maven and Gradle. Regarding Maven, we need to do register a listener in `maven-surefire-plugin`. This listener will be the class AllureJunit5 (located in the library `io.qameta.allure:allure-junit5`), which is basically a implementation of the JUnit 5's `TestExecutionListener`. As described in chapter 2, *What's New In JUnit 5*, `TestExecutionListener` is part of the Launcher API, and it is used to receive events about the test execution. All in all, this listener allows to Allure to compile the test information, while it is generated in the JUnit platform. This information is stored as JSON files by Allure. After that, we can use the plugin `io.qameta.allure:allure-maven` to generate the HTML5 from these JSON files. The commands are:

```
mvn test
mvn allure:serve
```

The content of our `pom.xml` should contain the following:

```xml
<dependencies>
    <dependency>
        <groupId>io.qameta.allure</groupId>
        <artifactId>allure-junit5</artifactId>
        <version>${allure-junit5.version}</version>
        <scope>test</scope>
    </dependency>
    <dependency>
        <groupId>org.junit.jupiter</groupId>
        <artifactId>junit-jupiter-api</artifactId>
        <version>${junit.jupiter.version}</version>
        <scope>test</scope>
    </dependency>
</dependencies>

<build>
    <plugins>
        <plugin>
            <artifactId>maven-surefire-plugin</artifactId>
            <version>${maven-surefire-plugin.version}</version>
            <configuration>
                <properties>
                    <property>
                        <name>listener</name>
                        <value>io.qameta.allure.junit5.AllureJunit5</value>
                    </property>
                </properties>
                <systemProperties>
                    <property>
                        <name>allure.results.directory</name>
```

```
                    <value>${project.build.directory}/allure-
  results</value>
                    </property>
                </systemProperties>
            </configuration>
            <dependencies>
                <dependency>
                    <groupId>org.junit.platform</groupId>
                    <artifactId>junit-platform-surefire-
  provider</artifactId>
                    <version>${junit.platform.version}</version>
                </dependency>
                <dependency>
                    <groupId>org.junit.jupiter</groupId>
                    <artifactId>junit-jupiter-engine</artifactId>
                    <version>${junit.jupiter.version}</version>
                </dependency>
            </dependencies>
        </plugin>
        <plugin>
            <groupId>io.qameta.allure</groupId>
            <artifactId>allure-maven</artifactId>
            <version>${allure-maven.version}</version>
        </plugin>
    </plugins>
</build>
```

The same process can be done using Gradle, this time using the equivalent plugin,
`io.qameta.allure:allure-gradle`. All in all, the content of our `build.gradle` file
should contain:

```
buildscript {
    repositories {
        jcenter()
        mavenCentral()
    }
    dependencies {
        classpath("org.junit.platform:junit-platform-gradle-
plugin:${junitPlatformVersion}")
        classpath("io.qameta.allure:allure-gradle:${allureGradleVersion}")
    }
}

apply plugin: 'io.qameta.allure'

dependencies {
    testCompile("org.junit.jupiter:junit-jupiter-
api:${junitJupiterVersion}")
```

```
    testCompile("io.qameta.allure:allure-junit5:${allureJUnit5Version}")
    testRuntime("org.junit.jupiter:junit-jupiter-
engine:${junitJupiterVersion}")
}
```

The following picture shows several screenshots of the Allure report generated using the above-mentioned steps (the final result is the same using Maven or Gradle). The project of this example is called `junit5-allure`, as usual hosted in GitHub.

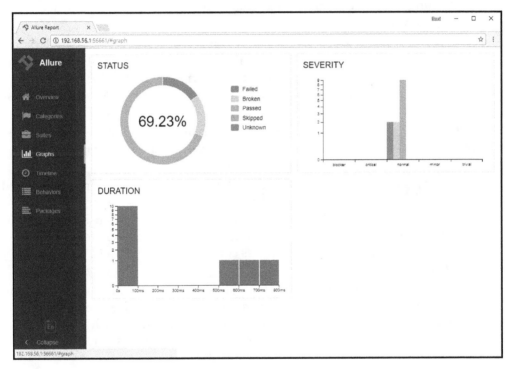

Allure reports generated in a JUnit 5 project

Defect-tracking systems

A defect-tracking system (also known as bug tracking system, bug tracker, or issue tracker) is a software system that keeps track of reported software defects in software projects. The main benefits of this kind of systems is to provide a centralized overview of development management, bug reporting, and even feature request. It is also common to maintain a list of pending items, often called backlog.

There are a bunch of defect-tracking systems available, both proprietary and open source. In this section, we make a brief of several of the most well-known:

- **JIRA** (`https://www.atlassian.com/software/jira`): It is a proprietary defect-tracking system created by Atlasian. In addition to bug and issue tracking, it provides managements capabilities such as SCRUM and Kanban boards, a language to query issues (JIRA Query Language), integration with external systems (for example, GitHub, Bitbucket), and an add-ons mechanism to extend JIRA with plugins from the Atlasian Marketplace (`https://marketplace.atlassian.com/`).
- **Bugzilla** (`https://www.bugzilla.org/`): It is an open source web-based, defect-tracking system developed by the Mozilla Foundation. Among its features, we can find a database designed to improve performance and scalability, query mechanism for searching defects, integrated e-mail capabilities, and user roles management.
- **Redmine** (`http://www.redmine.org/`): It is an open source, web-based defect-tracking system. It provides wikis, forums, time tracking, role-based access control, or Gantt charts for project management.
- **MantisBT** (`https://www.mantisbt.org/`): It is another open source, web-based defect tracking system designed to be simple but effective. Among its features, we can highlight its event-driven plugin system to allows extensions both official that third-party, multi-channel notification system (e-mail, RSS feed, Twitter plugin, and so on), or role-based access control.
- **GitHub issues** (`https://guides.github.com/features/issues/`): It is the tracking system integrated in each GitHub repository. The approach of GitHub issues is to provide a generic tracking system for defects, task scheduling, discussions, and even feature request using GitHub issues. Each issue can be categorized using a customizable label system, participators management, and notifications.

Static analysis

This book, which is finishing soon, has been focused on software testing. No surprises, JUnit is about testing. But as we seen in `Chapter 1`, *Retrospective on software quality and Java testing*, although software testing is the most commonly performed activities within **Verification & Validation (V&V)**, it is not the only type. The other important group of activities is static analysis, in which there is no execution of the software testing.

There are different activities that can be categorized as static analysis. Among them, the automated software analysis is an alternative quite inexpensive in terms of required effort, and it can help to increase the internal code quality significantly. In this chapter, we are going to review several automated software analysis tools, known as **linters**, namely:

- **Checkstyle** (`http://checkstyle.sourceforge.net/`): It analyzes Java code following different rules, such as missing Javadoc comments, the use of magic numbers, naming conventions of variables and methods, method's argument length and line lengths, the use of imports, the spaces between some characters, the good practices of class construction, or duplicated code. It can be used as Eclipse or IntelliJ plugin, among others.

- **FindBugs** (`http://findbugs.sourceforge.net/`): It looks for three types of errors within Java code:
  - Correctness bug: Apparent coding mistake (for example, class defines `equal(Object)` instead of `equals(Object)`.
  - Bad practice: Violations of recommended best practices (dropped exceptions, misuse of finalize, and so on).
  - Dodgy errors: Confusing code or written in a way that leads to error (for example, class `literal` never used, switch fall through, unconfirmed type casts, and redundant null check.

- **PMD** (`https://pmd.github.io/`): It is a cross-language static code analyzer, including Java, JavaScript, C++, C#, Go, Groovy, Perl, PHP, among others. It has a lot of plugins, including Maven, Gradle, Eclipse, IntelliJ, and Jenkins.

- **SonarQube** (`https://www.sonarqube.org/`): It (formerly just Sonar) is a web-based, open source continuous quality assessment dashboard. It supports a wide variety of languages, including Java, C/C++, Objective-C, C#, and many others. Offers reports on duplicated code, code smells, code coverage, complexity and security vulnerabilities. SonarQube has a distributed flavor called **SonarCloud** (`https://sonarcloud.io/`). It can be used for free in open source projects, providing a seamless integration with Travis CI through a few lines of configuration in `.travis.yml` (see the following snippet), including the SonarCloud organization identifier and secure token. These parameters can be obtained in the SonarCloud web administration panel, after associating out SonarCloud account with GitHub.

```
addons:
    sonarcloud:
        organization: "bonigarcia-github"
        token:
            secure: "encrypted-token"
```

After that, we simply need to call SonarCloud, using Maven or using Gradle:

```
script:
    - mvn test sonar:sonar
```

```
script:
    - gradle test sonarQube
```

The following picture shows the SonarCloud dashboard for the example application Rate my cat!, described in the last section of this chapter:

SonarCloud report for the application Rate my cat!

Another analysis static technique highly adopted in many software projects is **peer review**. This method is quite expensive in terms of time and effort required, but when correctly applied, it allows to maintain very good levels of internal code quality. Nowadays there is a wide range of tools aimed to ease the peer review process of software codebase. Among others, we find the following:

- **Collaborator** (`https://smartbear.com/product/collaborator/`): Peer code (and documentation) review propriety tool created by the company SmartBear.
- **Crucible** (`https://www.atlassian.com/software/crucible`): On-premises code review propriety tool for enterprise products, created by Atlassian.
- **Gerrit** (`https://www.gerritcodereview.com/`): Web-based code collaboration open source tool. It can be used with GitHub repository through GerritHub (`http://gerrithub.io/`).
- **GitHub pull request reviews** (`https://help.github.com/articles/about-pull-request-reviews/`): In GitHub, a pull request is a method for submitting contributions in third-party repositories. As part of the collaborative tools provided by GitHub, pull requests allows reviews and comments in a easy and integrated fashion.

Putting all pieces together

In this last section of the book, we are going to review some of the major aspects covered in this book with a practical example. To that aim, a complete application is developed together with different types of tests implemented with JUnit 5.

Features and requirements

The history of our application begins with a hypothetical person, which loves cats. This person owns a clowder, and he/she would like to get feedback about them from the external world. For that reason, this person (we can him/her our *client* from now on) contacts with us to implement a web application which satisfies his/her needs. The name for that application will be *"Rate my cat!"*. In a conversation with the client, we elicit a following list of features for the application to be developed:

- **F1**: Each user shall rate a list of cats by watching its name and picture.
- **F2**: The rate shall be done once per user using a star mechanism (from 0.5 to 5 stars per cat) and optionally comments could be included per cat.

As part of the analysis phase in our development process, those features are refined as a list of **functional requirements (FR)** as follows:

- **FR1**: The application presents a list of cats (composed by name and picture) to the end user.
- **FR2**: Each cat can be rated individually.
- **FR3**: The range for rating cats is an interval from 0.5 to 5 (stars).
- **FR4**: Optionally to the numeric rate per cat, users shall include some comments.
- **FR5**: Each end user only shall rate each cat (comments and/or stars) once.

Design

Since our application is quite simple, we decide to stop the analysis phase here, without modeling our requirements as use cases. Instead, we move on making a high-level architectural design of the web application using the classical three-tier model: presentation, application (or business) logic, and data tier. Regarding the application logic, as the following picture depicts, two components are needed. First one, called `CatService` is charge of all the rating actions as described in the requirements list. Second one, called `CookiesServices` is needed to handle HTTP Cookies, needed to implement FR5:

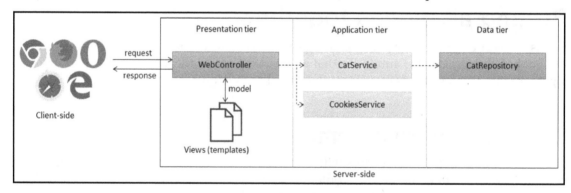

High-level architectural design for the application Rate my cat!

At this stage, in the development, we are able to decide the major technologies implied in the implementation our application:

- **Spring 5**: This will be the foundation framework for our application. Concretely, we use Spring MVC through Spring Boot to simplify the creation of our web application. Moreover, we use Spring Data JPA using a simple H2 database to persist the application data, and Thymeleaf (http://www.thymeleaf.org/) as template engine (for views in MVC). Finally, we also use the Spring Test module to make in-container integration tests in an easy way.
- **JUnit 5**: Of course, we cannot use a different testing framework than JUnit 5 for our tests cases. Moreover, to improve the readability of our assertions we use Hamcrest.
- **Mockito**: In order to implement unit test cases, we will use the Mockito framework, isolating the SUT from its DOCs in several out-of-container unit tests.
- **Selenium WebDriver**: We will also implement different end-to-end tests using Selenium WebDriver to exercise our web application from JUnit 5 tests.
- **GitHub**: Our source code repository will be hosted in a public GitHub repository.
- **Travis CI**: Our test suite will be executed each time a new patch is committed to our GitHub repository.
- **Codecov**: To track the code coverage of our test suite we will use Codecov.
- **SonarCloud**: To provide a complete assessment of the internal quality of our source code, we complement our test process with some automatic static analysis using SonarCloud.

The screenshot here shows the application GUI in action. It is not the main objective of this section to dig deeper in the implementation specifics of the application. Visit the GitHub repository of the application on `https://github.com/bonigarcia/rate-my-cat` for details about it.

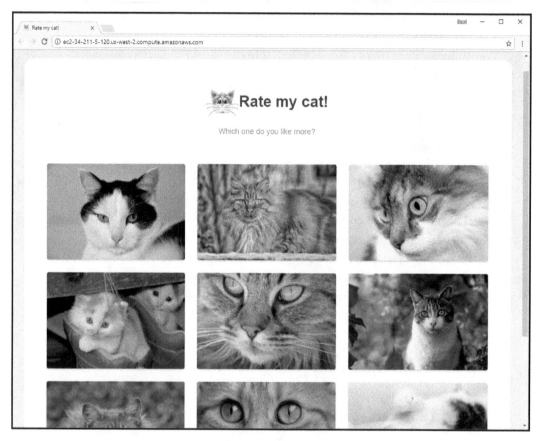

Screenshot of the application Rate my cat!

 The pictures used to implement this example have been downloaded from the free images gallery available on `https://pixabay.com/`.

Tests

Let's focus now on the JUnit 5 tests of this application. We implement three types of tests: unit, integration, and end to end. As introduced before, for the unit test, we use Mockito to exercise the SUT in isolation. We decide to unit test the two major components of our application (`CatService` and `CookiesServices`) using Java classes containing different JUnit 5 tests.

Consider the first test (called `RateCatsTest`). As can be seen the code, in this class we are defining the class `CatService` as the SUT (using the annotation `@InjectMocks`) and the class `CatRepository` (which is used by `CatService` with dependency injection) as the DOC (using the annotation `@Mock`). The first test of this class (`testCorrectRangeOfStars`) is an example of parameterized JUnit 5 tests. The objective of this test if to assess the rate method inside `CatService` (method `rateCate`). In order to select the test data (input) for this test, we follow a black-box strategy and therefore we use the information of the requirements definition. Concretely, *FR3* states the range of stars to be used in the rating mechanism for cats. Following a boundary analysis approach, we select the edges of the input range, that is, 0.5 and 5. The second test case (`testCorrectRangeOfStars`) also tests the same method (`rateCat`), but this time the test evaluates the SUT response when out-of-range inputs exercise the SUT (negative test scenario). Then, two more tests are implemented in this class, this time aimed to assess *FR4* (that is, using also comments to rate cats). Notice that we are using the JUnit 5 `@Tag` annotation to identify each test with its corresponding requirement:

```java
package io.github.bonigarcia.test.unit;

import static org.hamcrest.CoreMatchers.equalTo;
import static org.hamcrest.MatcherAssert.assertThat;
import static org.hamcrest.text.IsEmptyString.isEmptyString;
import static org.junit.jupiter.api.Assertions.assertThrows;
import static org.mockito.ArgumentMatchers.any;
import static org.mockito.Mockito.when;

import java.util.Optional;
import org.junit.jupiter.api.DisplayName;
import org.junit.jupiter.api.Tag;
import org.junit.jupiter.api.Test;
import org.junit.jupiter.api.extension.ExtendWith;
import org.junit.jupiter.params.ParameterizedTest;
import org.junit.jupiter.params.provider.ValueSource;
import org.mockito.InjectMocks;
import org.mockito.Mock;
import io.github.bonigarcia.Cat;
import io.github.bonigarcia.CatException;
```

```
import io.github.bonigarcia.CatRepository;
import io.github.bonigarcia.CatService;
import io.github.bonigarcia.mockito.MockitoExtension;

@ExtendWith(MockitoExtension.class)
@DisplayName("Unit tests (black-box): rating cats")
@Tag("unit")
class RateCatsTest {

    @InjectMocks
    CatService catService;

    @Mock
    CatRepository catRepository;

    // Test data
    Cat dummy = new Cat("dummy", "dummy.png");
    int stars = 5;
    String comment = "foo";

    @ParameterizedTest(name = "Rating cat with {0} stars")
    @ValueSource(doubles = { 0.5, 5 })
    @DisplayName("Correct range of stars test")
    @Tag("functional-requirement-3")
    void testCorrectRangeOfStars(double stars) {
        when(catRepository.save(dummy)).thenReturn(dummy);
        Cat dummyCat = catService.rateCat(stars, dummy);
        assertThat(dummyCat.getAverageRate(), equalTo(stars));
    }

    @ParameterizedTest(name = "Rating cat with {0} stars")
    @ValueSource(ints = { 0, 6 })
    @DisplayName("Incorrect range of stars test")
    @Tag("functional-requirement-3")
    void testIncorrectRangeOfStars(int stars) {
        assertThrows(CatException.class, () -> {
            catService.rateCat(stars, dummy);
        });
    }

    @Test
    @DisplayName("Rating cats with a comment")
    @Tag("functional-requirement-4")
    void testRatingWithComments() {
        when(catRepository.findById(any(Long.class)))
            .thenReturn(Optional.of(dummy));
        Cat dummyCat = catService.rateCat(stars, comment, 0);
        assertThat(catService.getOpinions(dummyCat).iterator().next()
```

```
        .getComment(), equalTo(comment));
}

@Test
@DisplayName("Rating cats with empty comment")
@Tag("functional-requirement-4")
void testRatingWithEmptyComments() {
    when(catRepository.findById(any(Long.class)))
        .thenReturn(Optional.of(dummy));
    Cat dummyCat = catService.rateCat(stars, dummy);
    assertThat(catService.getOpinions(dummyCat).iterator().next()
        .getComment(), isEmptyString());
}

}
```

Next, unit test evaluates the cookies service (*FR5*). To that aim, the following test use the class `CookiesService` as SUT, and this time we are going to mock the standard Java object, which manipulates the HTTP Cookies, that is, `javax.servlet.http.HttpServletResponse`. Inspecting the source code of this test class, we can see that the first test method (called `testUpdateCookies`) exercise the service method `updateCookies`, verifying whether or not the format of the cookies is as expected. Next two tests (`testCheckCatInCookies` and `testCheckCatInEmptyCookies`) evaluates the method `isCatInCookies` of the service using a positive strategy (that is the input cat corresponds with the format of the cookie) and a negative one (the opposite case). Finally, the last two tests (`testUpdateOpinionsWithCookies` and `testUpdateOpinionsWithEmptyCookies`) exercise the method `updateOpinionsWithCookiesValue` of the SUT following the same approach, that is, checking the response of the SUT using a valid and empty cookie. All these tests have been implemented following a white-box strategy, since its test data and logic relies completely in the specific internal logic of the SUT (in this case how the cookies are formatted and managed).

 This test does not follow pure white-box approach in the sense of its objective is to exercise all the possible paths within the SUT. It can be seen as white-box in the sense of it has been designed directly linked to the implementation rather than the requirements.

```
package io.github.bonigarcia.test.unit;

import static org.hamcrest.CoreMatchers.containsString;
import static org.hamcrest.CoreMatchers.equalTo;
import static org.hamcrest.CoreMatchers.not;
import static org.hamcrest.MatcherAssert.assertThat;
import static org.hamcrest.collection.IsEmptyCollection.empty;
```

```
import static org.mockito.ArgumentMatchers.any;
import static org.mockito.Mockito.doNothing;
import java.util.List;
import javax.servlet.http.Cookie;
import javax.servlet.http.HttpServletResponse;
import org.junit.jupiter.api.DisplayName;
import org.junit.jupiter.api.Tag;
import org.junit.jupiter.api.Test;
import org.junit.jupiter.api.extension.ExtendWith;
import org.mockito.InjectMocks;
import org.mockito.Mock;
import io.github.bonigarcia.Cat;
import io.github.bonigarcia.CookiesService;
import io.github.bonigarcia.Opinion;
import io.github.bonigarcia.mockito.MockitoExtension;

@ExtendWith(MockitoExtension.class)
@DisplayName("Unit tests (white-box): handling cookies")
@Tag("unit")
@Tag("functional-requirement-5")
class CookiesTest {
    @InjectMocks
    CookiesService cookiesService;
    @Mock
    HttpServletResponse response;

    // Test data
    Cat dummy = new Cat("dummy", "dummy.png");
    String dummyCookie = "0#0.0#_";

    @Test
    @DisplayName("Update cookies test")
    void testUpdateCookies() {
        doNothing().when(response).addCookie(any(Cookie.class));
        String cookies = cookiesService.updateCookies("", 0L, 0D, "",
          response);
        assertThat(cookies,
          containsString(CookiesService.VALUE_SEPARATOR));
        assertThat(cookies,
          containsString(Cookies.CAT_SEPARATOR));
    }

    @Test
    @DisplayName("Check cat in cookies")
    void testCheckCatInCookies() {
        boolean catInCookies = cookiesService.isCatInCookies(dummy,
            dummyCookie);
        assertThat(catInCookies, equalTo(true));
```

```
    }

    @DisplayName("Check cat in empty cookies")
    @Test
    void testCheckCatInEmptyCookies() {
        boolean catInCookies = cookiesService.isCatInCookies(dummy, "");
        assertThat(catInCookies, equalTo(false));
    }

    @DisplayName("Update opinions with cookies")
    @Test
    void testUpdateOpinionsWithCookies() {
        List<Opinion> opinions = cookiesService
            .updateOpinionsWithCookiesValue(dummy, dummyCookie);
        assertThat(opinions, not(empty()));
    }

    @DisplayName("Update opinions with empty cookies")
    @Test
    void testUpdateOpinionsWithEmptyCookies() {
        List<Opinion> opinions = cookiesService
            .updateOpinionsWithCookiesValue(dummy, "");
        assertThat(opinions, empty());
    }

}
```

Let's move on to the next type of tests: integration. For this type of test, we are going to use the in-container test capabilities provided by Spring. Concretely, we use the Spring test object `MockMvc` to evaluate the HTTP responses of our application from the client-side. In each test, different requests are exercised verifying if the responses (status code and content type) are as expected:

```
package io.github.bonigarcia.test.integration;

import static
org.springframework.test.web.servlet.request.MockMvcRequestBuilders.get;
import static
org.springframework.test.web.servlet.request.MockMvcRequestBuilders.post;
import static
org.springframework.test.web.servlet.result.MockMvcResultMatchers.content;
import static
org.springframework.test.web.servlet.result.MockMvcResultMatchers.status;

import org.junit.jupiter.api.DisplayName;
import org.junit.jupiter.api.Tag;
import org.junit.jupiter.api.Test;
```

```
import org.junit.jupiter.api.extension.ExtendWith;
import org.springframework.beans.factory.annotation.Autowired;
import org.springframework.boot.test.context.SpringBootTest;
import org.springframework.test.context.junit.jupiter.SpringExtension;
import org.springframework.test.web.servlet.MockMvc;

@ExtendWith(SpringExtension.class)
@SpringBootTest
@DisplayName("Integration tests: HTTP reponses")
@Tag("integration")
@Tag("functional-requirement-1")
@Tag("functional-requirement-2")

class WebContextTest {

    @Autowired
    MockMvc mockMvc;

    @Test
    @DisplayName("Check home page (GET /)")
    void testHomePage() throws Exception {
        mockMvc.perform(get("/")).andExpect(status().isOk())
            .andExpect(content().contentType("text/html;charset=UTF-8"));
    }

    @Test
    @DisplayName("Check rate cat (POST /)")
    void testRatePage() throws Exception {
        mockMvc.perform(post("/").param("catId", "1").param("stars", "1")
            .param("comment", "")).andExpect(status().isOk())
            .andExpect(content().contentType("text/html;charset=UTF-8"));
    }

    @Test
    @DisplayName("Check rate cat (POST /) of an non-existing cat")
    void testRatePageCatNotAvailable() throws Exception {
        mockMvc.perform(post("/").param("catId", "0").param("stars", "1")
            .param("comment", "")).andExpect(status().isOk())
            .andExpect(content().contentType("text/html;charset=UTF-8"));
    }

    @Test
    @DisplayName("Check rate cat (POST /) with bad parameters")
    void testRatePageNoParameters() throws Exception {
        mockMvc.perform(post("/")).andExpect(status().isBadRequest());
    }

}
```

Finally, we also implement several end-to-end tests using Selenium WebDriver. Inspecting the implementation of this test, we can see that this test is using two JUnit 5 extensions at the same time: `SpringExtension` (to start/stop the Spring context within the JUnit 5 tests' lifecycle) and `SeleniumExtension` (to inject WebDriver objects aimed to control web browsers in the test methods). In particular, we use three different browsers in one of the tests:

- PhantomJS (headless browser), to assess is the list of cats is properly rendered in the web GUI (FR1).
- Chrome, to rate cats using through the application GUI (FR2).
- Firefox, to rate cats using the GUI but getting an error as a result (FR2).

```java
package io.github.bonigarcia.test.e2e;

import static org.hamcrest.CoreMatchers.containsString;
import static org.hamcrest.CoreMatchers.equalTo;
import static org.hamcrest.MatcherAssert.assertThat;
import static
org.openqa.selenium.support.ui.ExpectedConditions.elementToBeClickable;
import static
org.springframework.boot.test.context.SpringBootTest.WebEnvironment.RANDOM_
PORT;

import java.util.List;
import org.junit.jupiter.api.DisplayName;
import org.junit.jupiter.api.Tag;
import org.junit.jupiter.api.Test;
import org.junit.jupiter.api.extension.ExtendWith;
import org.openqa.selenium.By;
import org.openqa.selenium.WebElement;
import org.openqa.selenium.chrome.ChromeDriver;
import org.openqa.selenium.firefox.FirefoxDriver;
import org.openqa.selenium.phantomjs.PhantomJSDriver;
import org.openqa.selenium.support.ui.WebDriverWait;
import org.springframework.boot.test.context.SpringBootTest;
import org.springframework.boot.web.server.LocalServerPort;
import org.springframework.test.context.junit.jupiter.SpringExtension;
import io.github.bonigarcia.SeleniumExtension;

@ExtendWith({ SpringExtension.class, SeleniumExtension.class })
@SpringBootTest(webEnvironment = RANDOM_PORT)
@DisplayName("E2E tests: user interface")
@Tag("e2e")
public class UserInferfaceTest {
    @LocalServerPort
    int serverPort;
```

```java
@Test
@DisplayName("List cats in the GUI")
@Tag("functional-requirement-1")
public void testListCats(PhantomJSDriver driver) {
    driver.get("http://localhost:" + serverPort);
    List<WebElement> catLinks = driver
        .findElements(By.className("lightbox"));
    assertThat(catLinks.size(), equalTo(9));
}


@Test
@DisplayName("Rate a cat using the GUI")
@Tag("functional-requirement-2")
public void testRateCat(ChromeDriver driver) {
    driver.get("http://localhost:" + serverPort);
    driver.findElement(By.id("Baby")).click();
    String fourStarsSelector = "#form1 span:nth-child(4)";
    new WebDriverWait(driver, 10)
        .until(elementToBeClickable
            (By.cssSelector(fourStarsSelector)));
    driver.findElement(By.cssSelector(fourStarsSelector)).click();
    driver.findElement(By.xpath("//*[@id=\"comment\"]"))
        .sendKeys("Very nice cat");
    driver.findElement(By.cssSelector("#form1 > button")).click();
    WebElement sucessDiv = driver
        .findElement(By.cssSelector("#success > div"));
    assertThat(sucessDiv.getText(), containsString("Your vote for
        Baby"));
}


@Test
@DisplayName("Rate a cat using the GUI with error")
@Tag("functional-requirement-2")
public void testRateCatWithError(FirefoxDriver driver) {
    driver.get("http://localhost:" + serverPort);
    driver.findElement(By.id("Baby")).click();
    String sendButtonSelector = "#form1 > button";
    new WebDriverWait(driver, 10).until(
        elementToBeClickable(By.cssSelector(sendButtonSelector)));
    driver.findElement(By.cssSelector(sendButtonSelector)).click();
    WebElement sucessDiv = driver
        .findElement(By.cssSelector("#error > div"));
    assertThat(sucessDiv.getText(), containsString(
        "You need to select some stars for rating each cat"));
}

}
```

In order to make easier the traceability of the test executions, in all the implemented test, we have selected meaningful test names using `@DisplayName`. In addition, for parameterized tests, we use the element name to refine the test name of each execution of the test, depending on the test input. The following screenshot of the execution of the test suite in Eclipse 4.7 (Oxygen):

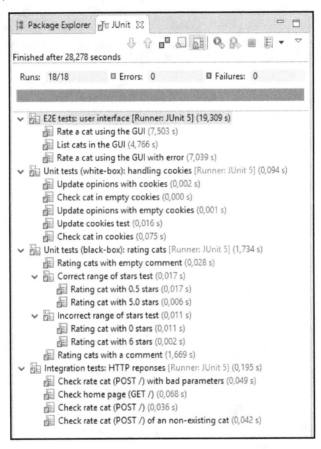

Execution of the test suite for the application Rate my cat! in Eclipse 4.7

As introduced before, we use Travis CI as build server to execute our tests during the development process. In the configuration of Travis CI (file `.travis.yml`), we setup two additional tools to enhance the development and test process of our application. On the one hand, Codecov provides a comprehensive test coverage report. On the other hand, SonarCloud provides a complete static analysis. Both tools are triggered by Travis CI as part of the continuous integration build process. As a result, we can evaluate both the coverage test and the internal code quality of our application (such as code smells, duplicated blocks, or technical debt) along with our development process.

The following picture shows a screenshot of the online report provided by Codecov (the report provided by SonarCloud was presented in the previous section of this chapter):

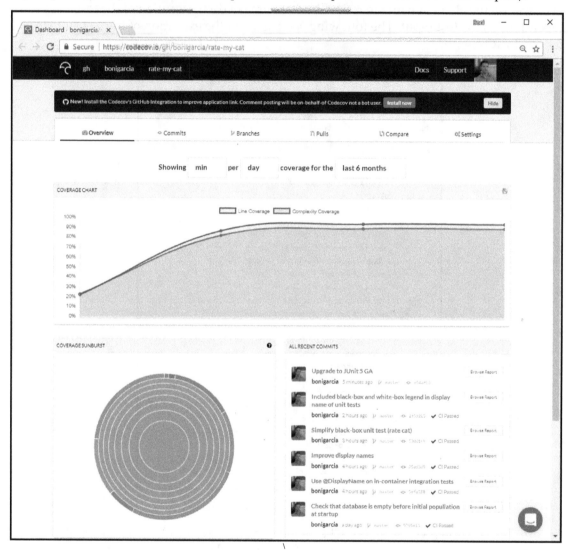

Codecov report for the application Rate my cat!

Last but not least, we are using several *badges* in the README of our GitHub repository. Concretely, we add badges for Travis CI (status of the last build process), SonarCloud (status of the last analysis), and Codecov (percentage of the last code coverage analysis):

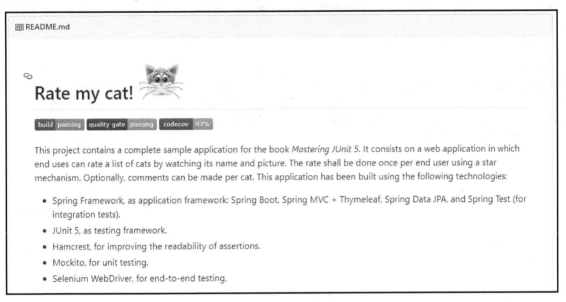

GitHub badges for the application Rate my cat!

Summary

In this chapter, we reviewed several concerns about the management side of the testing activities. First, we learned that testing can be made in different parts of the software development process (software lifecycle) depending on the test methodology: BDD (acceptance tests are defined before the requirement analysis), TDD (tests are defined before the design of the system), TFD (tests are implemented after the system design), and TLD (tests are implemented after the system implementation).

CI is a process more and more used in software development. It consists on the automated build and test of a codebase. This process is typically triggered with a new commit in a source code repository, such as GitHub, GitLab, or Bitbucket. CI is extended to Continuous Delivery (when releases are made to development environment) and to Continuous Deployment (when deployment to production environment is made continuously). We reviewed two of the most used build servers nowadays: Jenkins (*CI as a Service*) and Travis (in-premises).

There some other tools that can be used to improve the management of tests, for example, reporting tools (such as Maven Surefire Report or Allure) or defect tracking systems (such as JIRA, Bugzilla, Redmine, MantisBT, and GitHub issues). Automated static analysis is a great complement to testing, for example, using linters such as Checkstyle, FindBugs, PMD, or SonarQube, and also peer review tools such as Collaborator, Crucible, Gerrit, and GitHub pull requests reviews.

To close this book, the final section of this chapter presents a complete web application (named *Rate my cat!*) and its corresponding JUnit 5 tests (unit, integration, and end-to-end). It consists on a web applications developed and assessed using different technologies presented throughout the book, namely, Spring, Mockito, Selenium, Hamcrest, Travis CI, Codecov, and SonarCloud.

Index

Printed in the USA
CPSIA information can be obtained
at www.ICGtesting.com
LVHW070058231123
764659LV00008B/570